Florida

Preparing for

FCAT

Reading / Grade 7

Dana Chicchelly

AMSCO SCHOOL PUBLICATIONS, INC.
315 Hudson Street, New York, N.Y. 10013

About the Author

Dana Chichelly is a freelance writer and editor living and working in western Montana. She is a former middle school English Language Arts and French teacher and has taught in Arizona and Texas. She holds a Bachelor of Arts degree in English and French from Coe College in Cedar Rapids, Iowa and she received her post-baccalaureate teaching certification from the University of Arizona.

Consultant
Marian A. (Katy) Gordon
English Language Arts Teacher
Landmark Middle School
Jacksonville, FL

Reviewers
Susan Beecher
Secondary Reading Specialist
Orange County, FL

Ola Harb
English Language Arts Teacher
Bartow Middle School
Bartow, FL

Interior and Cover Design: A Good Thing, Inc.
Compositor: A Good Thing, Inc.
Illustration: Hadel Studio

Please visit our Web site at **www.amscopub.com**

When ordering this book, please specify:
either **R 123 W** *or* **PREPARING FOR FCAT READING, GRADE 7**

ISBN 1-56765-141-0

Copyright © 2006, Amsco School Publications, Inc.
No part of this book may be reproduced in any form without written permission from the publisher.

Printed in the United States of America
1 2 3 4 5 6 7 8 9 10   10 09 08 07 06

Contents

Introduction		v
About This Book		v
About the FCAT		vi
Diagnostic Test		**1**
Chapter 1	Reading Effectively	33
Chapter 2	Knowing the Difference	57
Chapter 3	Getting the Point	77
Chapter 4	The Author's "Why"	103
Lesson 1	*Author's Purpose*	*104*
Lesson 2	*Author's Point of View*	*118*
Chapter 5	Looking It Up	133
Chapter 6	Looking Into It	161
Chapter 7	Why Did That Happen?	185
Chapter 8	The Plot Thickens	205
FCAT Practice Test One		**235**
FCAT Practice Test Two		**265**
Index		**297**

Introduction

About This Book

The goal of this book is to help you get ready for the reading portion of the FCAT, Grade 7. It does this by reviewing many of the terms and ideas that you have already learned in your regular reading or English class. You might wonder, "Why should I go over all this stuff again?" The answer is that the more times you review a concept, the more you will understand it and the more likely you will be to remember it while taking the FCAT.

The eight chapters in this book each present one of the benchmark skills tested on the FCAT. The chapters review the skills you need to know for the test and give you plenty of examples. The **Try It Out** exercises walk you through a sample reading and test items. Then you will have a chance to practice the skills independently in the **On Your Own** exercises. At the end of the book are two Practice Tests, modeled after the actual FCAT.

This book also introduces you to FCAT Fred. Fred is a cartoon cat who considers himself an authority on the FCAT test (and on just about everything else!). He makes an appearance in every chapter to give you hints on taking the FCAT or strategies to use when answering questions.

Introduction

About the FCAT

The Florida State Board of Education adopted the Sunshine State Standards in 1996. These standards identify the skills and essential knowledge that students should possess. The state then developed the Florida Comprehensive Assessment Test (FCAT) to determine whether students are meeting these standards

All students in grades 3 through 10 take the reading and mathematics portions of the FCAT. Students in grades 4, 8, and 10 also take the writing portion; and students in grades 5, 8, and 10 also take the science portion. This book is about the reading portion of the FCAT, Grade 7.

The test questions are based on the following benchmarks.

Grade Seven Benchmarks

The Student:

LA.A.1.3.2   Uses a variety of strategies to analyze words and text, draw conclusions, use context and word structure clues, and recognize organizational patterns.

LA.A.2.2.7   Recognizes the use of comparison and contrast in a text.

LA.A.2.3.1   Determines the main idea or essential message and identifies relevant details, facts, and patterns of organization.

LA.A.2.3.2   Identifies the author's purpose and/or point of view in a variety of texts and uses the information to construct meaning. (Includes **LA.A.2.2.2**: Identifies the author's purpose in a simple text, and **LA.A.2.2.3**: Recognizes when a text is primarily intended to persuade.)

LA.A.2.3.5   Locates, organizes, and interprets written information for a variety of purposes, including classroom research, collaborative decision making, and performing a school or real-world task. (Includes **LA.A.2.3.6**: Uses a variety of reference materials, including indexes, magazines, newspapers, and journals and tools, including card catalogs and computer catalogs, to gather information for research topics, and **L.A.A.2.3.7**: Synthesizes and separates collected information into useful components using a variety of techniques, such as source cards, note cards, spreadsheets, and outlines.)

LA.A.2.3.8   Checks the validity and accuracy of information obtained from research, in such ways as differentiating facts and opinion, identifying strong vs. weak arguments, and recognizing that personal values influence the conclusions an author draws.

LA.E.2.2.1   Recognizes cause-and-effect relationships in literary text. (Applies to fiction, nonfiction, poetry, and drama.)

LA.E.2.3.1   Understands how character and plot development point of view, and tone are used in various selections to support central conflict or a story line. (Includes **L.A.E.1.3.2:** Recognizes complex elements of plot including setting, character development, conflicts and resolutions.)

Multiple-Choice Questions

All questions on the FCAT, Grade 7 will be in multiple-choice format. The multiple-choice questions will have four possible answer choices, and only one of them will be considered the best answer. The four choices will be labeled A, B, C, D or F, G, H, I.

Here are some strategies for choosing the right answer to a multiple-choice question:

- See if you can answer the question before you even read the possible answers. If your answer is one of the four choices, it is very likely correct.
- Read the possible answers and see if you can rule any of them out because you *know* they are incorrect.
- If you have time, write a short outline of the reading selection or make a list of the important information.
- See if the question itself has a clue that will lead you to the answer.
- Can't figure out the answer to one of the questions? Then move on to other questions for that reading rather than spending all your time on that one item. After you finish answering the other questions, go back to the one you skipped. Sometimes the information in later questions will actually help you figure out the answers to questions that came earlier.
- If you find you have spent a long time on one question, don't worry. Other questions will probably take less time to answer, and you will be able to make up for the time you spent figuring out the tricky ones.

No matter how far you have to go to prepare for the FCAT, be confident that you will get there by taking just one step at a time. Good luck on your journey!

Diagnostic Test

Read the article "Adventure on the Everglades Trail" before answering Numbers 1 through 8.

Adventure on the Everglades Trail

by Christopher Percy Collier

My companion and I are three days into a four-day trip along the Everglades Trail, a new driving route that strings together 20 natural areas spread across 300 miles of Florida's greater Everglades watershed. We've just spent the night in Hell's Bay on a chickee, a wooden platform completely surrounded by water, four miles from the nearest road. After polishing off this paddle, we'll head north—past miles and miles of native saw grass, through sugar cane and winter vegetable fields, past canals and culverts and dikes—on our way to hop a swamp buggy at the headwaters where the Everglades is born.

But before we can pull this canoe out of the water after a half day of sitting on hard seats, before we can go one more paddle stroke down this serpentine, mangrove-entangled passage way, we have to wait for a large snake—suspiciously resembling a cottonmouth moccasin—to vacate the water trail ahead.

Explore the Everglades Trail and you never know what you'll find lurking around the bend. Over the past three days, we've seen dozens of alligators, scores of wading birds, and enough plant species to fill a field guide to Everglades botanicals. Out here, bobcats can cover up to 50 miles a day in search of prey. Prehistoric fish—like the creepy, toothsome Florida gar—proliferate in oxygen-deprived swamps, while shark, barracuda and snapper crowd brackish bays. Forty-three species of mosquito swarm about. There are salamanders the length of toy poodles and pelicans with 9-foot wingspans. Royal palms that would be at home on Hollywood Boulevard grow wild beside swollen cypress trunks shrouded in Spanish moss and soaked in cool, bourbon-colored water.

The 4-million-acre Everglades is more or less one huge superlative. One of the largest wetlands in the Western Hemisphere (roughly the size of Rhode Island and

Connecticut combined), it contains the largest concentration of orchids, the largest concentration of native royal palms and the biggest swath of continuous saw-grass prairie in the United States. It's considered the country's most noteworthy breeding ground for tropical wading birds and serves as a primary source of drinking water for the Sunshine State.

But superlatives aside, the greater Everglades watershed has been put through the wringer—by a century's worth of canals, dikes, locks, levees and drainage ditches. Trying to understand how this ecosystem operates, as well as how it has been altered and what's being done to restore it, is enough to make your head spin.

One hundred years ago, the Everglades was twice its current size. When summer rains fell, the water languidly pushed south, steadily creeping down through South Florida, spilling over Lake Okeechobee to flow in sheets 50 miles wide, crawling toward the Gulf of Mexico. The Everglades teemed with plants and wildlife: Saw grass flourished; fish thrived; wading-bird populations were 10 times what they are now. Then came the changes that have led many to point out that the *real* Everglades—the fabled "river of grass"—has all but vanished. Canals were dug. Wetlands were drained. Farmers planted sugar cane. More and more houses were built as people began moving to Florida in droves. East-west roads created a barrier to water flow.

In 1928 a hurricane flooded Lake Okeechobee, killing 1,800 people. Soon after, a mound of earth was built around the southern rim and eventually encircled the 467,000-acre lake. Demand for water for irrigation and human consumption inspired the creation of a water-management system with 1,000 miles of canals and 720 miles of levees, which wreaked further havoc on the Everglades ecosystem. Less water now enters the remaining Everglades natural areas, out of sync with the natural ebb and flow of the seasons, and it's less clean. There is less food for wading birds to feed on. And as water containing phosphorous—an ingredient used in fertilizers—enters protected areas, invasive cattails overtake native saw grass.

The leading plan to save the Everglades—the Comprehensive Everglades Restoration Plan (CERP), now under way—has been called the largest ecosystem restoration ever attempted. It's an $8 billion project with 60-some parts that will take more than three decades to complete. If it works, appropriate volumes of clean water will enter the remaining natural areas at the right times. More storm-water treatment facilities will be constructed. Water will be stored in aquifers before re-entering the water supply. Canals will be filled. In short, the entire Everglades will be replumbed to improve drinking water, restore a more natural flow to the Everglades and revive the ecosystem.

Now answer Numbers 1 through 8 using the Answer Sheet on page 31. Base your answers on the article "Adventure on the Everglades Trail."

1. How is the Everglades different today than it was one hundred years ago?

   A. It is much larger.
   B. It is much smaller.
   C. It has more floods.
   D. It has more saw grass.

2 Why did people build a mound of earth around Lake Okeechobee?

    F. They wanted to irrigate the land for farming.

    G. They wanted to prevent another deadly flood.

    H. They wanted to make a reservoir for drinking water.

    I. They wanted to restore the natural ebb and flow of the lake.

3 With which statement would the author MOST likely agree?

    A. The Everglades is almost completely destroyed.

    B. The Everglades is nearly as healthy as it used to be.

    C. The Everglades is a threat to Florida's growing population.

    D. The Everglades is a unique ecosystem that needs protection.

4 Read the sentence below.

> The Everglades teemed with life: Saw grass flourished; fish thrived; wading-bird populations were 10 times what they are now.

What does the word *flourished* mean?

    F. died off

    G. grew well

    H. did poorly

    I. crowded out

5 Which word BEST describes the tone of the article's first two paragraphs?

    A. relaxing

    B. terrifying

    C. humorous

    D. adventurous

6 What is the MAIN idea of the paragraph that begins "Explore the Everglades Trail and you never know what you'll find lurking around the bend"?

    F. The Everglades Trail is a twisty, winding waterway.

    G. The Everglades Trail is made up of swamps and bays.

    H. The Everglades has many dangerous species of animals.

    I. The Everglades is filled with a variety of wildlife and plants.

7 How does the author support the idea that the real Everglades has all but vanished?

    A. by writing about his recent trip on the Everglades Trail
    B. by listing natural events that have changed the Everglades
    C. by explaining why the Everglades is "one huge superlative"
    D. by telling how human-made changes have affected the Everglades

8 What can you infer from the fact that the author waited for a snake to pass by before paddling on?

    F. The author is a snake expert.
    G. The author is terrified of all snakes.
    H. The cottonmouth is a dangerous snake.
    I. The cottonmouth is an endangered species.

Read the article "Looking Good, Eating Right" before answering Numbers 9 through 16.

Looking Good, Eating Right
by Dr. Charles A. Salter

How Does One Develop an Eating Disorder?

The causes of eating disorders are not always clear. There may be genetic or biochemical factors in some cases. There may be psychological problems from early childhood or the present (such as school or family conflicts) that trigger the problem. Often, the psychological trap that immediately precedes anorexic or bulimic behavior is the double pressure to enjoy life through food and yet remain ultra-slim.

Society all around us encourages self-indulgence in food and drink as one of the main ways to enjoy life. For example, almost any popular magazine, newspaper, or TV show has ads showing attractive food that makes your mouth water at first glance. The characters in movies and TV shows are often shown indulging themselves with a bewildering array of high-fat snacks and treats. In real life, no party or ceremonial event would be complete without a table full of tasty food items. To be part of the action, to be popular, you are supposed to eat, eat, eat. . . .

But in real life most people, if they keep consuming like that, just keep putting on more and more weight. They then find themselves in conflict with another dominant pressure in society—to stay slim and trim. Models in ads—even those hawking food—and actors in shows—even those shown gorging themselves on fatty foods—are usually physically fit and quite thin.

All of these incompatible pressures put teens in a terrible bind. A person with a very high metabolism rate may be able to overeat and not gain weight. But the vast majority of us are not so lucky. Even people in the high-metabolism category usually find their rate slowing and their weight increasing over the years. The "solution" that some teens choose is to deny themselves all the time so as to keep temptation at bay. But soon, hunger and food boredom lead to a binge. Feeling guilty over the binge, they desperately seek a way out. For instance, they make themselves throw up, or they double their resolve to eat less in the future. Over time they develop anorexia or bulimia.

Why do some teens develop eating disorders while others don't? Some experts relate the problem to childhood traumas, disturbed family relationships, chemical imbalances in the brain, or distorted self-images. But speculation about the causes often does not help much unless sufficient time is spent with a psychiatrist or psychologist to explore those causes thoroughly. Someone who already has a full-fledged eating disorder or has traumatic conflicts pushing him or her strongly toward unhealthy eating should consult a professional immediately.

Treatment of Eating Disorders

Once an eating disorder has become firmly established, there is no easy cure. Someone who's never suffered anorexia and never known an anorexic might be tempted to think, "It's simple—just tell them to eat more!"

Unfortunately, it's not that simple. Even when anorexics have been brought into the hospital and are receiving physical care, many don't improve much. Some will go to extraordinary lengths to deceive family members and doctors, pretending to change but not really doing so. Some others will begin to improve under the intense scrutiny possible in a hospital, but as soon as they are released they will go straight back to the disordered eating behavior again.

Prevention of Eating Disorders

Since treatment for eating disorders is difficult, the best approach is prevention. And successful prevention depends on keeping a healthy self-image and on maintaining a balanced diet.

> **Maintain a Healthy Self-Image.** As we saw earlier, our society's obsession with thinness, together with a constant emphasis on the theme that rich food means pleasure, puts many teens in a bind. Being drawn to excessive eating on the one hand and self-denial on the other can trigger anorexia or bulimia—or both. Anorexics, in particular, seem to feel that no matter how much weight they lose, they are still too fat. When asked to draw themselves, some draw an image of a body much plumper than any mirror or photograph would show them.
>
> Therefore, it is important for each person in our society to try to maintain a healthy and realistic self-image. Don't compare yourself with the models and actors in the media. Set your sights more realistically by comparing yourself with family and friends, if anyone. Better yet, try to find your own strengths and weaknesses without comparing yourself with others at all. In short, don't try to be someone else. Try to be the best person you can uniquely be.

Maintain a Balanced Diet. Prolonged self-denial is the typical first step toward an eating disorder. Eventually, cravings for what you've denied yourself become unbearable, and you react with either a binge or overly fierce self-control. The answer is not, of course, to indulge in all the snacks and treats you fancy. Instead, to avoid that first step that leads to cravings, strive for a good and healthy diet. Such a diet is based primarily on grain products, fruits, and vegetables, with moderate amounts of meat and dairy products and with small amounts of snacks and desserts. Research demonstrates that this kind of diet leaves you more alert and energetic, with no uncontrollable cravings.

In fact, some research by Stephanie Dalvit-McPhillips found that even among those who have already developed bulimia, this kind of diet can help them to overcome the tendency to binge. She studied 28 bulimic patients for two and a half years. When chowing down their usual unbalanced diet, they indulged in frequent binges. But when operating on a good diet, they not only stopped the binges completely but even lost weight on the average.

You really can live more happily and healthily with a sound, balanced diet.

Now answer Numbers 9 through 16 using the Answer Sheet on page 31. Base your answers on the article "Looking Good, Eating Right."

9 What organization method does the author use in the section "How Does One Develop an Eating Disorder?"

A. time order
B. spatial order
C. cause and effect
D. comparison and contrast

10 Which of the author's opinions is supported by the fact that many ads show mouth-watering food?

F. People should eat a balanced diet.
G. Society pressures people to be thin.
H. People should set realistic weight goals.
I. Society encourages people to eat too much.

11 How are real people who eat a lot DIFFERENT from the models who eat a lot in TV ads?

A. They gain weight.
B. They eat a balanced diet.
C. They stay in better shape.
D. They have a better self-image.

12 According to the article, how does society help cause eating disorders?

　　F. by pressuring people to both eat a lot and be thin
　　G. by showing models on TV who lead healthy lifestyles
　　H. by encouraging people to celebrate events with parties
　　I. by causing psychological problems in early childhood

13 Read the sentence below.

> The "solution" that some teens choose is to deny themselves all the time so as to keep temptation at bay.

Why did the author put the word *solution* in quotation marks?

　　A. to show that he is using a quotation from another author
　　B. to show that it is very difficult to treat eating disorders
　　C. to show that it is important to find a solution to eating disorders
　　D. to show that teens' denying themselves food is not really a solution

14 Read the sentence below.

> Some will go to extraordinary lengths to deceive family members and doctors, pretending to change but not really doing so.

What does the word *deceive* mean?

　　F. trick
　　G. please
　　H. hide from
　　I. agree with

15 What can you conclude from the article about snacks and desserts?

　　A. They are the best foods to eat for high energy.
　　B. They are the first step that leads to an eating disorder.
　　C. They should never be eaten by people with eating disorders.
　　D. They should be eaten in small amounts to help avoid cravings.

16 What is the author's MAIN purpose in this article?

　　F. to describe a new treatment for eating disorders
　　G. to persuade people with eating disorders to seek help
　　H. to discuss the family relationships that cause eating disorders
　　I. to explain the causes of eating disorders and how to prevent them

Read the article "History of Chocolate" before answering Numbers 17 through 24.

History of Chocolate

The story of chocolate, as far back as we know it, begins more than 2,000 years ago in equatorial Central America where the Mayan Indians held cocoa beans in high regard. Images of cocoa pods were carved into the walls of their elaborate stone temples, and Mayan writings refer to cacao as "food of the gods." It was the Mayans who first created a beverage from crushed cocoa beans that was enjoyed by royalty and shared at sacred ceremonies.

Chocolate's importance in the Aztec Empire also is clearly recorded. The Aztecs called the prized drink they made from cocoa beans "chocolatl," which means "warm liquid." Like the earlier Mayans, the Aztecs drank the unsweetened beverage during special ceremonies. Montezuma II, a royal monarch of the Aztecs, maintained great storehouses filled with cocoa beans and reportedly consumed 50 or more portions of chocolatl daily from a golden goblet. Cocoa beans, however, weren't only consumed. They also were used as a form of currency. According to records of the time, a rabbit could be purchased for four cocoa beans.

Europe was first introduced to the principal ingredient of chocolate when Christopher Columbus brought a handful of the dark, almond-shaped beans back to Spain from his last voyage to the Caribbean islands in 1502. He presented to King Ferdinand and Queen Isabella many strange and wonderful objects from the lands he explored. Included among them were cocoa beans, placed before royalty as little more than a curiosity. They appeared most unpromising. The King and Queen of Spain never dreamed how important cocoa beans would become. It remained for Hernando Cortes, the Spanish explorer, to grasp the commercial possibilities of cocoa beans.

Chocolate Travels to Spain

When Cortes arrived in what is now known as Mexico in 1519, the Aztecs mistakenly believed that he was the reincarnation of a former god-king who had been exiled from the land. They did not realize that Cortes was seeking Aztec gold that was rumored to exist. Montezuma greeted the Spanish explorers with a large banquet, which included cups of a bitter chocolate drink. By the time the Aztecs realized their mistake, the Spanish had begun to overpower them. Within three years, Cortes and his followers brought about the fall of the Aztec empire.

During this time, Cortes realized the economic potential for cocoa beans. He experimented with chocolatl, adding cane sugar to make it more agreeable to Spanish tastes. He also established additional cacao plantings in the Caribbean region before returning to Spain.

Back in Spain, the new version of chocolatl found favor with the wealthy, and continued to undergo flavor refinements. Newly imported spices, such as cinnamon and vanilla, were added to the drink. Ultimately, someone decided the drink would taste better if served steaming hot, creating the first hot chocolate, which quickly won followers among the Spanish aristocracy. Spain proceeded to plant more cacao trees in its overseas colonies in Ecuador, Venezuela, Peru and Jamaica to ensure an ample supply of cocoa beans. Remarkably, the Spanish were able to keep their ventures in cocoa cultivation and their creation of early cocoa drinks a secret from the rest of Europe for nearly one hundred years.

Chocolate Spreads Across Europe

Spanish monks were assigned the task of processing the cocoa beans. It may have been these monks who let out the secret by discussing cocoa with their French counterparts. Then in 1580, the first cocoa processing plant was established in Spain. It did not take long before chocolate was acclaimed throughout Europe as a delicious, health-giving drink. For a while it reigned as the chosen beverage at the fashionable Court of France. Chocolate drinking spread across the English Channel to Great Britain, and in 1657 the first of many famous English Chocolate Houses appeared.

Mass production of cocoa became possible with the invention of a perfected steam engine which mechanized the cocoa grinding process. By 1730, cocoa had dropped in price from three dollars or more per pound to within financial reach of all.

The invention of the cocoa press in 1828 was another major breakthrough in cocoa production. This not only helped reduce prices even further, but more importantly, improved the quality of the beverage by squeezing out about half of the cocoa butter (the fat that occurs naturally in cocoa beans) from the ground-up beans, leaving behind a cake-like residue that could be further processed into a fine powder. From then on, chocolate drinks had more of the smooth consistency and the recognizable flavor of those enjoyed today.

The 19th century witnessed two more revolutionary developments in the history of chocolate. In 1847, an English company introduced the first solid eating chocolate made by combining melted cocoa butter with sugar and cocoa powder. This chocolate had a smooth, velvety texture and quickly replaced the old coarse-grained chocolate that formerly dominated the world market. The second development occurred in 1876 in Vevey, Switzerland, when Daniel Peter devised a way of adding milk to chocolate, creating the product we enjoy today known as milk chocolate.

Chocolate Comes to America

In the United States of America, the production of chocolate proceeded at a faster pace than anywhere else in the world. It was in pre-revolutionary New England—1765, to be exact—that the first chocolate factory was established in this country. During World War II, the U.S. government recognized chocolate's role in the nourishment and group spirit of the Allied Armed Forces, so much so that it allocated valuable shipping space for the importation of cocoa beans. Many soldiers were thankful for the chocolate bars, which gave them the energy to carry on until more food rations could be obtained. Today, the U.S. Army's Meals Ready to Eat contain chocolate bars and chocolate candies, and chocolate has been taken into space as part of the diet of U.S. astronauts.

Now answer Numbers 17 through 24 using the Answer Sheet on page 31. Base your answers on the article "History of Chocolate."

17 How does the author support the idea that cocoa beans were important to the Mayans?

　　A. by describing the history of the cocoa bean
　　B. by giving the meaning of the word *chocolatl*
　　C. by explaining how cocoa beans were used for money
　　D. by telling how cacao was called the "food of the gods"

18 Which culture gave chocolate its name?

　　F. the Aztecs
　　G. the Mayans
　　H. the Spanish
　　I. the Mexicans

19 Why did Hernando Cortes have more success than Christopher Columbus in getting people to like chocolate?

　　A. He added sugar to it.
　　B. He sold it for less money.
　　C. He served it as a beverage.
　　D. He served it as a hot drink.

20 What effect did both the steam engine and cocoa press have on cocoa?

　　F. They both made cocoa taste better.
　　G. They both gave cocoa a smoother texture.
　　H. They both helped make cocoa cheaper to buy.
　　I. They both sped up the cocoa-grinding process.

21 Read the sentence below.

> The second development occurred in 1876 in Vevey, Switzerland, when Daniel Peter devised a way of adding milk to chocolate, creating the product we enjoy today known as milk chocolate.

What does the word *devised* mean?

　　A. learned
　　B. planned
　　C. invented
　　D. remembered

㉒ How was the production of chocolate in the United States DIFFERENT from its production in any other country?

    F. It began more slowly.
    G. It happened more quickly.
    H. It occurred after World War II.
    I. It started in response to soldiers' needs.

㉓ Read the sentence below.

During World War II, the U.S. government recognized chocolate's role in the nourishment and group spirit of the Allied Armed Forces, so much so that it allocated valuable shipping space for the importation of cocoa beans.

What can you infer from this sentence?

    A. Chocolate is nutritious and it makes people feel good.
    B. Chocolate has more psychological than nutritious benefits.
    C. The government wasted valuable space shipping chocolate.
    D. The government sold chocolate to help fund World War II.

㉔ What organization method does the author use in this article?

    F. time order
    G. spatial order
    H. cause and effect
    I. question and answer

Read the passage from *My Story* before answering Numbers 25 through 32.

from MY STORY
by Rosa Parks

When I got off from work that evening of December 1, I went to Court Square as usual to catch the Cleveland Avenue bus home. I didn't look to see who was driving when I got on, and by the time I recognized him, I had already paid my fare. It was the same driver who had put me off the bus back in 1943, twelve years earlier. He was still tall and heavy, with red, rough-looking skin. And he was still mean-looking. I didn't know if he had been on that route before—they switched the drivers sometimes. I do know that most of the time if I saw him on a bus, I wouldn't get on it.

I saw a vacant seat in the middle section of the bus and took it. I didn't even question why there was a vacant seat even though there were quite a few people standing in the back. If I had thought about it at all, I would probably have figured maybe someone saw me get on and did not take the seat but left it vacant for me. There was a man sitting next to the window and two women across the aisle.

The next stop was the Empire Theater, and some whites got on. They filled up the white seats, and one man was left standing. The

---

The Author

Rosa Parks was born in Tuskegee, Alabama, but grew up and made her home in Montgomery. She worked as a seamstress in a department store, and her husband, Raymond, was a barber.

Many people think Parks's refusal to give up her seat was her first act of protest. It was not. She was a member of the local NAACP chapter and served as its secretary. Following the successful boycott, Parks and her husband moved to Detroit, Michigan, where she worked for U.S. Representative John Conyers for a number of years.

driver looked back and noticed the man standing. Then he looked back at us. He said, "Let me have those front seats," because they were the front seats of the black section. Didn't anybody move. We just sat right where we were, the four of us. Then he spoke a second time: "Y'all better make it light on yourselves and let me have those seats."

The man in the window seat next to me stood up, and I moved to let him pass by me, and then I looked across the aisle and saw that the two women were also standing. I moved over to the window seat. I could not see how standing up was going to "make it light" for me. The more we gave in and complied, the worse they treated us.

I thought back to the time I used to sit up all night and didn't sleep, and my grandfather would have his gun right by the fireplace, or if he had his one-horse wagon going anywhere, he always had his gun in the back of the wagon. People always say that I didn't give up my seat because I was tired, but that isn't true. I was not tired physically, or no more tired than I usually was at the end of a working day. I was not old, although some people have an image of me as being old then. I was forty-two. No, the only tired I was, was tired of giving up.

The driver of the bus saw me still sitting there, and he asked was I going to stand up. I said, "No." He said, "Well, I'm going to have you arrested." Then I said, "You may do that." These were the only words we said to each other. I didn't even know his name, which was James Blake, until we were in court together. He got out of the bus and stayed outside for a few minutes, waiting for the police.

As I sat there, I tried not to think about what might happen. I knew that anything was possible. I could be manhandled or beaten. I could be arrested. People have asked me if it occurred to me then that I could be the test case the NAACP had been looking for. I did not think about that at all. In fact, if I had let myself think too deeply about what might happen to me, I might have gotten off the bus. But I chose to remain.

The *Response*

After Parks's arrest, members of the African-American community rallied behind her. They, too, had grown tired of the Jim Crow laws and the mistreatment by whites. They decided to stage a boycott of Montgomery buses. African-Americans would not ride the buses in Montgomery until the city ended its segregated seating system. It was a yearlong struggle, but Montgomery officials finally agreed to end segregation on its buses. Dr. Martin Luther King Jr., who had led the boycott, emerged as a national leader in the civil rights movement. He and other ministers from Montgomery formed the Southern Christian Leadership Conference, which would become a leading civil rights organization.

Now answer Numbers 25 through 32 using the Answer Sheet on page 31. Base your answers on the passage from *My Story*.

25 Why did Rosa Parks dislike the bus driver?

    A. because he was rude

    B. because he looked mean

    C. because he made her get off the bus once

    D. because he always made her change seats

26 What was the MAIN conflict Parks faced in the passage?

    F. She had to get off the bus after too many people got on.

    G. She had to decide whether or not to give up her seat to a white person.

    H. She had to overcome her fear of being arrested for disobeying the driver.

    I. She had to ride a bus driven by a man with whom she had already had trouble.

27 Why did Parks disobey the bus driver?

    A. She was exhausted from work.

    B. She thought the driver was rude.

    C. She was old and had trouble walking.

    D. She was tired of the way blacks were treated.

28 What is the theme of the passage?

    F. It is important to stand up for your rights.

    G. It is better to try and fail than not to try at all.

    H. It is hard for one person to make a difference.

    I. It is easy to take for granted the rights we have.

29 What do both the passage and the sidebar "The Author" tell you about people's understanding of Rosa Parks?

    A. They have many mistaken beliefs about her.

    B. They have little understanding of her early struggles.

    C. They have no idea she was a member of the NAACP.

    D. They underestimate how determined she was to bring about change.

30 How does the sidebar "The Response" support the passage?

    F. It tells when the event in the passage took place.

    G. It describes how the Jim Crow laws were created.

    H. It explains why Parks reacted the way she did in the passage.

    I. It shows the significance of the event Parks describes in the passage.

31. Which pair of words BEST describes Rosa Parks?

   A. pushy and rude
   B. calm and peaceful
   C. worried and scared
   D. brave and determined

32. What is the MOST likely reason that the city of Montgomery finally agreed to end segregation on buses?

   F. The city saw how unfairly it had treated blacks.
   G. The city felt ashamed for having a woman like Rosa Parks arrested.
   H. The city realized it was losing money when blacks refused to ride the buses.
   I. The city grew tired of having to arrest blacks who did not give up their seats.

Read the article "Cloud Cover" before answering Numbers 33 through 40.

Cloud Cover

by Nick Walker

You have only to look up into the sky to try your luck at weather forecasting. Clouds give us a clue about what is going on in our atmosphere and how the weather might change in the hours or even days to come. Each type of cloud forms in a different way, and each brings its own kind of weather.

Cool Condensation

Clouds are water. As you probably know, we can find water in three forms: liquid, solid and gas. Water as a gas is called water vapor. Clouds form when water vapor turns back into liquid water droplets. That is called condensation. It happens in one of two ways: when the air cools enough, or when enough water vapor is added to the air. You've seen the first process happen on a summer day as drops of water gather on the outside of a glass of iced tea. That's because the cold glass cools the air near it, causing the water vapor in the air to condense into liquid. Unlike the drops on the side of your glass though, the droplets of water in a cloud are so small that it takes about one million of them to form a single raindrop. Most clouds form this way, but the cooling comes not from ice in a glass, but as the air rises and cools high in the sky. Each tiny cloud droplet is light enough to float in the air, just as a little cloud floats out from your breath on a cold day.

Too Clean for Clouds?

Our air has to be just a little bit dirty for clouds to form. That's because water vapor needs a surface on which to condense. Fortunately, even the cleanest air has some microscopic particles of dust, smoke, or salt for water droplets to cling to, so the air is rarely too clean for clouds to form.

Cloud Classifications

Meteorologists name clouds by how high in the sky they form and by their appearance. Most clouds have two parts to their name.

Usually the first part of the name has to do with the height and the second part refers to the appearance.

If clouds form at the highest levels, they get the prefix "cirro" as the first part of their name. Middle clouds get the prefix "alto." Low clouds don't get a prefix.

There are two cloud appearance types: cumulus and stratus, which are also the basic names of the low clouds. Sometimes they appear higher in the atmosphere and

> **Word Up**
> *Cumulus:* In Latin, this means "heap." Cumulus clouds look like a heap of cotton balls or whipped cream.
> *Stratus:* It's Latin for "covering" or "blanket." Stratus clouds look like a flat blanket in the sky.
> *Cirrus:* It's Latin for "curl." Cirrus clouds look like curls of white hair.

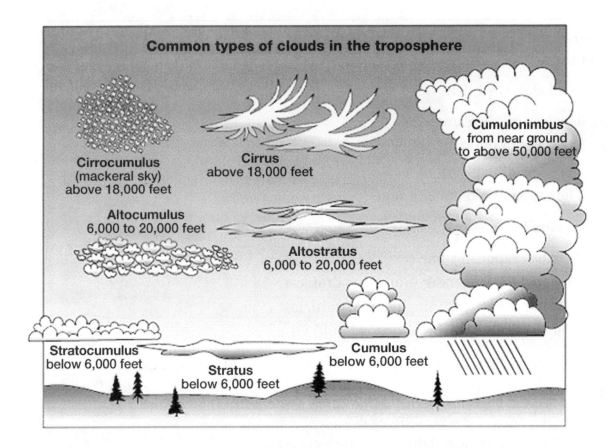

get a combination name with a prefix. For example, middle cumulus clouds are called "altocumulus," and high stratus clouds are "cirrostratus." If a cloud produces rain or snow, it gets either "nimbo" at the beginning or "nimbus" at the end.

Cumulus clouds are billowy globs that are low, have flat bases, and look a little like cauliflower. They are at least as tall as they are wide and form on sunny days from pockets of rising air. Their constantly changing outlines are fun to watch because they can take the shapes of almost anything, including animals and faces. Cumulus clouds usually signal fair weather. If they build into the middle or high part of the atmosphere, they get the name "cumulonimbus." A cumulonimbus cloud is tall, deep and dark and can bring lightning, heavy rain, and even severe weather, such as hail, damaging winds, or tornadoes. It is a sign of rapidly rising and sinking air currents.

Stratus clouds are layered and cover most of the sky. They are much wider than they are tall. If you see them in broken or puffy layers, they are stratocumulus clouds. If you see them in thin high layers that turn the sky solid white, they're cirrostratus clouds. The tiny prisms of ice in a cirrostratus layer can bend the sun's light. As a result, often you can see a halo or veil of rainbow colors around the sun. When stratus clouds are very thick, they become dark nimbostratus clouds, which can produce rain, drizzle or snow.

Cirrus clouds are high and thin and made entirely of ice crystals. Forming above 20,000 feet in the atmosphere, they often look like wisps of white hair. Cirrus clouds, which are a sign of warm moist air rising up over cold air, are sometimes an early signal that thickening clouds could bring light rain or snow within one or two days.

Try to learn the names of the different clouds, and the next time you look up into the sky, take notice of what kind of clouds you see. And if you try, you might be able to guess what kind of weather they will bring.

Now answer Numbers 33 through 40 using the Answer Sheet on page 31. Base your answers on the article "Cloud Cover."

33 How are all clouds ALIKE?

   A. They are all the same size.
   B. They are all the same shape.
   C. They are all made up of water.
   D. They are all predictors of rain.

34 How is a cloud created?

   F. by water vapor turning into a gas
   G. by water vapor turning into water droplets
   H. by water droplets turning into ice particles
   I. by water droplets turning into a liquid form

35 Why does the author compare a person's breath on a cold day to a cloud?

   A. to show how clouds form
   B. to tell how tiny water droplets are
   C. to demonstrate how light cloud droplets are
   D. to explain how water vapor condenses

36 What can you learn from both the article and the "Word Up" section?

   F. the position of different clouds in the sky
   G. the appearance of different types of clouds
   H. ways to predict the weather from clouds
   I. the language that gave different cloud types their names

37 What is the author's purpose?

   A. to explain why clouds come in different shapes and sizes
   B. to show the value of being able to predict the weather from clouds
   C. to teach the reader about clouds and how they can be used to predict weather
   D. to persuade the reader that clouds are an important part of Earth's weather system

38 How are stratus clouds DIFFERENT from cumulus clouds?

   F. They spread out across the sky.
   G. They are as tall as they are wide.
   H. They bring hailstorms and tornadoes.
   I. They take on the shapes of animals and faces.

39 What two characteristics of clouds do meteorologists use to name clouds?

    A. how high they are and what they look like

    B. how wide they are and what color they are

    C. how tall they are and what kind of weather they bring

    D. how dense they are and what water form they are made of

40 What causes a halo of rainbow colors around the sun?

    F. ice prisms from a cirrostratus cloud

    G. hailstorms from a cumulonimbus cloud

    H. water vapor from an altocumulus cloud

    I. water droplets from a stratocumulus cloud

The Wolf and the Cow

by Emily Sohn

A gray wolf prowls the underbrush. It stops for a moment and raises its head. It looks about alertly. It bares its sharp teeth. Its golden eyes glint in the sunlight.

Like lions, tigers, eagles, and sharks, the wolf is a predator. It hunts other animals for food. Some people admire the wolf. Others fear it.

Visitors to zoos or animal parks tend to think that wolves, tigers, and other predators are pretty cool. Ranchers who are trying to protect their cattle have a very different reaction. They tend to like only one kind of predator: the dead kind.

Will Holder used to have the same reaction that most ranchers do. As a kid growing up on a ranch in Arizona, Holder learned early on that wolves, coyotes, and mountain lions were supposed to be evil, ever poised to pounce on a herd of innocently grazing cattle.

"What you did when you saw coyotes run across the road was to jump out of the pickup and shoot them," Holder says.

As the years passed, Holder started to wonder if killing predators actually helped protect livestock. He asked his parents when a coyote had ever killed a ranch animal. His mother could remember just one incident, which had occurred during a drought in the 1950s.

Was it really necessary to shoot coyotes? Holder asked himself.

So, when Holder started his own ranch, he took a different approach. Instead of chasing predators away, he allowed them to live on the same land as his cattle do.

Holder still keeps a close eye on his livestock. He uses various strategies to give predators fewer chances to grab a farm animal. And it seems to work. After eight years of ranching, Holder has yet to lose a cow to a predator.

Many of Holder's neighbors think he's crazy. But the idea of "predator-friendly" ranching is catching on. Perhaps predators, livestock, and people can live in harmony, after all.

Conflict

The message of living in harmony is becoming more urgent. Conflicts between people and predators are becoming more common because development and population growth are bringing people and wildlife closer together.

From tigers in India to lions in Africa, many of Earth's fiercest and most magnificent creatures are rapidly heading toward extinction.

"This problem is happening all over the world with basically every type of predator," Adrian Treves says. He's a conservation ecologist with the Wildlife Conservation Society.

When predators show up, farmers get angry, Treves says. "The most common response is to kill wildlife."

Now, however, science is starting to suggest that predators have a far worse reputation than they deserve.

In an article in a book coming out later this year, Treves presents evidence that killing cougars, wolves, and bears benefited livestock on only a third of ranches that were studied. Even in these cases, the benefits lasted for just a short time.

Livestock Threats

Still, it's easy to see why ranchers might hate predators, even if they just suspect that the animals pose a threat to their livestock. The quality of their cattle or sheep directly impacts how much money they make. So, anything that endangers their animals endangers their ability to put food on the table.

Scientists take a less personal view. They focus instead on the importance of biodiversity—the enormous variety of life on earth.

In that spirit, every species has value, Treves says, and every species is worth protecting for its own sake.

Each species is connected to many others, he says. So, if you destroy one, you end up affecting the entire balance of nature.

In Wisconsin, for example, wolves eat white-tailed deer. Wisconsin's wolves are in trouble, though, and the deer population has exploded as a result. All these deer have to eat something, and their diet now includes rare plant species, which are in turn becoming extinct.

People are paying a price for the imbalance, too—with chewed-up gardens and damaging collisions between cars and the hefty animals.

Predator Havens

Predator-friendly farming might be the answer, Holder says. He was inspired to try it when scientists began reintroducing wolves in Arizona.

Holder's first reaction was negative. "Reflexively, we thought, 'No. They're going to eat the cattle. The last thing we need is more of them,'" he says.

"Then, we started to recognize a lot of the little things that make up the big picture of how the environment works," Holder says. "We recognized there was a role that the wolves could play."

Holder also developed strategies that made his cattle less tempting targets. To outwit a predator, he says, you have to think like a predator.

Holder likes to go out into the fields and just watch what wolves do. Then, he uses what he sees to prevent attacks from happening in the first place.

Holder has noticed, for instance, that wolves like to eat without a lot of hassle.

So, he spends a lot of time with his cattle and moves them around a lot. He also keeps his cows clustered together. Attacking a large group is a lot less appealing to a predator than attacking a single cow.

The extra effort pays off, Holder says. There are now between 100 and 120 wolves living near his ranch, he says, but none has ever eaten any of his cows.

And people are willing to pay much more for his organic, predator-friendly beef than they would for ordinary meat in a grocery store, partly because they know their money is helping protect biodiversity.

Learning to live together will take a lot of effort and a large dose of cooperation, Treves says. Eventually, though, maybe everyone will get along—wolves, tigers, people, and all.

Now answer Numbers 41 through 48 using the Answer Sheet on page 31. Base your answers on the article "The Wolf and the Cow."

41 How did Will Holder's opinion of predators change over time?

    A. He grew to hate predators more than ever.

    B. He started to believe that predators were useless animals.

    C. He began to wonder how much harm predators really do.

    D. He began to think that predators were more important than livestock.

42 What is the MAIN idea of the article?

    F. Some scientists believe that predators do not deserve their bad reputation.

    G. Many ranchers do not believe that "predator-friendly" ranching is possible.

    H. It will be difficult to persuade people not to kill predators living near them.

    I. It might be possible for predators, people, and livestock to coexist peacefully.

43 Why are there now more conflicts between people and predators than in the past?

    A. because people are losing more livestock to predators

    B. because people are moving into places where predators live

    C. because predators are experiencing a population explosion

    D. because predators are moving into areas where they never used to live

44 How might Adrian Treves's job influence his opinion of predators?

    F. It might cause him to believe that all predators hurt livestock.

    G. It could make him more likely to think that predators are good.

    H. It might lead him to think that ranchers' rights are most important.

    I. It could make him less likely to think that predators ever attack livestock.

45 In what way are Treves and Holder ALIKE?

    A. They are both ranchers concerned about predators.

    B. They are both authors of books that support biodiversity.

    C. They are both scientists working to reintroduce predators.

    D. They are both supporters of "predator-friendly" ranching.

46 Why has the deer population in Wisconsin exploded?

    F. There are not enough wolves to eat the deer.

    G. There are too many wolves being struck by cars.

    H. There are rare plant species for the deer to enjoy.

    I. There are many gardens for the deer to eat from.

47 What is another word that uses the prefix -im with the same meaning as in *imbalance*?

    A. important

    B. immediate

    C. impossible

    D. imagination

48 What conclusion can be drawn from the author's statement, "There are now between 100 and 120 wolves living near his ranch, he says, but none has ever eaten any of his cows"?

    F. The statement is an opinion.

    G. The statement is a fact.

    H. The author's personal beliefs are clear in this statement.

    I. The author believes that wolves are a threat to livestock.

Read the two folktales "Forsaken Brother" and "How Sun, Moon, and Wind Went Out to Dinner" before answering Numbers 49 through 56.

Forsaken Brother

One summer evening, scarcely an hour before sunset, the father of a family lay in his lodge, dying. Weeping beside him were his wife and three children. Two of them were almost grown up; the youngest was but a small child. These were the only human beings near the dying man, for the lodge stood on a little green mound away from all others of the tribe.

A breeze from the lake gave the sick man a brief return of strength. He raised himself a little and addressed his family.

"I know that I will leave you soon. Your mother, my partner of many years, will not stay long behind. She will soon join me in the pleasant land of spirits. But, O my children, my poor children! You have just begun life. All unkindness and wickedness are still before you.

"I have contented myself with the company of your mother and yourselves for many years, in order to keep you from evil example. I will die content, my children, if you will promise me to love each other. Promise me that on no account will you forsake your youngest brother. I leave him in your charge. Love him and hold him dear."

Time wore heavily away. Five long moons passed, and when the sixth moon was nearly full, the mother also died. In her last moments she reminded the two older children of their promise to their father. Willingly they renewed their promise to take care of their little brother. They were still free from any selfishness.

The winter passed away, and spring came. The girl, the oldest, directed her brothers. She seemed to feel an especially tender and sisterly affection for the youngest, who was sickly and delicate. The older boy, however, already showed signs of selfishness. One day he spoke sharply to his sister.

"My sister, are we always to live as if there were no other human beings in the world? Must I never associate with other men? I am going to visit the villages of my tribe. I have made up my mind, and you cannot prevent me."

"My brother," replied his sister, "I do not say no to what you wish. We were not forbidden to associate with others, but we were commanded never to forsake each other. If we separate to follow our own selfish desires, will we not be compelled to forsake our young brother? Both of us have promised to take care of him."

Making no reply, the young man picked up his bow and arrows, left the wigwam, and returned no more.

For many moons the girl took kindly care of her little brother. At last however, she too began to weary of their solitude and wished to escape from her duty. Her strength and her ability to provide food and clothing had increased through the years, but so had her desire for company. Her solitude troubled her more and more, as the years went slowly by. At last, thinking only of herself, she decided to forsake her little brother, as the older brother had already done.

One day, she placed in the lodge all the food she had gathered. After bringing a pile of wood to the door, she said to her young brother, "Do not stray far from the lodge while I am gone. I am going to look for our brother. I shall soon be back."

Then taking her bundle, she set off for the villages. She found a pleasant one on the shore of a lake. Soon she became so much occupied with the pleasures of her new life that her affection for her brother gradually left her heart. In time, she was married. For a long time, she did not even think of the sickly little brother she had left in the woods.

In the meantime the older brother had settled in a village on the same lake, not far from the graves of their parents and the solitary home of the little brother.

As soon as the little fellow had eaten all the food left by his sister, he had to pick berries and dig roots. Winter came on, and the poor child was exposed to its cold winds. Snow covered the earth. Forced to leave the lodge in search of food, he strayed far without shelter. Sometimes he passed the night in the crotch of an old tree and ate the fragments left by wolves.

Soon he had to depend for his food entirely on what the wolves did not eat. He became so fearless that he would sit close to them while they devoured the animals they had killed. His condition aroused the pity of the animals, and they always left something for him. Thus he lived on the kindness of the wolves until spring came. As soon as the lake was free from ice, he followed his new friends and companions to the shore.

Now it happened that his brother was fishing in his canoe, far out on the same lake, when he thought he heard the cry of a child. "How can any child live on this bleak shore?" he said to himself. He listened again, and he thought he heard the cry repeated. Paddling toward the shore as quickly as possible, he saw and recognized his little brother. The young one was singing, "My brother, my brother! I am now turning into a wolf. I am turning into a wolf!"

At the end of his song, he howled like a wolf. His brother, approaching, was shocked to find him half a wolf and half a human being. Leaping to the shore, the older brother tried to catch him in his arms. Soothingly he said, "My brother, my brother, come to me!"

But the boy fled, still singing as he ran, "I am turning into a wolf! I am turning into a wolf!" And at the end of his song he howled a terrifying howl.

Conscience-stricken, feeling his love return to his heart, the older brother called to him, "My brother, O my brother! Come back to me!"

But the nearer he came to the child, the more rapidly the change to a wolf took place. Still the younger brother sang his song, and still he howled. Sometimes he called on his brother, and sometimes he called on his sister. When the change was complete, he ran toward the wood. He knew that he was a wolf. "I am a wolf! I am a wolf!" he cried, as he bounded out of sight.

The older brother, all the rest of his life, felt a gnawing sense of guilt. And the sister, when she heard what had happened to her little brother, remembered with grief the promise she had solemnly made to their father. She wept many tears and never ceased to mourn until her death.

How Sun, Moon, and Wind Went Out to Dinner

by Joseph Jacobs

One day Sun, Moon, and Wind went out to dine with their uncle and aunt, Thunder and Lightning. Their mother (one of the most distant Stars you see far up in the sky) waited alone for her children's return.

Now both Sun and Wind were greedy and selfish. They enjoyed the great feast that had been prepared for them, without a thought of saving any of it for their mother. But the gentle Moon did not forget her. Of every dainty dish that was brought round, she placed a small portion under one of her beautiful long fingernails, that Star might also have a share in the treat.

On their return, their mother, who had kept watch for them all night long with her little bright eye, said, "Well, children, what have you brought home for me?" Then Sun (who was eldest) said, "I have brought nothing home for you. I went out to enjoy myself with my friends—not to fetch a dinner for my mother!" And Wind said, "Neither have I brought anything home for you, Mother. You could hardly expect me to bring a collection of good things for you, when I merely went out for my own pleasure." But Moon said, "Mother, fetch a plate, see what I have brought you." And shaking her hands she showered down such a choice dinner as never was seen before.

Then Star turned to Sun and spoke thus, "Because you went out to amuse yourself with your friends, and feasted and enjoyed yourself, without any thought of your mother at home—you shall be cursed. Henceforth, your rays shall ever be hot and scorching, and shall burn all that they touch. And men shall hate you, and cover their heads when you appear."

And that is why the Sun is so hot to this day.

Then she turned to Wind and said, "You also who forgot your mother in the midst of your selfish pleasures—hear your doom. You shall always blow in the hot dry weather, and shall parch and shrivel all living things. And men shall detest and avoid you from this very time."

And that is why the Wind in hot weather is still so disagreeable.

But to Moon she said, "Daughter, because you remembered your mother, and kept for her a share in your own enjoyment, from henceforth you shall be ever cool, and calm, and bright. No noxious glare shall accompany your pure rays, and men shall always call you 'blessed.'"

And that is why the moon's light is so soft, and cool, and beautiful even to this day.

Now answer Numbers 49 through 56 using the Answer Sheet on page 31. Base your answers on the folktales "Forsaken Brother" and "How Sun, Moon, and Wind Went Out to Dinner."

49 What problem do the older children face in "Forsaken Brother"?

- A. They made a promise to take care of their younger brother.
- B. They had to take care of their brother, whom they did not like.
- C. They lost their father and mother before they could survive alone.
- D. They told their father and mother they would not associate with others.

50 When the first spring came, how was the sister in "Forsaken Brother" DIFFERENT from the older brother?

- F. She felt more love for the younger brother.
- G. She felt more ready to go visit the other villages.
- H. She felt less concern for the younger brother's needs.
- I. She felt less obligated to keep her word to her parents.

51 How did the sister in "Forsaken Brother" change over time?

- A. She became weak and lazy.
- B. She turned mean and angry.
- C. She grew lonely and restless.
- D. She became kind and thoughtful.

52 How did the older brother in "Forsaken Brother" feel when he found the younger brother on the shore of the lake?

- F. angry
- G. happy
- H. relieved
- I. ashamed

53 Why did the author write "Forsaken Brother"?

- A. to show that people need to take care of themselves
- B. to explain why it is not always easy to keep a promise
- C. to demonstrate that sisters make better caretakers than brothers
- D. to teach the importance of taking care of one's family members

54 In "How Sun, Moon, and Wind Went Out to Dinner," which word describes both Sun and Wind?

- F. helpful
- G. uncaring
- H. grateful
- I. spoiled

55 What happened to Moon as a result of how she treated her mother?

- A. She became dark.
- B. She became hated.
- C. She became cursed.
- D. She became beautiful.

56 What is the theme of both folktales?

- F. People should think of others' needs as well as their own.
- G. People should follow their desires.
- H. People should not be surprised when others let them down.
- I. People should not rely on other people to get what they need.

Chapter One

Reading Effectively

Benchmark: L.A.A.1.4.2

The student uses a variety of strategies to analyze words and text, draw conclusions, use context and word structure clues, and recognize organizational patterns.

Chelsea was getting ready to audition for a school play. The role she hoped to get was that of Julie, whom the script described as "a girl who loves to dress 'retro-seventies.'" Chelsea wasn't sure what that meant, until she remembered from her vocabulary lessons that as a prefix, *retro-* means "past." She finished practicing Julie's lines from the play, then asked her mother if she could borrow some of the clothes from the 1970s she'd been hanging onto. When Chelsea showed up at the audition looking like she'd just stepped off a disco dance floor, the drama teacher was thrilled. Knowing she looked the part, Chelsea gave a great audition and was given the role of Julie.

Even though Chelsea had never seen the word "retro-seventies" before, she was able to figure out what it meant. In her language arts classes, Chelsea had learned how to use prefixes and suffixes to figure out a word's meaning. This turned out to be an important skill. Instead of knowing only the vocabulary words she had been taught in class, she was able to figure out the meaning of many unknown words on her own.

33

WHY STUDY THIS?

On the FCAT, you will find the same types of reading materials as you do in everyday life. You might, for example, be asked to read a magazine article about a new medical breakthrough. Or you might find yourself reading a newspaper story about the discovery of ancient treasures. Poems, textbook readings, short stories, and even letters are among the many forms of writing you will run into. These are all made up of words, so a strategy that helps you figure out word meanings is a valuable tool.

Understanding, however, is more than just figuring out the meanings of words. In order to understand something, you must evaluate, analyze, synthesize, and draw conclusions about the information in the text. This is called reading *actively*.

For example, suppose you read the statement, "The bald eagle is the largest and most beautiful bird in the world." If you are reading actively, you might have these thoughts about what you just read:

- Analyze: "Wait a minute! Did they say the bald eagle is a 'large' bird or the 'largest' bird? Let's see . . . They say it's the 'largest.'"
- Synthesize: "I'm pretty sure my science book said that the California condor is really big, and I know from that TV special I saw that ostriches are huge."
- Evaluate: "I'm not sure this writer got the facts straight!"
- Draw conclusions: "The writer says that the bald eagle is the 'most beautiful' bird. He or she must really love bald eagles."

Active readers use the power of *inference* to understand what they read.

Inference

As you read, you gather and process information. When you add this new information to what you already know, you are able to make *inferences* and draw conclusions. These inferences and conclusions help you understand the selection's meaning and purpose.

Think Of It This Way

> Information from the selection + Your own knowledge ⟶ Inference

To infer is to add information you read to your own knowledge and experience to make an educated guess. Making inferences means reaching an understanding about what you read that is not printed right there on the page.

Here is an example:

> **Statement:** Jessica frosts a cake and places 14 candles on top.
> **Inference:** The cake is for someone's birthday.

Although inferences are based on facts, they go far beyond facts. Often, you can draw more than one inference from a single statement or set of facts. You must use your judgment to come up with the inference that makes the most sense. Here's an example:

> **Fact:** Miguel went to school and found the doors locked, the lights out, and no one there.
>
> **Inference A:** Miguel forgot that it was a school holiday.
>
> **Inference B:** School was canceled because of a power outage.
>
> **Inference C:** Miguel mistakenly thought it was Monday, not Sunday.

Can you infer another explanation why no one was at school?

Your inference: _____

As you can see, all of these inferences could be true. Yet logic tells you that only one is actually true. Your job as a reader is to make the correct inference. Luckily, the material you read will usually give you enough clues so that making the correct inference is easy. The techniques you will learn in this chapter will help you analyze words, sentences, and paragraphs in anything you read.

Technique 1: Analyzing Word Parts

Many words in the English language are actually combinations of words (or parts of words) from other languages, such as Latin or Greek.

Key Concepts

- **Prefix:** A *prefix* is a word part that can be placed in front of a word. A prefix changes the word's meaning.
- **Suffix:** A *suffix* is a word part that can be placed at the end of a word. A suffix changes the word's meaning.
- **Root:** The *root* is the main part of the word, to which prefixes or suffixes may be added. Sometimes a root can stand alone as a word.

Some words are formed with a prefix at the front, a suffix at the end, and another word part between them. The part of the word between the prefix and the suffix is called the *root*. Here are some examples of the way words can be built in the English language.

> root + suffix = word (Examples: doable, thinking, trying)
> prefix + root = word (Examples: redo, rethink, retry)
> prefix + root + suffix = word (Examples: redoing, rethinking, retrying)

See if you can find the seven prefixes and suffixes in this sentence:

> The weatherman restated his forecast and my hopeful heart sank: The coach would probably be postponing the game.

In the next section you will find lists of some of the most commonly used prefixes and suffixes. Learn as many of these word parts as you can. The more prefixes and suffixes that you know, the better you will be able to figure out unfamiliar words.

Prefixes

Sometimes you identify word meanings by taking a word apart without even realizing it. For example, when you see the word *replay*, you can probably assume automatically that it means "play again." You know this because you have seen the prefix re- in so many words, such as *repeat* or *reconnect*. Your best chance of identifying words and increasing your vocabulary through the use of prefixes is to memorize the word parts and be familiar with how they are used.

COMMONLY USED PREFIXES AND THEIR MEANINGS

Number-Related Prefixes

prefix	meaning	example	explanation
semi-	half	semicircle	*half* of a circle
uni-	one	unicycle	*one*-wheeled cycle
bi-	two	bicycle	*two*-wheeled cycle
tri-	three	tricycle	*three*-wheeled cycle
dec-	ten	decimal	system of *tens*
cent-	one hundred	centimeter	*hundredth* of a meter

Time-Related Prefixes

prefix	meaning	example	explanation
ante-	before	antecedent	coming *before*
fore-	before	forethought	think of something *before* it happens
pre-	before	predate	date *before*
post-	after	postdate	date *after*
re-	again	recycle	use *again*
retro-	past	retroactive	active after a *past* date

Position-Related Prefixes

prefix	meaning	example	explanation
circum-	around	circumnavigate	sail *around*
para-	beside	parallel lines	*beside* each other
peri-	around	periscope	tool for viewing *around* something

Other Commonly Used Prefixes

prefix	meaning	example	explanation
co-	together	coordinate	move *together*
contra-	against	contradict	argue *against*
hyper-	extremely	hyperactive	*extremely* active
in-	not	incapable	*not* able to
non-	not	nonessential	*not* important
pro-	forward	proceed	go *forward*
sub-	under	submarine	*under* the sea
trans-	across	transport	bring *across*

Suffixes

What is the difference between *joyful* and *joyless*? Look at the suffixes. With the suffix *-ful*, the word means that there is joy. With the suffix *-less*, the word means that there is no joy. One small suffix added to the end of a word can make a very big difference. A suffix also can change a word's part of speech. It can, in other words, change a verb to an adverb. It can also change present tense to past tense, or singular to plural. Here are some examples:

Word	Part of Speech	Add Suffix	New Word	New Part of Speech
quick	adjective	-ly	quickly	adverb
travel	verb (present tense)	-ed	traveled	verb (past tense)
alligator	noun (singular)	-s	alligators	noun (plural)

COMMONLY USED SUFFIXES AND THEIR MEANINGS

Noun Suffixes (People)

suffix	meaning	example	explanation
-ant	person who	servant	*person who* serves
-ent	person who	student	*person who* studies
-er	person who	runner	*person who* runs
-ist	person who	dentist	*person who* works with teeth
-ster	person who	youngster	*person who* is young
-ee	person who	employee	*person who* is employed

Noun Suffixes (Places or Things)

suffix	meaning	example	explanation
-ance	act of	acceptance	*act of* accepting
-ation	state of	starvation	*state of* starving
-cy	state of	literacy	*state of* being literate
-ion	action, result	fusion	*act of* being fused together
-ity	state of	nobility	*state of* being noble
-ment	state of	disappointment	*state of* being disappointed
-ty	state of	safety	*state of* being safe

Adjective Suffixes

suffix	meaning	example	explanation
-able	able, likely	capable	*able* to do something
-en	made of	wooden	*made of* wood
-ful	full of	thankful	*full* of thanks
-ish	like	childish	*like* a child
-like	like	dreamlike	*like* a dream
-ly	like	motherly	*like* a mother
-less	without	hopeless	*without* hope
-y	showing	wavy	*showing* waves

Try to match the prefixes and suffixes on the left with their meanings on the right (without looking back at the tables!).

1. cent-   _____ state of
2. -ster   _____ beside
3. contra-   _____ person who
4. -ty   _____ one hundred
5. para-   _____ against

Technique 2: Using Context Clues

What if you are reading and you come across an unfamiliar word that you can't identify by its prefix or suffix? This is when your ability to infer, or draw conclusions, comes in handy.

Without realizing it, you are still learning new words. Often you learn them through *context*, or the words around the unfamiliar word. For example, if you see the word *intrepid* on a vocabulary list, and you are not familiar with it, you need to look up its definition in order to understand it. However, if you hear the word *intrepid* used in context, you might be able to guess its meaning. The sentence, "Mayor Peterson awarded two intrepid firefighters with the mayor's Medal of Courage for entering a burning house to rescue a mother dog and her litter of puppies," gives you a clue to the meaning of the word *intrepid*. You know that to enter a burning house requires bravery. Also, the sentence says the firefighters were receiving a Medal of Courage. You can therefore guess that *intrepid* means "brave." The context of the word has helped you to understand its meaning.

Often a writer includes a description of the unfamiliar word in a sentence. Here are some sentences that are designed to explain the meaning of an unfamiliar word. As you read each example, use the other words in the sentence to help you figure out the meaning of the underlined word. You can check the list of definitions under the examples to see if you are correct.

1. Some species of monkeys are <u>semiarboreal</u>, coming down from the treetops fairly often in the course of the day. _____

2. Kim's old neighborhood is experiencing an amazing <u>renaissance</u>, with new homes, shops, and businesses popping up everywhere. _____

3. Chris's brother was disappointed that no one noticed his new mustache, but it was so wispy that the change in his appearance was <u>imperceptible</u>. _____

4. After getting hired at Burger Hut, Justin's schedule became <u>burdensome</u> as he struggled under the weight of his homework, chores, and job commitments. _____

5. Libertyville is celebrating its <u>centennial</u> with a parade featuring 100 floats, one for each year of the town's existence. _____

Reading Effectively

Definitions

1. <u>semiarboreal</u>: living only part of the time in trees
2. <u>renaissance</u>: a renewal; act of being reborn or being given new life
3. <u>imperceptible</u>: unnoticeable
4. <u>burdensome</u>: overwhelming, heavy
5. <u>centennial</u>: one-hundred-year anniversary

Sometimes a writer uses contrast to describe an unfamiliar word in a sentence. In these cases, it should be clear from the context that the word you do not know means the opposite of the words you know. Here are some sentences that use contrast or opposites to describe other words.

1. In my theater class, Mrs. Grant would not allow us to make <u>disparaging</u> remarks about another student's performance; we could give only encouraging feedback. _____

2. Life in <u>antebellum</u> Georgia was much different from life there after the war. _____

3. Lupita was the most <u>loquacious</u> girl I had ever met, but it was impossible to get more than two words out of her brother Mario. _____

4. Bill and his neighbor settled their disagreement in an <u>amicable</u> manner, without exchanging a single unpleasant word. _____

5. Sam's <u>jubilation</u> at winning the football championship turned to sadness when he learned that the quarterback on the opposing team had been seriously injured. _____

Definitions

1. <u>disparaging</u>: insulting, sharply critical
2. <u>antebellum</u>: before war
3. <u>loquacious</u>: talkative
4. <u>amicable</u>: friendly, pleasant
5. <u>jubilation</u>: happiness

In every profession, there are special words used to describe certain things that only people who are in that profession are expected to understand. These special words are called "technical terms." For example, in medicine there are words for diseases and medications that doctors and nurses need to understand. Lawyers and legal secretaries must be familiar with the language used in contracts. Anyone who works with computers must know the many terms that are used in computer-related conversations. When a writer writes for people who do not know these technical terms, he or she often explains the term in the context of the sentence.

Here are examples:

1. <u>Amphibians</u>, such as frogs and salamanders, begin life in the water and use gills to breathe; as adults, they are able to live out of the water, using lungs to breathe the air. _____

2. Before moving to a foreign country, pet owners should research the country's <u>quarantine</u> policy to find out how long their furry friend will have to be kept by government authorities to make sure it has no infectious diseases. _____

3. As you write your research paper, be sure to use your own words to avoid <u>plagiarizing</u> what others have written. _____

4. When the man who really ran into the fire hydrant turned himself in, Ross was <u>acquitted</u> and released from jail. _____

5. In Louisiana, some people speak a <u>dialect</u> of French called Cajun, which is a fascinating mixture of French, English, Indian, and African words, grammar, and pronunciation. _____

Definitions

1. <u>amphibians</u>: animals that live in water and breathe with gills when young, but live on land and breathe with lungs as adults

2. <u>quarantine</u>: a time period in which animals are isolated to prevent the spread of disease
3. <u>plagiarizing</u>: stealing the words and ideas of others and pretending they are your own
4. <u>acquitted</u>: found not guilty
5. <u>dialect</u>: a regional variety of language

SEEING IT IN ACTION

Now let's use some of the concepts you have learned in this chapter. Read the following paragraph and answer the questions that follow.

Which Puppy for You?

Yes! After weeks and weeks of <u>incessant</u> nagging, morning, noon, and night, you have finally convinced your parents that you need a dog. But, of the hundreds of breeds of dogs out there, how do you know which one is right for you? You might think that the basset hound is the most adorable creature on four paws, but did you know that they are <u>notorious</u> for heavy drooling? That's not what I'd like to be known for! So, before you fall in love with the first puppy you see, do some homework to find out the positive and negative characteristics of the breed you're considering. Also, think about your own personality: Do you have the tendency to spend weekends sprawled on the couch watching sports? Then be sure to get a dog who has a similar "couch potato" personality, rather than one who'd rather be out there chasing a ball himself than watching people chase them on TV. And be ready to make room on the couch for him!

1. What does the word *incessant* mean as used in this passage?

    A. annoying
    B. intelligent
    C. thoughtful
    D. nonstop

2. What does the word *notorious* mean as used in this passage?

    F. famous for something bad
    G. admired for a special trait
    H. respected for a certain talent
    I. feared for a good reason

The best way to answer the first question is to test each answer choice to see if it makes sense. Remember, other words in the sentence can clue you in to the definition of the unknown word. First, look at the sentence that contains the word:

> "After weeks and weeks of <u>incessant</u> nagging, morning, noon, and night, you have finally convinced your parents that you need a dog."

The word *incessant* is an adjective: It tells what your nagging was like. Now look for clues in the rest of the sentence that will help you figure out what *incessant* means:

> The nagging went on for "weeks and weeks."
> The nagging took place "morning, noon, and night."

These clues should help you figure out the meaning of *incessant*. Another clue is the prefix *in-*, which means "not." From this prefix, you know that the correct answer will have something to do with the idea of not doing something. Keep this in mind as you try out all the answers in the question to see which one makes the most sense. The right answer choice will be the one that makes sense when plugged into the sentence below:

> After weeks and weeks of _____ nagging, morning, noon, and night, you have finally convinced your parents that you need a dog.

Does it make sense that the writer's nagging was annoying? Yes, but remember that the word has the prefix *in-*. Being annoying doesn't have anything to do with *not* doing something, so A is incorrect. Is nagging usually thought of as an intelligent thing to do? No, it's usually not a smart way to get what you want, so B is incorrect. Nagging is not a very thoughtful way to treat people either, so C is incorrect. After trying out each of these answers, you may conclude that D, nonstop, is correct. It even has the prefix *non-*, which also means "not"!

Reading Effectively

To answer Question 2, you need to read the next sentence in the passage to find a clue to what *notorious* means:

> "You might think that the basset hound is the most adorable creature on four paws, but did you know that they are <u>notorious</u> for heavy drooling? That's not what I'd like to be known for!"

The writer doesn't want to be known for "heavy drooling." The answer that best matches this idea is F, famous for something bad. Trying out the other answers lets you know for sure that F is the correct answer.

Read "You Want to Be *What* When You Grow Up?" Then answer the questions that follow.

You Want to Be *What* When You Grow Up?

When most men get ready for work, they put on a suit and tie or other serious *garb*, such as a uniform. When Barry Anderson gets ready for work, he puts on a bull costume, complete with horns and a tail. Anderson is one of an elite group of people who have chosen the unique career path of professional team mascot.

Anderson got his start at the University of Montana, where he performed for Montana Grizzly fans as Monte, a break-dancing, back-flipping bear. He threw himself into the role with such enthusiasm that he won the Capitol One National Mascot of the Year award in 2002 and caught the attention of professional sports teams. Now, as a mascot for the Chicago Bulls basketball team, Anderson continues to fire up fans with his comic cheerleading, tricky stunts, and sly dance moves.

When team mascots first began entertaining at sporting events, coaches worried that they would be too distracting for fans. They soon realized that mascots did not *detract from* the games, but instead made the games even more enjoyable and exciting.

Being a team mascot can be quite lucrative: Mascots for professional basketball teams can make over $100,000 a year. But there are drawbacks. Mascots are sometimes injured, either from stunts, or from interactions with angry fans or team players. In 1995, Phoenix Suns' player Charles Barkley slugged Denver Nuggets' mascot Rocky the Mountain Lion, after the mascot pretended to challenge Barkley to a boxing match. (They later made up.) But if you love sports, enjoy being the center of attention, and don't mind dressing up as a giant stuffed animal, then you might consider a career as a professional team mascot.

1. What does the word *garb* mean as used in the passage?

    A. litter

    B. shoes

    C. clothing

    D. briefcase

FCAT Fred Says:

Don't be fooled by choice A, litter! The word *garb* might look like the word *garbage*, but they're two entirely different things (unless you're into the grunge look!).

2. What does the phrase *detract from* mean?

    F. make fun of

    G. give importance to

    H. help improve upon

    I. take away from

Now read to see how one student answered these questions.

1. The sentence tells about men going to work wearing a suit and tie, a uniform, or other such garb. A suit, a tie, and a uniform are all kinds of clothing. Therefore, the meaning of the word garb is "clothing."

2. The prefix de- in detract means "away" or "from." Choice I has both of these words in it, and "take away from" makes more sense than the other answers. Therefore, the answer is "take away from."

THE AMERICAN COWBOY
by Amy Bunin Kaiman

Read the article "The American Cowboy" before answering Numbers 1 through 8.

No other figure in American history has been as integral to myth, legend, and romance as the American cowboy. The story of this lone figure, rugged and free, has been sung, told, written, filmed, and painted. The image of the rough-and-ready cowboy, with his horse for company and his cattle to protect, has captured the hearts of the American people. The reality of the cowboy's experience, however, was often quite different from the myth.

Cattle were introduced to the New World by the Spanish in the seventeenth century. The first cowboys were actually Mexicans, who were trained by Spanish cattlemen, or *vaqueros*. The Spanish tradition still lingers in the language of the cowboy trade. The lariat, used for roping cattle, comes from the Spanish *la reata*. The heavy leather leggings, or chaps, that cowboys wore to protect their breeches came from the Spanish *chapparal*, and the ponies' bridles were called "hackamores," from the Spanish *jaquima*. The Spanish left their mark on the cowboy's clothing as well. High-heeled durable leather boots, designed to slip easily into stirrups, were worn by the Spanish *vaqueros* long before "cowboy boots" came into vogue. The bandanna, a multi-purpose scrap of cloth, was also worn by *vaqueros*. Later, cowboys found that the bandanna could be used for a handkerchief, a sling, a lunch holder, or a face mask to protect them from the dust raised by thousands of hooves beating on dry ground.

The original cowboys had a fairly low-key job. They stayed primarily on the large Spanish-style ranches that flourished throughout Texas and much of the Southwest. The real heyday of the cowboy, however, began shortly after the Civil War. Cowboys were needed to drive the cattle from Texas to railheads in the Midwest, where the cattle were loaded onto trains and shipped to Kansas City, Chicago, and St. Louis. Although the legend of the lonesome cowboy seems as old as America, the actual period of cowboys on the trail was only about 20 years, from the 1860 to the 1880s.

The cowboys who rode the ranges during those 20 years were the ones who left their mark on American history and mythology. They came from all over the country, particularly the South where young single men were looking for work. Many black Americans found opportunity and acceptance on the open range. The

Western ranches were one of the few places after the Civil War where hiring was based on the ability to perform the job well, rather than on skin color or family origin.

The cowboy's work began in the spring. The first job was to round up the cattle and herd them into pens. The cattle were then separated by their brands, the marks burned into their sides by hot irons. Young calves had to be branded with the same symbol as their mothers. Each ranch in Texas had its own distinctive brand registered with the Cattleman's Association. Unbranded cattle could be claimed and branded by any rancher who found them. An enterprising cowboy named Sam Maverick built so many herds this way that unbranded cattle became known as "mavericks."

After roundup and branding, the cowboys saddled up their ponies and hit the trail. Small herds of about 1,000 cattle could be handled by 4 or 5 cowhands, but they often joined up with larger groups and traveled together. The cattle were driven as much as 1,500 miles through the open range, a journey that could take several months. Cowboys were not paid until they reached the railhead, and they were known for their wild celebrations at the end of the trail. Some of the more ambitious cowboys took their pay in cattle and became ranchers themselves.

Now answer Numbers 1 through 8. Base your answers on the article "The American Cowboy."

1 What can you infer about the *vaqueros* from the design of their boots?

- **A.** They rode horses to herd cattle.
- B. They were skilled leather craftsmen.
- C. They often worked in snowy weather.
- D. They risked being injured by the cattle.

2 Why did cowboys MOST likely have to drive their cattle to railheads in the Midwest?

- F. Midwest railheads were more reliable.
- G. There were very few railheads in Texas.
- H. Railheads in the Midwest were more convenient.
- **I.** It cost less to ship cattle from Midwest railheads.

3 What is another word that uses the suffix *-ance* with the same meaning as in *acceptance*?

- A. distance
- **B.** instance
- C. freelance
- D. performance

Reading Effectively

4 What does the word *distinctive* mean as used in the sentence below?

Each ranch in Texas had its own distinctive brand registered with the Cattleman's Association.

- F. unique ✓
- G. familiar
- H. colorful
- I. permanent

5 If a person were called a *maverick*, what phrase would also describe his or her personality?

- A. tense and worried
- B. careful and cautious ✓
- C. kind and considerate
- D. free and independent

6 What is the MOST likely reason cowboys were not paid until they reached the railhead?

- F. so that they would not spend all their money along the way
- G. so that they could be paid based on how they did on the trail ✓
- H. to make sure that everyone received the same amount of pay
- I. to make sure they would not quit in the middle of the cattle drive

7 Which two words from the article have about the same meaning?

- A. primarily/shortly
- B. opportunity/origin ✓
- C. history/mythology
- D. enterprising/ambitious

8 What is another word that uses the prefix *un-* with the same meaning as in *unbranded*?

- F. united
- G. unusual ✓
- H. universe
- I. unnoticed

Read the article "Triumph of the Imagination: The Story of Writer J. K. Rowling" before answering Numbers 1 through 8.

TRIUMPH OF THE IMAGINATION: THE STORY OF WRITER J. K. ROWLING

by Lisa A. Chippendale

Despite being unemployed, Joanne [Rowling] had little opportunity to write. Her infant daughter required almost constant care, and she hated writing in her freezing, gloomy apartment. She didn't give up, however. She just found a creative solution. Every day she put Jessica in her baby carriage and walked around Edinburgh until Jessica fell asleep. Then she would head for a local café, buy a cup of espresso and a glass of water, and write for a few hours while Jessica slept nearby.

Not all café owners appreciated her sitting for hours in their establishment, having ordered only one cup of coffee. Joanne began to frequent Nicolson's Café, a new coffeehouse partly owned by her brother-in-law. The staff was kind to her and let her sit for hours, nursing her coffee and her water as she painstakingly churned out page after page of Harry Potter's story in long hand. When she ran out of paper, she would scribble her ideas on napkins.

Joanne continued to revise relentlessly. In fact, she later admitted in an interview for BBC Online that only once did she write a chapter completely right the first time through. "That was the chapter in *Philosopher's Stone* when Harry learns to fly. I remember vividly—the old story we've heard a million times, my daughter fell asleep, it was a beautifully sunny day, I sat in a café, and wrote that chapter from beginning to end. And I think I changed two words."

After nearly a year Joanne finished her manuscript and began the long process of typing it. She used a cheap manual typewriter, which she had scrimped to buy for $63, or the computer lab at the college where she was taking her teaching classes. "I was terrified that people would discover that I wasn't doing my course work," she said in *Telling Tales*. She had to type up two copies of the manuscript because she didn't have any spare money for photocopying it, which would have cost quite a bit. A typical children's novel is about 40,000 words—and *Harry Potter and the Philosopher's Stone* was twice that long.

Finally, in 1995, after five years of writing and rewriting, Joanne was finished with the novel. She could hardly believe it. Now it was time to take the next step: getting published. After spending some time in the library looking up agents and publishers, Joanne chose one of each.

After weeks of waiting, Joanne was disappointed when she received both copies of her manuscript back with rejection letters. Undaunted, Joanne sent three sample chapters out to another agent, Christopher Little, whom she picked because she liked his name.

Her package landed on the desk of Bryony Evans, Christopher Little's office manager. She was intrigued by the story, although the agency did not normally handle children's books. Soon she asked Rowling to send in the rest of the manuscript. Rowling complied, and Evans quickly read the entire book. She loved it.

On her recommendation Christopher Little read the book, finishing it in one night, and the agency wrote back to Rowling within days. They offered to represent the manuscript and requested some minor revisions. Evans wanted Neville, a bumbling but kindhearted friend of Harry's, to play more of a role. Little wanted Joanne to explain Quidditch more thoroughly.

Joanne ranks receiving Little's letter as one of the high points of her life. After opening it, she read it eight times. According to Evans, Rowling wrote back and said, "That's brilliant because I like Neville, and, oh great, I can put the rules of Quidditch back in."

Still, Joanne knew that representation by an agent didn't guarantee a sale to a publisher. She would have to be patient. Plus, Little cautioned her not to expect much money.

Children's books rarely earned their authors more than $3,000 to $4,000. That didn't bother Rowling. All she wanted was to be able to make ends meet so she could keep on writing.

Now answer Numbers 1 through 8. Base your answers on the article "Triumph of the Imagination: The Story of Writer J. K. Rowling."

1 Why were most café owners unhappy that Joanne spent time writing in their cafés?

   A. She bothered other customers with her writing.
   B. Her daughter upset customers with her crying.
   C. They didn't make much money off her as a customer.
   D. They didn't know she would some day be a famous author.

2 What does the word *frequent* mean as used in the sentence below?

   Joanne began to frequent Nicolson's Café, a new coffeehouse partly owned by her brother-in-law.

   F. many times
   G. few occasions
   H. visit a place rarely
   I. go to a place often

3 What is another word that uses the prefix *re-* with the same meaning as in *revise*?

   A. regret
   B. review
   C. resting
   D. receive

4 What is another word that uses the suffix *-ly* with the same meaning as in *vividly*?

   F. holy
   G. early
   H. family
   I. gently

5 Why was Joanne "terrified" that people would find out she was typing her book in the school's computer lab?

   A. because she was not a student at that school
   B. because the computers were for schoolwork only
   C. because she felt guilty for not doing her homework
   D. because she didn't want others to read her book yet

6 Read the sentences below.

   Soon she asked Rowling to send in the rest of the manuscript. Joanne complied and Evans quickly read the entire book.

   What does the word *complied* mean?

   F. refused to do
   G. offered to do
   H. did as requested
   I. complained about

7 What is the MOST likely reason that Christopher Little finished Joanne's book in one night?

   A. He liked it so much he couldn't put it down.
   B. He wanted to give Joanne an answer as quickly as possible.
   C. The book was very short compared to most children's books.
   D. The book was not the kind that his company normally handled.

8 Why did Joanne read Little's letter eight times?

   F. She had trouble understanding Little's letter.
   G. She was happy and excited to receive Little's letter.
   H. She wanted to make sure she revised her book correctly.
   I. She could not believe her book would now be published.

Read the article "Manatees" before answering Numbers 1 through 8.

Manatees

Manatee Introduction and Background

The geological time scale for the Earth covers the past three and one half billion years. The period of time when manatees appeared (50 to 60 million years ago) is known as the Eocene, and it is very recently compared with the evolution of better-known creatures such as the dinosaurs.

Manatees are large marine mammals, streamlined in shape, with adults averaging 1,000 to as much as 1,500 pounds in weight, and an adult length of about 12 feet. Manatees and their living relatives today inhabit coastal estuarine systems within the boundaries of the tropics.

Manatee migration in North Florida is seasonal and prompted chiefly by changes in water temperature. In South Florida, however, a second reason for manatee migration takes precedence, which is the need for fresh or low salinity drinking water.

Near the middle of Florida's West Coast, a tributary called the Crystal River flows for about seven miles into the Gulf of Mexico. At the headwaters of the river are several major springs, from which hundreds of millions of gallons of clear, 72-degree water flows year-round.

When winter begins, and the waters of the Gulf of Mexico turn colder, two hundred or more manatees migrate up the river to Kings Bay, Florida, where they expect to find shelter in the relatively warm, fresh water.

In recent years the influx of manatees has increased significantly, a fact that may be related to environmental troubles manatees are facing in other parts of the state.

For regional manatees, finding warm waters is a matter of survival-to stay in the cold Gulf of Mexico could mean catching a respiratory illness, the most common natural cause of death among the manatee.

Many of these gentle creatures also spend their summers in the Crystal River area, but at that time of year they tend to widely disperse in the adjacent waters of the Gulf of Mexico, and are difficult to find.

Since Kings Bay supports the largest wintertime concentration of manatees in the United States, it has become a popular destination for tourists interested in learning more about these charming wild animals.

Manatees, People, and the Buddy System

The manatee is generally a very curious animal, and often seems to seek playful activity with man and inanimate objects. They like to scratch themselves on poles, boat bottoms, and ropes. They touch, bump, scratch, roll over, and behave in ways that humans find irresistibly charming.

In recent years, manatee-gathering places such as Crystal River have become extremely popular destinations for people who want to experience an encounter with a huge, wild, marine animal.

Yet most manatees do not seek interaction with people. They often move away when swimmers approach, and manatee females, or cows, are especially careful to not let strangers come too close to their calves.

Pursuing or harassing the manatees constitutes a breach of federal endangered-species protection laws, and is punishable by heavy fines.

These protection efforts were necessary in Florida because people sometimes behaved in ways that we now believe were highly inappropriate—pursuing animals in boats, trying to hold or "ride" the animals, and even sadistically injuring or killing them. In other parts of the world, manatees are hunted for food, but those days are probably over here in the U.S.

Still, manatee interactions with people continue to be a troublesome subject.

Because of the widespread concern for the protection of the manatees, each winter the U.S. Fish and Wildlife Service sets aside marked sanctuary areas in the Crystal River where boats, swimmers and divers are prohibited. However, there is relatively little difficulty seeing the manatees, since many of the animals roam freely outside the sanctuaries and are friendly with people.

But all visitors are asked to become educated on proper and legal behavior around the manatees, and when enforcement officers observe violations, fines are issued. Naturally, some long-time residents resent the restricted areas and sanctuaries, and consider all forms of behavior management or limited access a loss of freedom. Fortunately, the manatees themselves are so charming that most folks who observe and learn about them are pleased to cooperate with protection efforts.

Now answer Numbers 1 through 8. Base your answers on the article "Manatees."

1 What does the phrase *takes precedence* mean as used in the sentence below?

In South Florida, however, a second reason for manatee migration takes precedence, which is the need for fresh or low salinity drinking water.

   A. is unknown

   B. is less obvious

   C. is understandable

   D. is more important

2 What is another word that uses the prefix *in–* with the same meaning as in *influx*?

   F. include

   G. inactive

   H. informal

   I. incorrect

Reading Effectively

3 Which illness does the article suggest that manatees can catch in the Gulf of Mexico?

　　A. rabies
　　B. a cold
　　C. the flu
　　D. allergies

4 Read the sentences below.

The manatee is generally a very curious animal, and often seems to seek playful activity with man and inanimate objects. They like to scratch themselves on poles, boat bottoms, and ropes.

What does the word *inanimate* mean?

　　F. not real
　　G. not living
　　H. underwater
　　I. unbreakable

5 What can you infer about manatee females by how they react to swimmers that approach them?

　　A. They are easily tamed.
　　B. They are very friendly.
　　C. They are good mothers.
　　D. They are often dangerous.

6 Read the following sentence.

Pursuing or harassing the manatees constitutes a breach of federal endangered-species protection laws, and is punishable by heavy fines.

What does the phrase *a breach of* mean?

　　F. an interest in
　　G. a breaking of
　　H. an honoring of
　　I. a confusion about

7 What is another word that uses the suffix *-some* with the same meaning as in *troublesome*?

　　A. lonesome
　　B. foursome
　　C. handsome
　　D. chromosome

8 Read the following sentence.

> Because of the widespread concern for the protection of the manatees, each winter the U.S. Fish and Wildlife Service sets aside marked sanctuary areas in the Crystal River where boats, swimmers and divers are prohibited.

What does the word *prohibited* mean?

- F. not allowed
- G. not protected
- H. encouraged
- I. discouraged

MAKING SENSE OF IT

In this chapter you learned the building blocks of active reading. These concepts will be visited time and again in the upcoming chapters. Feel free to refer back to the tables listed in this chapter. Reviewing them often will help you to learn the material covered.

> Information from the selection + Your own knowledge ⟶ Inference
>
> **Prefix:** A *prefix* is a word part that can be placed in front of a word. A prefix changes the word's meaning.
>
> **Suffix:** A *suffix* is a word part that can be placed at the end of a word. A suffix changes the word's meaning.
>
> **Root:** The *root* is the main part of the word, to which prefixes or suffixes may be added. Sometimes a root can stand alone as a word.
>
> root + suffix = word
> (Examples: doable, thinking, trying)
>
> prefix + root = word
> (Examples: redo, rethink, retry)
>
> prefix + root + suffix = word
> (Examples: redoing, rethinking, untried)

Chapter Two

Knowing the Difference

Benchmark: L.A.A.2.2.7

The student recognizes the use of comparison and contrast in a text.

"Okay, okay, let me think about it, and I'll let you know tomorrow morning at school." Brandon put down his cell phone and picked up a notepad and pencil. That was his best friend Ramón calling to see if he was going to try out for the wrestling team. Brandon had been planning to go out for wrestling with Ramón, but then he had seen a poster at school advertising auditions for the school's choral group, Locomotion. Brandon had heard that the choral group was a lot of fun and that this winter they were traveling to California for a choral competition.

On the notepad, Brandon drew a three-column table. At the top of the second and third columns he wrote "Wrestling" and "Locomotion." In the first column, he listed the reasons why he wanted to do an after-school activity: have fun, make new guy friends, meet girls, travel in state, and travel out of state. Then he used the table to compare the activities. He saw that both wrestling and the choral group would be fun, but if he joined the wrestling team he would probably make guy friends but would not meet many girls. He would also have the chance to travel around the state, but probably not out of state. On the other hand, joining Locomotion gave him everything he was looking for in an after-school activity. That decided it. But now, how to break the news to Ramón?

As you can see from Brandon's example, the ability to compare and contrast can come in handy when it's time to make a decision. For Brandon, the decision involved choosing between two activities. For you it might mean choosing which book to read, which CD to buy, or even which multiple-choice answer is correct on the FCAT.

WHY STUDY THIS?

The world needs critical thinkers, people who can judge similarities and differences. For instance, clothing store buyers use these skills to choose between different fashions to sell at their stores. Teachers compare and contrast different textbooks in order to better teach their students. Even a stop at a vending machine requires you to use these skills. Would you buy a can of Shockwave soda (with "*twice* the sugar and *all* the caffeine!") or a bottle of Nature's Goodness sparkling mineral water ("as pure as the driven snow!")?

On the FCAT, the stories, articles, and other reading selections demand that you be a skilled critical thinker. Many of the multiple-choice questions will ask you to compare and contrast one or more of the following elements:

Element	Sample FCAT Question
Character	How are Tom Sawyer and Huck Finn alike?
Tone	How is the tone of "Casey at the Bat" different from the tone of *The Raven*?
Theme	Which of these statements expresses the theme of both *Island of the Blue Dolphins* and *Julie of the Wolves*?
Organizational pattern	How does the organization of "Computer Mania" differ from that of "I Didn't Recognize You Without Your Laptop"?
Author's purpose	How are the authors' purposes the same in both the story and the poem?
Point of view	How does the point of view in *The Outsiders* differ from the point of view in *The Incredible Journey*?
Setting	How are the settings of both the poem and the story alike?
Plot	How does the ending of *The Red Pony* differ from the ending of *The Yearling*?

Don't worry if you are unfamiliar with some of these text elements; the chapters ahead will cover them all.

Key Concepts

- **Compare:** to identify similarities (Examples: Life is like a river. Both my little sister and my big brother drive me crazy! Jack London's *Call of the Wild* and *White Fang* are equally good.)
- **Contrast:** to identify differences (Examples: My math class is interesting; however, I almost always fall asleep in my history class. Unlike most *normal* people, Jenna actually enjoyed doing the dishes. Spanish differs from English in that you always pronounce all the letters in a word; whereas in English, some words, such as *knife* and *numb*, have silent letters.)

THINK OF IT THIS WAY

There are some key words that authors use to signal that a comparison or contrast is being made.

Words that signal a comparison					
as	like	likewise	similar	just like	same
also	alike	resembles	just as	equally	both

Words that signal a contrast			
however	in contrast	instead	different from
although	yet	unlike	on the other hand
whereas	differs from	on the contrary	

While the ability to identify similarities and differences is important, it is only the first step in the decision-making process. The next step involves organizing this information into something useful.

SEEING IT IN ACTION

Remember Brandon? When he was faced with a problem that required him to compare and contrast, he used a table to help him organize the information. The comparison table he drew on his notepad probably looked something like this:

Reasons for Doing an After-school Activity	Wrestling	Locomotion
Have fun	Yes	Yes
Make new guy friends	Yes	Yes
Meet girls	No	Yes
Travel in-state	Yes	Yes
Travel out of state	No	Yes

But a comparison table is good for more than just comparing two activities. It can help you when you read, as well. Read the two paragraphs that follow and then note how a comparison table can be used to answer questions that follow.

Selecting a Kayak

When selecting a kayak, the most important consideration is function. Not all kayaks are alike. They are crafted in different styles to make them perform best in specific paddling situations. How do you plan to use your kayak? Do you want to whale-watch or explore islands that are some distance apart? Then choose a sea kayak. Sea kayaks are longer and skinnier than other kayaks, and they have a deeper hull. This allows the boat to cut through the water more easily and lets you go farther and faster without tiring. They have a closed cockpit, meaning that the paddler sits inside the boat and uses a spray skirt to keep water from swamping the kayak. They also have roomy waterproof hatches for storing cameras, backpacks, and other gear you might need for longer voyages.

On the other hand, if you long to "shoot the rapids," a white-water kayak is for you. Like a sea kayak, white-water kayaks have a closed cockpit, andpaddlers use a spray skirt. But white-water kayaksdiffer from sea kayaks in that they are shorter and much more maneuverable than sea kayaks. This is a nice feature when you're hurtling downriver toward a giant boulder! However, they do not have the deep hull of a sea kayak. The flat bottom of a white-water kayak makes it very "squirrelly" on flat water and, therefore, exhausting to paddle across a lake. But whether you choose a sea kayak or a white-water kayak, you will reap the same benefits: improved strength and stamina, the chance to get outdoors and enjoy the natural world, and most of all, the pure fun and enjoyment of kayaking.

Now look at how you can use a comparison table to answer the following questions.

1. How are sea kayaks and white-water kayaks similar?

   A. Both kayaks are good for floating rivers.
   B. Both kayaks are good for paddling on lakes.
   C. Both kayaks have large hatches for storing gear.
   D. Both kayaks have a closed cockpit and a spray skirt.

The best way to find the correct answer to this question is to compare each of the categories that are listed in the answer choices. These can be put in a simple table:

Category	Sea Kayaks	White-water Kayaks
Good for floating rivers		
Good for paddling on lakes		
Large hatches for storing gear		
Closed cockpit and spray skirt		

Now compare the kayaks using the categories on the left side of the table. Ask yourself the following questions:

- Are both sea kayaks and white-water kayaks good for floating rivers? No. Therefore, choice A is not the correct answer.
- Are both sea kayaks and white-water kayaks good for paddling on lakes? No. Therefore, choice B is not the correct answer.
- Do both kayaks have large hatches for storing gear? No. Therefore, choice C is not the correct answer.
- Do both kayaks have a closed cockpit and spray skirt? Yes. Therefore, choice D is the correct answer.

2. How do sea kayaks and white-water kayaks differ?

    F. Sea kayaks do not build strength.

    G. White-water kayaks do not build stamina.

    H. White-water kayaks let the paddler enjoy nature.

    I. Sea kayaks are not as good at making quick turns.

To answer this question, you can make another table just like the one on page 61.

Category	Sea Kayaks	White-water Kayaks
Build strength		
Build stamina		
Let the paddler enjoy nature		
Good at making quick turns		

This question is a little bit trickier than Question 1, because you are not looking for similarities. You are also being asked to judge how certain things differ. By reading the article, you can see that the two types of kayak differ in several ways. Then check each answer choice to see if it is true or false.

- Does just one type of kayak build strength? No. Therefore, choice F is false.
- Does just one type of kayak build stamina? No. Therefore, choice G is false.

Knowing the Difference 63

- Does just one type of kayak let the paddler enjoy nature? No. Therefore, choice H is false.
- Is one kayak better than another at making turns? Yes. The white-water kayak is more "maneuverable." Therefore, choice I is true.
- Since choice I is the only one that is true, it is the correct answer.

FCAT Fred Says:

On the FCAT you will not only be asked to compare text elements. You will also be required to compare information in tables, maps, diagrams, and other illustrations.

This skill came in very handy when I was buying my first cell phone. In the section that follows, check out the advertisement I used to compare phones.

Try It Out

Examine the advertisements below. Then read how one student answered the questions that follow.

BRAND A

Lightning Wireless

- Up to 5 hours talk time
- 500-number capacity
- Digital camera phone
- Downloadable ring tones
- Folds to fit in your pocket
- External-caller ID

$79.99 (FREE with 2-year plan agreement)

Limit 4 phones per customer

BRAND C

Star Wave Wireless

- Up to 9 hours talk time
- 700-number capacity
- Digital camera and video phone
- Downloadable ring tones
- Folds to fit in your pocket
- External-caller ID
- Voice Dialing

Limit 5 phones per customer

$199.99 ($49.99 with 2-year plan agreement)

BRAND B

Talkster Communications

- Up to 7 hours talk time
- 500-number capacity
- Digital camera phone
- Speakerphone
- Folds to fit in your pocket
- External-caller ID

$99.99 (FREE with 2-year plan agreement)

Limit 4 phones per customer

Now read to see how one student figured out answers to the questions that follow.

1. How are Brands A and C ALIKE?

    A. Both phones have the same price.
    B. Both phones have external-caller ID.
    C. Both phones are video-camera phones.
    D. Both phones have the same amount of talk time.

"Hmm. I think I better make a table. I'll put the two brands at the top and write the categories down the left side. Wait, what are the categories? Oh, yeah! They're the answer choices."

1. the price of the phones
2. whether the phones have external-caller ID
3. whether the phones are video-camera phones
4. the amount of talk time.

"Then I just fill in the table based on the cell-phone ads. Here we go . . ."

Category	Brand A	Brand C
Price	$79.99	$199.99
External-caller ID	Yes	Yes
Video-camera phone	No	Yes
Talk time	5 hours	9 hours

"Now I can compare the phones, starting with the first category. Let's see."

- Are the prices the same for Brand A and Brand C? No. Therefore, choice A is not right.
- Do both brands have external-caller ID? Yes. Therefore, choice B is the correct answer.
- Are both brands video-camera phones? No. Therefore, choice C is wrong.
- Do both brands have the same amount of talk time? No. Therefore, choice D is wrong, too.

Knowing the Difference

"Now I'm on the second question. What does it want to know?"

2. How do Brands B and A DIFFER?

   F. Only Brand B fits in your pocket.
   G. Only Brand A is a digital camera phone.
   H. Only Brand A has downloadable ring tones.
   I. Brand B has a higher number capacity.

"I'll make another table like the first one."

Category	Brand A	Brand B
Fits in your pocket	Yes	Yes
Digital camera phone	Yes	Yes
Downloadable ring tones	Yes	No
Number capacity	500 numbers	500 numbers

"So, is each choice true or false?"

- Do they both fit in your pocket? Yes. Therefore, choice F is false.

- Are they both digital camera phones? Yes. Therefore, choice G is false.

- Does only Brand A have downloadable ring tones? Yes. Therefore, choice H is true.

- Does Brand B have a higher number capacity than Brand A? No. Therefore, choice I is false.

- Since choice H is the only one that is true, it must be the correct answer.

"There! Piece of cake!"

Key Concepts

- **Comparison** shows how things are the *same* or *alike*.
- **Contrast** shows how things are *different*.

On Your Own: Read the article "Extrovert or Introvert?" before answering Numbers 1 through 8.

EXTROVERT
or Introvert?
by Dana Chicchelly

Madison burst through the front door of the apartment, yelling, "WE'RE HOME!" Her sister Maggie followed her inside. Their mother came in from the balcony where she had been watering her pansies and petunias.

"So how was it?" she asked. "How was your first day of school?"

"It was so awesome!" Madison exclaimed. "Kennedy is a much better school than Jefferson. All my classes are packed with people, and you can barely make it from one class to the next in time because the hallways are totally jammed! I've already made friends with six girls. One of them, Jules, is on the cheerleading squad and she's going to help me practice for try-outs. And this one boy, Luke, his parents are throwing a back-to-school party for all the kids in the neighborhood, and he invited me to go! I have to call Jules!" Madison ran out to the balcony with her cell phone. They could already hear her chatting away.

"How about you, Maggie? What do you think of the school?"

Maggie shrugged and said, "Um, I don't know, it's okay, I guess." And with that she went to her bedroom, shut her door, took out her journal, and began to write: "Dear Diary: Alone at last! I thought I was going to lose it on my way to sixth period, when that girl shoved past me in the hall. I think I'll like this school, though. There are enough people that I just might find someone I can relate to. Later."

Even though they are sisters, Madison and Maggie couldn't be more different personalitywise. Madison is a prime example of what psychologists call an extrovert, while Maggie is clearly an introvert. Madison was charged up with excitement from a day surrounded by people, while Maggie took refuge in her bedroom for a little time alone to regroup and to reflect on her day.

Extroverts

Extroverts like Madison are the "life of the party." Outgoing, talkative, and sociable, they enjoy other people's company. They draw their energy from being with other people and become even more talkative and animated the more time they spend with others. They are most interested in what is happening in the outer world and do not dwell on their own thoughts and feelings. In fact, they may not know what they think and feel about something until they talk it over with another person.

Introverts

Introverts like Maggie, on the other hand, may not show up for the party at all, unless they know that they will have at least one close friend to talk to. Introverts tend to be reserved and quiet, which leads some people (mainly extroverts!) to label them shy or antisocial. However, it isn't that introverts do not enjoy other people; they just prefer quality over quantity. An introvert would much rather carry on an in-depth conversation with a close friend than make silly, meaningless small talk with a group of strangers.

In fact, being around people for long periods of time saps introverts of their energy. To get reenergized, introverts seek out solitude—a little time away from other people so that they can recharge their battery. Introverts use this alone time to think things over. Whereas extroverts focus on the world outside themselves, introverts focus on the inner world of thoughts and feelings. Rather than talking out their feelings with another person, as an extrovert would do, an introvert will think out or even write out his or her feelings. It is only after reflecting on their thoughts and feelings that introverts will act, as opposed to an extrovert's tendency to act first and think later.

Majority Rules?

The American population is made up of about 75 percent extroverts and 25 percent introverts. Does this mean that extroverts are better than introverts? Of course not! While certain professions do tend to favor people who are friendly and outgoing (salesperson, politician, teacher), there are other professions in which an introvert's ability to think and feel deeply are clearly assets (writer, artist, actor). And just think of a world made up entirely of either extroverts or introverts. It would be a very noisy, or very quiet, planet!

Conflicts can arise, however, when there is a lack of understanding between the two personality types. An extrovert may feel hurt when an introvert retreats to another room for some time alone. An introvert may seethe with resentment at the extrovert who hogs a conversation. But by learning a little of how the other personality type "ticks," extroverts and introverts can find ways to defuse these conflicts. They may even learn to value the qualities the other personality type possesses which they themselves lack, and declare, *"Vive la différence!"*

Now answer Numbers 1 through 8. Base your answers on the article "Extrovert or Introvert?"

 How was Maggie's opinion of the school hallways DIFFERENT from Madison's opinion?

    A. She thought they were fun.

    B. She thought they were crowded.

    C. She thought they were annoying.

    D. She thought they were dangerous.

2 What did Maggie and Madison agree on?

    F. They both thought Jefferson was a better school.
    G. They both thought they would like the new school.
    H. They both thought they would make a lot of friends.
    I. They both thought they would find one good friend.

3 How do large groups of people affect introverts differently than they do extroverts?

    A. They drain introverts' energy.
    B. They make introverts more lively.
    C. They help introverts feel less shy.
    D. They help introverts to be more outgoing.

4 Read the sentence below.

To get reenergized, introverts seek out solitude—a little time away from other people so that they can recharge their battery.

What does the word *solitude* mean?

    F. being alone
    G. taking a break
    H. getting some rest
    I. doing some thinking

5 How are extroverts DIFFERENT from introverts?

    A. They like to be alone.
    B. They think first and then act.
    C. They focus on the outer world.
    D. They prefer talking with one close friend.

6 How are the professions of salesperson, politician, and teacher ALIKE, according to the article?

    F. They are good professions for extroverts.
    G. They are the best professions for introverts.
    H. They are professions that require deep thinking.
    I. They are professions that require good writing skills.

7 How does the number of introverts in America compare to the number of extroverts?

    A. There are a lot more extroverts than introverts.
    B. There are slightly more introverts than extroverts.
    C. There are slightly fewer introverts than extroverts.
    D. There is about an equal number of extroverts and introverts.

8 Read this excerpt from the article.

> Introverts tend to be reserved and quiet, which leads some people (mainly extroverts!) to label them shy or antisocial. However, it isn't that introverts do not enjoy other people; they just prefer quality over quantity. An introvert would much rather carry on an in-depth conversation with a close friend than make silly, meaningless small talk with a group of strangers.

What can you infer about the author from this excerpt?

F. The author is probably an introvert.
G. The author is most likely an extrovert.
H. The author prefers being around extroverts.
I. The author enjoys extroverts as much as introverts.

Read the article "In the Beginning" and the poem "The Base Stealer" before answering Numbers 1 through 9.

In the Beginning
by Lawrence S. Ritter

Baseball has been providing us with fun and excitement for more than a hundred and fifty years. The first game resembling baseball as we know it today was played in Hoboken, New Jersey, on June 19, 1845. The New York Nine beat the New York Knickerbockers that day, 23-1.

The game was played according to rules drawn up by Alexander J. Cartwright, a surveyor and amateur athlete. It is a myth that Abner Doubleday invented baseball. It was Alexander Cartwright, not Abner Doubleday, who first laid out the present dimensions of the playing field and established the basic rules of the game.

The first professional baseball team was the Cincinnati Red Stockings, who toured the country in 1869 and didn't lose a game all year. Baseball began to attract so many fans that in 1876 the National League was organized—the same National league that still exists today.

Although the game as it was played in 1876 was recognizable as baseball—nobody would confuse it with football or basketball—it was quite a bit different from baseball as we know it now. For example, pitchers had to throw underhand, the way they still do in softball; the batter could request the pitcher to throw a "high" or "low" pitch; it took nine balls, rather than four, for a batter to get on base on balls; and the pitching distance was only forty-five feet to home plate.

The rules were gradually changed over the following twenty years, until by about 1900 the game was more or less the same as it is today. In 1884, pitchers were permitted to throw overhand; in 1887, the batter was no longer allowed to request a "high" or "low pitch; by 1889, it took only four balls for a batter to get a base on balls; and, in 1893, the pitching distance was lengthened to the present sixty feet, six inches.

Players didn't start to wear gloves on the field until the 1880s. At first, they wore only a thin piece of leather over the palm of the hand, with five holes cut out for the fingers to go through. By the 1890s, however, the gloves began to look like today's baseball gloves, although they were not nearly as large.

Nowadays, the glove is much larger than it used to be, and the ball is not caught in the palm of the hand but trapped in the glove's webbing, between the thumb and forefinger. Since the mid-1950s, the glove has become more of a net with which to snare the ball rather than just a protective covering for the hand.

If a ball, like a foul ball or a home run, went into the stands, the ushers would try to get it back, sometimes offering whoever had it a free pass to another game. If they succeeded in getting it back, it would be returned to the field, and the game would continue with the same ball. Now, of course, close to a hundred baseballs are used in an average big league game.

Until the early 1900s, one umpire took care of the entire field. Typically, he would call balls and strikes from behind the catcher until a man got on base, and then move out and call balls and strikes from behind the pitcher so he could be closer to the bases in case of an attempted steal.

With only one umpire, there was plenty of opportunity for mischief. Tim Hurst, a famous umpire in the 1890s, who knew all the tricks of the trade, once called a player out who slid across home plate in a cloud of dust even though no one was even trying to tag him. Tim had been looking toward right field and second base all the while, but then he whirled around and yelled, "You're out!"

"What do you mean I'm out?" the player screamed. "They didn't even make a play on me." "You never touched third base," Tim shouted back.

"Of course I did," the player responded. "And anyway, how do *you* know? You weren't even watching."

"That's just it," the umpire said. "For when I wasn't watching, you got home *too* fast!"

Needless to say, Tim Hurst won the argument, as have almost all umpires before and since.

In 1901, a second major league, the American League, was established alongside the twenty-five-year-old National League. Many of the stars of the National League jumped over to the new American League because they were offered higher salaries. Ballplayers didn't make the kind of money in those days that they make now, of course, but even then dollars and cents played an important role in professional baseball.

After some initial hard feelings, the pennant winners of the two major leagues met each other in 1903 in the first modern World Series. The stage was set for a great and long-lasting rivalry, one that continues to this very day.

Knowing the Difference

The Base Stealer
by Robert Francis

Poised between going on and back, pulled
Both ways taut like a tightrope-walker,
Fingertips pointing the opposites,
Now bouncing tiptoe like a dropped ball
Or a kid skipping rope, come on, come on,
Running a scattering of steps sidewise,
How he teeters, skitters, tingles, teases,
Taunts them, hovers like an ecstatic bird,
He's only flirting, crowd him, crowd him,
Delicate, delicate, delicate, delicate—now!

Now answer Numbers 1 through 9. Base your answers on the article "In the Beginning" and on the poem "The Base Stealer."

1 How was baseball pitching in 1876 DIFFERENT from pitching today?

  A. The baseball was thrown overhand.
  B. The baseball was thrown underhand.
  C. The pitcher had to throw the ball farther to home plate.
  D. The batter could ask for an overhand or an underhand ball.

2 How are today's baseball gloves the same as those used from the 1880s to the mid-1950s?

  F. They are used as a net to catch the ball.
  G. They are used to protect the hand from injury.
  H. They are made to catch the ball between the thumb and forefinger.
  I. They are made out of thin leather with holes cut out for the fingers.

3 What can you infer from the article about what happens today when a ball is struck into the stands?

  A. The ball is kept by the person who finds it.
  B. The ball is returned by the person who finds it.
  C. A person who catches a ball gets a game pass.
  D. A person who refuses to return the ball is fined.

4 How are the article and the poem ALIKE?

- F. They both explain the rules of baseball.
- G. They both tell how base-stealing was invented.
- H. They both describe an event from a baseball game.
- I. They both show how baseball has changed over time.

5 How was the new American League DIFFERENT from the National League?

- A. It paid its players more money.
- B. It hired players who had never played professionally.
- C. Its players had a chance to play in the World Series.
- D. Its players made as much money then as they do now.

6 Read the sentence below.

After some initial hard feelings, the pennant winners of the two major baseball leagues met each other in 1903 in the first modern World Series.

What does the word *initial* mean in the sentence above?

- F. first
- G. letter
- H. angry
- I. shared

7 How are the fourth and eighth lines of the poem ALIKE?

- A. They both describe how the player runs to the next base.
- B. They both show how fearful the player is between bases.
- C. They both use repetition to imitate the sounds of the game.
- D. They both use a comparison to show how the player acted.

8 According to the article, what do umpires today have in common with umpires in the early years of baseball?

- F. They win almost all arguments with players.
- G. They stay behind the catcher for the whole game.
- H. They must watch over the whole field by themselves.
- I. They can call players out only if they see them break a rule.

9 Which word would both the author of "In the Beginning" and the author of "The Base Stealer" use to describe baseball?

- A. exciting
- B. evolving
- C. historical
- D. confusing

Read the article "Animal Fat" before answering Numbers 1 through 9.

Animal Fat

by Stephen James O'Meara

Riddle #1: What land mammal is larger than the largest land mammal?

Give up? Well, first of all, trunks down, the African elephant is Earth's largest land mammal. So, what's the answer to the riddle? . . . (tap those tusks, please) . . . An overweight elephant!

It's not a joke.

In the wild, an elephant can weigh in at a whopping 6.5 tons. It can consume nearly 2 percent of its body weight in just 12 hours; it can also drink about 70 gallons of water per day. In fact, elephants spend about 75 percent of their day just eating. But wild elephants are *not* fat. They're just big. (An African elephant may measure 30 feet in length and stand 13 feet tall.) But being big does *not* mean being fat. There *is* a difference.

Elephants are not big because they eat so much. It's just the opposite. To maintain its massive body, a wild elephant *has* to eat so much. But it's not an idle eater. Elephants will walk 20 to 50 *miles* every day to forage for food. Walking is their exercise, and it helps them maintain a healthy physical condition. Indeed, a healthy elephant in the wild may live to the ripe old age of 70!

Those kept in zoos reach only half that age! Although many factors contribute to the premature death of zoo elephants, one major concern is that captive elephants do not get to travel the sorts of vast distances (and therefore receive appropriate levels of physical exercise) that wild elephants do.

The result: Zoo elephants are massively overweight—being up to 50 percent heavier than their counterparts in the wild! And overweight elephants tend to develop disorders of the feet, joints, ligaments, and skin, causing discomfort and suffering. Overweight zoo elephants in the United Kingdom are not alone. U.S. zoos also have had problems with overweight elephants.

But the plight of the zoo elephant is understandable. It's a containment issue. Wild elephants roam over distances as much as 60 to 100 times larger than typical zoo housing for elephants. Most zoos, however, are in cities, where they serve the most people—but where space is most limited.

While zoo officials and elephant researchers have been tackling this weighty issue, yet another recent study announced that zoo elephants are not the only animals with weight problems. . . . Read on!

Riddle #2: What do a zoo elephant, a human living in the United States, a dog, and a cat all have in common?

If you said, "Obesity," you're right! Their eating habits are "weigh" out of range.

One recent study has shown that as many as 25 percent of dogs and cats in the Western world are obese! What's more, obesity in pets is on the rise!

What's going on?

According to Dan Christian of the Purina Pet Institute—overfeeding is primarily to blame.

Obesity is the most common nutritional disorder in dogs and cats, especially as they age. Aside from genetic factors (some breeds of pets are more prone to obesity than others), an obese pet is most likely a physically inactive pet (all rest and no play) that either consumes more food than the body uses or is fed table scraps and treats high in calories.

Other studies have placed pet obesity in the range of 28 to 50 percent in the United States. Practicing veterinarians say that it's closer to 50 or 60 percent.

The findings, actually, should not be shocking-especially if the theory is true that says dogs and their owners begin to resemble one another after living together for a few years. In 2001, the Centers for Disease Control and Prevention (CDC) found that more than 44 million Americans are considered obese, reflecting an increase of 74 percent since 1991. Indeed, an overweight owner is twice as likely to have an overweight pet as a non-overweight owner.

There's a grave danger in this news. Obese pets, like obese people, are more likely to develop diseases such as diabetes and heart disease. The likelihood of obesity increases with the pet's age and occurs more frequently in neutered animals.

So shower your pets with love, not food. And if you love your pet, make sure that they have a healthy diet and get plenty of exercise. Remember that an obese pet suffers with its added weight. Obesity increases the likelihood of joint pain and degenerative bone disease. It can cause or worsen high blood pressure, cancer, and heart disease.

There's an old adage that says, "Diet and exercise are the keys to living." Indeed, many experts believe that regular exercise is the single most important thing a human can do to improve overall health and well-being. Now it appears that this advice holds true for your pet as well.

Now answer Numbers 1 through 9. Base your answers on the article "Animal Fat."

1 How does the life expectancy of a zoo elephant differ from that of a wild elephant?

    A. Zoo elephants live longer.

    B. Zoo elephants live fewer years.

    C. Zoo elephants live almost the same number of years.

    D. Zoo elephants live shorter lives, but with fewer health problems.

Knowing the Difference

2 How are zoo elephants in the U.K. and zoo elephants in the U.S. ALIKE?

F. They are extremely overweight.
G. They walk up to 20 miles a day for exercise.
H. They are not fed enough to maintain their weight.
I. They need to roam farther distances than wild elephants.

3 Which health problem do obese pets have in common with overweight elephants?

A. diabetes
B. joint pain
C. foot problems
D. skin disorders

4 What can you infer from the fact that obese pet owners are more likely to have obese pets than non-obese pet owners?

F. Obese pet owners tend to choose breeds that are more likely to get obese.
G. Non-obese pet owners do not feed their pets table scraps and high-calorie treats.
H. Non-obese pet owners are more careful about their own weight and that of their pets.
I. Obese pet owners care less about their pets' health than non-obese pet owners do.

5 According to the article, what is the MOST important factor for good health and well-being in both pets and humans?

A. eating a healthy diet
B. eating a low-calorie diet
C. avoiding high-calorie foods
D. exercising regularly

6 Read the sentences below.

U.S. zoos also have had problems with overweight elephants. But the plight of the zoo elephant is understandable.

What does the word *plight* mean?

F. escape
G. weight
H. troubles
I. experiences

7 How are older pets DIFFERENT from younger pets?

    A. They get half as much daily exercise.

    B. They are more likely to become obese.

    C. They eat healthier diets with fewer treats.

    D. They are less likely to have heart disease.

8 How has the health of Americans changed since 1991?

    F. More Americans have diabetes.

    G. More Americans are overweight.

    H. Americans are eating more nutritious food.

    I. Americans are less likely to get heart disease.

9 According to the article, which of the following varies by breed of dog or cat?

    A. their ideal weight

    B. their risk of cancer

    C. their need for a nutritious diet

    D. their need for plenty of exercise

MAKING SENSE OF IT

In this chapter you learned that the FCAT will ask you to compare characters, story settings, authors' purposes, main ideas, themes, organizational structure, style, poems, articles, and stories. You may also be required to compare tables, maps, and other illustrations.

- **Comparison** shows how things are similar or the same.
- **Contrast** Contrast shows how things are different.
- Key words used in comparisons are *as, like, likewise, similar, same, also, resembles, alike, equally,* and *both*.
- Key words used in contrasts are *however, in contrast, instead, but, on the other hand, differs from, unlike, yet, although, still, on the contrary,* and *different from*.

Chapter Three

Getting the Point

> **Benchmark: L.A.A.2.3.1**
>
> The student determines the main idea or essential message in a text and identifies relevant details, facts, and patterns of organization.

Welcome to **Gator's Skate Park!**

GSP is an adult-supervised park and is open from 10 A.M. to 8 P.M.

For safety reasons, all skaters must have a liability release form signed by a parent or guardian, wear required safety gear, and obey all rules and regulations (see Park Supervisor for a copy of the official Rules and Regulations).

Skaters who do not comply with the park rules will be asked to leave immediately and will not be allowed re-admittance without permission of the Park Supervisor.

Tony pointed out the car window to the sign.

"Mom, just read the sign, would you please?" Mrs. Mendoza unpuckered her worried brow so that she could squint to read the sign instead.

" . . . will not be allowed re-admittance . . ." she finished the last sentence half-aloud.

"So would you please sign the release form? You can tell from the sign that they're really into safety at this place. I'll *be* okay!"

"Okay, I'll sign the form, but this first time, I'm going in there with you."

"Mom, no, you can't . . . You're not serious! You *are* serious! Mom! C'mon! No! . . . Well, *okay* then, if that will make you feel better!"

"It *will*."

Fortunately for Tony, his mother was able to find the main idea of the sign outside the skate park. Its message, that the skate park was a safe place for skateboarders to have fun, convinced Mrs. Mendoza to sign the release form.

Why Study This?

Words are everywhere. You see them on television, bulletin boards, Web sites, cereal boxes, street signs, and in shop windows, newspapers, and books. Knowing how writers use words to get their most important point across will help you get the most out of what you read every day, everywhere.

Key Concepts

- **Main Idea:** the most important point an author makes
- **Details:** points made by an author that support his or her main idea(s)
- **Organizational Methods:** ways of organizing information in writing; using a certain organizational pattern can help support an author's main idea

Main Idea

Ideas are all-important in reading and writing. Authors organize their writing around ideas. In fact, every paragraph that an author writes is actually a group of sentences about a central idea. That idea holds the paragraph together and expresses what the paragraph is about. This is called the *main idea*.

Suppose you are reading an article about tsunamis. The first paragraph might be about how tsunamis are formed. The main idea in that paragraph might be that tsunamis are created when earthquakes occur on the ocean floor. Other paragraphs in the article might describe the effects of tsunamis, major tsunamis that took place in the last hundred years, and the devastating Indian Ocean tsunami of 2004. So each paragraph can have its own main idea.

In addition to the main ideas that pop up in each paragraph, *the article itself* has a main idea, an overall main point the writer is trying to convey. In this case, it could be that the writer wants the reader to understand that tsunamis are an example of a powerful force of nature that people cannot prevent or control. Each of the paragraphs in the text will support this larger main idea.

How can you identify the main idea in a paragraph or passage? You might start by asking yourself the following questions:

> - What is the main point the writer makes?
> - What is the most important idea?
> - What idea summarizes the entire passage?

Don't confuse a main idea with a topic. A *topic* tells you what the paragraph or passage is *about*. The title or heading of a passage usually lets you know what the topic is. A topic is *general* while the main idea is more *specific*.

> **Topic:** Tsunamis
> **Main Idea:** Tsunamis are a powerful force of nature.

Stated vs. Implied Main Idea

Usually, a main idea is easy to find because it is clearly stated: One sentence (or group of sentences) tells you what the main point of the paragraph or passage is. Finding an implied main idea is trickier. An implied main idea is not directly stated. You have to figure it out based on what is suggested in the passage. In other words, you have to read between the lines. Careful readers can usually find an implied main idea by paying attention to *details*.

Suppose that your best friend said to you, "You know what? Next Saturday's my birthday. Last month I went to this *really* great surprise birthday party for my cousin. It was *so* much fun. I love surprise parties. But no one's ever thrown a surprise party for me. Never! Not even once. Can you believe that?"

Even though your friend doesn't say it outright, it's easy to tell what she's implying: She would like you to throw her a surprise birthday party.

FCAT Fred Says:

Here's a match up game you can use to help you figure out the main idea. Just follow these steps:

1. Choose the sentence that you believe states the main idea of a passage.
2. Read each sentence in the passage, checking to see if it supports the main idea sentence you chose.

So, can you figure out the main idea *I'm* trying to get across? My stomach is growling. I'm ready to eat my own tail! Is that a cobweb I see on my food dish?"

What is FCAT Fred's problem?
- **A.** Fred is sick.
- **B.** Fred is tired.
- **C.** Fred is lonely.
- **D.** Fred is hungry.

Details

As already discussed, a well-written paragraph always contains a main idea that is clearly stated or implied. In either case, the main idea is always *supported* by *details*. These details elaborate on the main point the author is making. Details are either factual or sensory.

Factual details are often used to explain or clarify points about a topic and can be proved, or verified, by using an outside source, like an encyclopedia or the

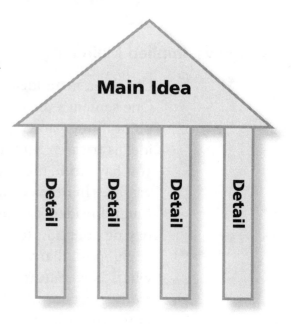

Getting the Point

Internet. (For more on verifying information, see Chapters 5 and 6). Factual details answer questions such as **where? when? how? who? what? which?** or **why?** and are useful in explaining or clarifying points about a particular topic.

Sensory details, however, give readers a vivid idea about how something *looks, feels, sounds, smells,* or *tastes*. Writers often use sensory details in fiction and nonfiction to give life to the people and places they write about.

Can you find at least three factual details and three sensory details in the following passage?

> My mother's bakeshop was located on, coincidentally enough, Bakers Street. The small, old-fashioned brick building was nestled between the new bank and an insurance company—an oasis of warmth and hominess. Every morning, on my way to school, I would drop by for a cup of hot chocolate as I finished my homework. Sitting at my favorite old wooden table by the front window, I would bask in the sunlight streaming in, soak up the aroma of cinnamon rolls and fresh-brewed coffee, and half-listen to the old-time country music playing on the radio in the kitchen. Lingering as long as I dared, I would gather up my books at the last possible minute. Then, with a farewell hug from my mother, I was off to school, ready to face whatever the day might bring.

Factual details (What? Where? When? Who? Why? How?)

_____

_____

Sensory details (How did the bakeshop look? What sounds are heard? How does it feel to be there? What tastes and smells does the narrator experience?)

_____

_____

What is the topic of this passage?

_____

Based on the factual and the sensory details, what do you think is the main idea of the passage?

_____

_____

SEEING IT IN ACTION

Read the paragraph in the box that follows and see if you can spot the main idea.

> Watching the water moccasin gliding through the swampy water straight toward me, I felt fear as I had never felt it before. My right arm, which had been in the middle of casting my fishing line to the splash made by a five-pound bass, was frozen in midair. My left hand clutched my waders at belly level; maybe it had tried to catch my breath before it was sucked out of me in one big *whoosh* at the sight of the poisonous snake. I couldn't breathe. I couldn't scream.

Were you able to find the main idea? In this case, it can be found in the very first sentence:

Watching the water moccasin gliding through the swampy water straight toward me, I felt fear as I had never felt it before.

But what about the *other* sentences in the paragraph? What purpose do they serve? Let's look at them a little more closely:

- My right arm, which had been in the middle of casting my fishing line to the splash made by a five-pound bass, was frozen in midair.

- My left hand clutched my waders at belly level; maybe it had tried to catch my breath before it was sucked out of me in one big *whoosh* at the sight of the poisonous snake.
- I couldn't breathe.
- I couldn't scream.

What do these sentences have in common? The answer is simple: They all provide **details** that support, or back up, the main idea (that *I felt fear as I had never felt it before*).

FCAT Fred Says:

When answering FCAT main idea questions, use the "Try it on for Size" technique. When you try on clothes in a store, you'll find that some are too big, some are too small, and others are juuust right. The same goes for answer choices on the FCAT. Read each answer choice and ask yourself, "Is this answer too broad, too narrow, off the topic entirely, or is it juuust right?" This technique really helps when you're figuring out the main idea of the whole passage. The test writers might write an answer that is too broad, resembling a topic rather than a main idea. Or they might write an answer that is too narrow, related to just one part of the passage. Or they might even write an answer that is off topic and only vaguely related to the passage.

Now read how one student analyzed the answer choices for a main idea question on the previous reading passage.

What is the main idea of the passage on page 82?

A. The narrator is on a fishing trip. (*Too broad. A fishing trip is the topic, but it is not the main idea.*)

B. The narrator is fishing and, in the middle of casting for a bass, sees a snake. (*Too narrow. These are all details, but this choice doesn't give the overall main idea the writer was trying to get across.*)

C. Big bass can be found in swampy water. (*Off topic. The passage mentions bass, but it is not the main idea of the passage.*)

D. The narrator is paralyzed with fear after seeing a snake. (*Juuust right!*)

THINK OF IT THIS WAY

A web is a helpful tool for organizing the main idea and details in a reading selection. This web uses the paragraph about the fishing trip.

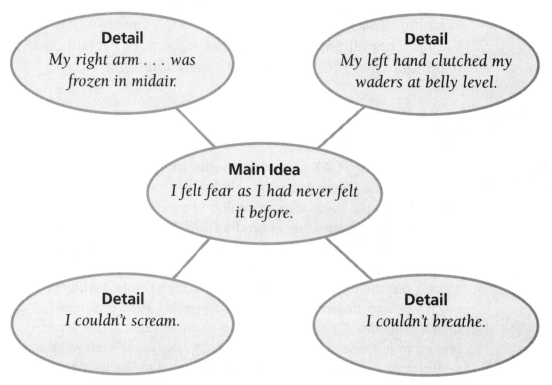

Now try your hand at creating a web for the main idea and details in the paragraph that follows.

As I opened the door to the bedroom that I shared with my twin sister, Kate, I knew something was up. For one thing, I actually *could* open the door. Usually, there were so many piles of laundry and books and other clutter (mainly Kate's) that just getting into the room was an adventure. I walked in and was amazed to see that all the books had been put back in the bookcase, and it looked like, yes, the bookcase had been dusted. Equally amazing was the fact that the usual piles of laundry had been magically transformed into two tidy stacks of freshly washed jeans, T-shirts, and other clothing, one stack on Kate's bed, and one stack on mine. And was that Kate bent intently over the ironing board, ironing one of *my* blouses with a feverish intensity?

"Okay," I said. "What do you want?"

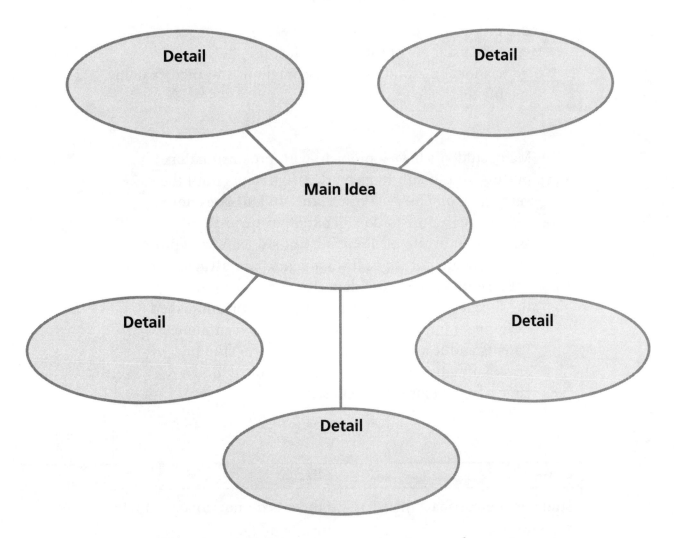

Keep in mind that you can customize a web to suit your needs. If a paragraph has fewer or more details than our web does, add bubbles to the web, or draw your own with fewer bubbles.

Methods of Organization

Authors use many different methods to organize information. If you know which organizational method the author is using, you will better understand the information you read. Here are four common methods of organization:

Cause and Effect

In a passage that is organized according to cause and effect, the author tells what happened (effect) and why it happened (cause). Several causes might be given for one effect, or the passage might describe several effects of one cause. (For

more on cause and effect, see Chapter 7.)
Here is an example of cause and effect used as an organizational method. Read the paragraph and then examine the table that follows.

> Many students have a problem with procrastination, putting off difficult homework assignments until the very last moment. As a result, the student does not have enough time to do a good job or turns the assignment in late or not at all. But students who procrastinate are not lazy. Most students procrastinate because they aren't confident that they can complete the dreaded assignment. Sadly, each late or unfinished assignment hurts a student's confidence even more. Parents and teachers can help students to stop procrastinating by showing them how to break down large assignments into small steps.

Cause	Effect(s)
Students procrastinate on assignments.	Students do not do a good job; students turn in assignments late; students do not turn in assignments at all.
Students are not confident they can complete an assignment.	Students procrastinate.
Students turn in late or unfinished assignments.	Students' confidence is hurt even more.
Parents and teachers show students how to break down big assignments into small steps.	Students stop procrastinating.

Comparison and Contrast

A passage of comparison and contrast focuses on how two or more things are alike and different. Sometimes an author compares a familiar item with something that is less well-known.

Getting the Point

Use a comparison table to map the differences and similarities in the following paragraph. (For more on comparing and contrasting and using comparison tables, see Chapter 2.)

> No two teachers could have been more different than Mr. Ambrose and Ms. Clark. Mr. Ambrose wore a suit and tie every day to class. Ms. Clark almost always wore jeans and a T-shirt. When taking attendance, Mr. Ambrose insisted that we reply, "Present!" in a serious tone of voice. But in Ms. Clark's class, she encouraged us to answer in funny voices. I usually said "Pwesent!" in my best Elmer Fudd imitation. After attendance, Mr. Ambrose would deliver his lecture from a podium, while we took notes. When he finished the lecture, he would have us do an assignment from the textbook. Ms. Clark, on the other hand, would stroll around the room during her lecture, sometimes sitting down in an empty desk and pretending to lecture to just one student. After her lecture, she would have us either play a learning game or work on a project.

Spatial Order

An author uses spatial order when he or she describes something in a logical order. For example, he might describe a tall building from bottom to top, a painting from left to right, or a Thanksgiving buffet from nearby to far away. Imagine that an author wants to describe a barn. If she first talks about the chickens in front of the barn, then describes the hay inside the barn, then jumps back outside to talk about the color of the barn and then goes back inside the barn to describe the horses' stables, you'll be in for a confusing ride. A better approach would be to describe everything outside the barn that she wants to discuss, and then to venture inside the barn to describe the hayloft and the stables. The details should be given in some logical spatial order, so that it's easy for the reader to follow along.

How is the following paragraph spatially ordered?

I was talking to my friend Renee by the punch bowl when the doorbell rang. "That must be Josh!" I ran to the door, flung it open, and gasped. Josh was standing there dressed in full clown regalia: He had on bright red floppy shoes, baggy polka-dot pants, a pink shirt with giant yellow daisies on it, orange suspenders, a red clown nose, clown make-up, and a fuzzy, flame-red clown wig. Josh peered into the house at everyone who was dressed in normal clothes and said, "I thought you said it was a costume party!"

Time Order

Time order is perhaps the most common way to organize information. This type of organization arranges events chronologically, or in the order in which they occur. Some important words that signal time order (also called **chronological order**) in a piece are: *first, second, next, last, finally, then, later, earlier,* and *before.*

There! I had finally put the finishing touches on the report for my computer science class. I was especially happy with that last line: "Computers may be smart, but they'll never outsmart humans." I moved the cursor arrow up to the toolbar and clicked on the printer icon. Nothing happened. Hmm . . . this had never happened before. What to do? First, I tried clicking on the printer icon again. Again, nothing happened. Next, I did Command + P. Nothing. Finally, I went to the File menu and selected Print. The print window came up! Success! I hit the return button to select Print . . . and my computer crashed! Guess who had forgotten to save a backup copy of the file? At that moment I realized I would have to change the last line of my report.

Organizational Methods

In addition to the methods described above, authors frequently organize their writing in the following ways:

Flashback: The author starts with a situation and then "flashes back" to earlier events.

> Dylan walked into Adams Elementary School and felt the memories rush over him like kids stampeding to get outside at recess . . . "Red Rover, Red Rover, send Dylan right over!" "Mrs. Thompson! Dylan took the ball and he won't give it back!"

Bulleted list: This is effective in drawing the reader's attention to important points.

Whenever you bake, it's important to follow these guidelines:

- Measure your ingredients precisely.
- Preheat your oven to the temperature specified in the recipe.
- Set the timer for the minimum time stated in the recipe; you can always bake under-baked cookies a bit longer, but you cannot "unbake" burnt cookies.

Foreshadowing: Early on, the author gives subtle hints of things that will happen later in the text.

> I had a funny feeling about Jake the first time I met him, as if I could only half trust the guy. But I didn't realize until the last play of the last football game of my senior year how right my first impression had been.

Question/Answer: The author asks a question in the first paragraph or two and then goes on to answer it.

> What is biology? Biology is the study of living organisms. There are many different branches of biology, including botany, zoology, and microbiology.

Argument/Support: The author takes a stand on an issue and then supports it with details.

> It is outrageous that the Jordanville City Council plans to shut down the Starlight Teen Dance Palace! Just because a few teens caused some trouble is no reason to close the only place in town where teenagers can go to hear good music, to dance, and to hang out with their friends.

FCAT Fred Says:

On the FCAT, you might find other main idea questions besides "What is the main idea of this passage?" Some of the other kinds of questions you will find are: What was the main idea of the first paragraph? Why did the story end the way it did? How does the organization of the article help to support the author's main idea? What is a good title for this article? (They really love throwing that one at you!)

Let me tell you a little story and see how you do on the FCAT question that follows it:

> Once upon a time, there was an incredibly handsome cat named Fred. Fred was not only the most handsome cat in the neighborhood, but he was also the smartest. He was so smart that cats from all over would come to see Fred to ask for help with problems they could not figure out on their own. Sometimes smart-aleck cats would ask him hard questions just to see if they could stump him, but Fred managed to answer them all. Until one day, Samuel, the most smart-alecky cat of them all, said, "So, Fred, answer me this: When is a door not a door?"
>
> Fred was stumped. He had no idea when a door was not a door. He knew how to unlatch the lock on a screen door, and he knew how to meow to get humans to open doors, but he did not know when a door was not a door. Fred slunk away, ashamed.
>
> For the next week, he could not get the riddle out of his mind. It tormented him so much that he could not sleep, eat, or make weird chattering noises at the birds just outside the living room window. He spent the whole day meowing to get his owner to let him out and then meowing to get back in.
>
> Finally, his owner said, "Look, Fred, I'm going to put this jar of peanut butter in the door to keep it open. That way you can come and go without PESTERING ME ANYMORE!"
>
> As Fred jumped over the peanut butter to get out, it came to him. He raced out of the yard and hunted throughout the neighborhood until he found Samuel. Panting, he proudly exclaimed: "A door ... is not a door ... when it is ajar!"

Getting the Point

What would be a good title for this story?

    A. "All's Well that Ends Well"

    B. "The Cat Who Cried 'Wolf!'"

    C. "Once a Genius, Always a Genius"

    D. "A Friend in Need Is a Friend Indeed"

The answer is **C** (naturally!).

Key Concepts

- *Topic* and *main idea* are not the same thing.
- A **topic** is what the passage is about.
- The **main idea** is the most important point that an author wants to make about the topic. It can be *stated directly* or *implied*.
- **Details** and **organization** work to support the author's *main idea*.
- Authors use many different **methods of organization**. Some are:

      Cause and effect

      Comparison and contrast

      Spatial order

      Time order

      Flashback

      Bulleted list

      Foreshadowing

      Question/Answer

      Argument/Support

Read the article "Conquering Mount Everest" before answering Numbers 1 through 9.

Conquering Mount Everest

by Phyllis Raybin Emert

Climbing to the top of Mount Everest was the major goal in George Mallory's life. It was all he thought about, as if Everest itself had issued a personal challenge to him. Everest was the focus of Mallory's life . . . and the cause of his death.

Mount Everest is the tallest mountain in the world, rising 29,035 feet into the air. That's more than 5 1/2 miles up, higher than many airplanes fly. Everest is located in the central Himalayas on the border between Tibet and Nepal.

Officially, Sir Edmund Hillary and Tenzing Norgay were the first men to reach the top of Mount Everest on May 29, 1953. But some believe that George Mallory was actually the first man to stand on that summit, nearly thirty years earlier.

Mallory was among the very first group to attempt to climb Everest in May and June of 1921. But snowstorms and winds of up to one hundred miles per hour thwarted their attempt.

Another expedition tried in 1922, and Mallory was among them. A sudden avalanche swept down on the climbers, and seven men plunged over the edge of a five-hundred-foot glacier cliff. One survivor said, "The others saved themselves by swimming the breaststroke in the snow."

Mallory's last attempt to climb Mount Everest took place in 1924. Six camps were set up on the mountain at various elevations. Camp Five was located at 25,000 feet, and Camp Six was established at 27,000 feet, only 2,100 feet shy of the summit.

The thirty-seven-year-old Mallory was determined to reach the top. On June 8, along with twenty-two-year-old Andrew

Irvine, an excellent athlete and an experienced mountain climber, Mallory left Camp Six to fulfill his goal.

The expedition's geologist, Noel Odell, was at Camp Five observing the summit with a strong telescope. The summit was covered in clouds. Suddenly, at 12:50 P.M., the clouds parted to reveal two moving black spots. Odell saw that the spots were Mallory and Irvine, and they were only about 800 feet from the top of Everest!

Could they reach the summit and return to Camp Six by dark? Odell believed they were several hours behind schedule, although they seemed to be moving without any trouble. But soon, a sudden snowstorm came up and the men were lost from sight. It was the last time Mallory and Irvine were ever seen.

Odell searched for two hours with no luck. He kept shouting throughout the night and the next day in an attempt to guide the two back. Finally, on June 19, the expedition leader declared Mallory and Irvine dead. Their bodies were never found.

Many questions remain. Did the sudden storm cause the men to turn back so close to their goal? Knowing George Mallory's zeal, it is not likely.

Did one of them slip and fall? Roped together, the two climbers may have fallen to their deaths on the slopes of the mountain. Perhaps they knew they couldn't get back to camp by nightfall. Did they take shelter, fall asleep, and die from the intense cold?

And most important, did the two men reach the summit? Odell testified that they were only 800 feet from the top. Were they really the first to conquer Mount Everest, not Hillary and Norgay?

It is very likely that the bodies of Mallory and Irvine are still very well preserved in the high altitude of Everest, even after so many years. If their cameras (as well as their bodies) are ever recovered, and the film can be developed, perhaps the world would know whether these two were the first to reach the top.

In 1924 Odell declared, "Considering the position they had reached on the mountain, I am of the opinion that Mallory and Irvine must have reached the summit."

Did they or didn't they? It may never be known. Mallory once wrote, "We expect no mercy from Everest," and he was right.

Now answer Numbers 1 through 9. Base your answers on the article "Conquering Mount Everest."

1 Which detail BEST supports the idea that climbing Mount Everest was the major goal of Mallory's life?

    A. He took experienced mountain climbers with him on his expeditions.

    B. He and the other climbers set up six camps on the mountain to help them reach the top.

    C. He took along a camera to prove that he and Irvine had reached the mountain summit.

    D. He made another attempt to climb Mount Everest even after he was almost killed in an avalanche.

2 What organization method does the author use in the first paragraph?

    F. flashback

    G. foreshadowing

    H. question/answer

    I. argument/support

3 What can you infer from the fact that Hillary and Norgay were officially the first people to reach Mount Everest's summit?

    A. Their bodies were found at the summit by later climbers.

    B. They took a photographer along to take photos for evidence.

    C. They must have made it back alive after reaching the summit.

    D. They were better mountain climbers than Mallory and Irvine.

4 What is the MAIN idea of the article?

    F. It is a mystery whether Mallory and Irvine died during their climb to the top.

    G. It is unknown whether Mallory and Irvine made it to the top of Mount Everest.

    H. It is a fact that Mallory and Irvine were the first to reach Mount Everest's summit.

    I. It is certain that Hillary and Norgay were the first to reach the top of Mount Everest.

5 What organization method does the author use for the article as a whole?

    A. time order

    B. spatial order

    C. cause and effect

    D. comparison/contrast

Getting the Point

6 Read the sentence below.

Camp Five was located at 25,000 feet, and Camp Six was established at 27,000 feet, only 2,100 feet shy of the summit.

What does the phrase *shy of* mean in the sentence?

F. next to
G. beyond
H. short of
I. far from

7 How many times did Mallory attempt to reach the summit of Mount Everest?

A. 1
B. 2
C. 3
D. 4

8 What is the MAIN idea of the paragraph that begins with the sentence: "Odell searched for two hours with no luck"?

F. Odell tried his best to find Mallory and Irvine.
G. Odell never gave up hope of finding Mallory and Irvine.
H. Mallory and Irvine must have died during their climb.
I. Mallory and Irvine did not respond to Odell's shouting.

9 Which detail BEST supports the idea that Mallory and Irvine did reach the summit?

A. Irvine was an experienced mountain climber.
B. Camp Six was set up very close to the summit.
C. Odell saw them only 800 feet from the summit.
D. Mallory had already tried to climb Everest in the past.

Read the article "Mars Mission Offers Clues in Hunt for New Worlds" before answering Numbers 1 through 9.

Mars Mission Offers Clues in Hunt for New Worlds

by Randal Jackson

Is there another Mars out there? Within the next decade or so, NASA plans to develop space telescopes with super-sharp vision that can detect planets like Mars or Earth around other stars. In the meantime, learning as much as we can about our terrestrial next-door neighbors will help us understand what to look for, according to scientists at NASA's Jet Propulsion Laboratory.

While more than 100 planets have been discovered outside our Solar System, all of them are gaseous giants like Jupiter and Saturn. NASA's search for life beyond our Solar System hinges on eventually detecting smaller, rocky planets. As far as we know, these are the only type of planets that could harbor liquid water on the surface, considered essential to life.

But which are we most likely to find—another Mars, or another Earth, or perhaps a Venus? That remains an open question, according to Vikki Meadows, an astrobiologist at JPL.

"It may be that Earths are unusual, or common. Terrestrial Planet Finder is an experiment we have to run in order to find out," Meadows said.

One of the goals of the Mars Exploration Rover mission is to determine the past climate history of Mars. Knowing what Mars was like before it became the barren, static world we see today would help scientists recognize a younger version of Mars should it turn up out there among the stars.

The Viking mission, which placed two landers on Mars in the 1970s, told scientists that the planet has undergone massive alterations since its formation. Scientists believe it was once a warm, wet world with plate tectonics, active volcanoes, and a magnetic field that could protect the surface from deadly radiation.

But after about 1 billion years, its chances of becoming another Earth were over. Because of its relatively puny mass (about one-tenth that of Earth), Mars didn't have enough gravity to hang onto some of the conditions favorable to life. It cooled quickly. It lost much of its atmosphere. It froze solid. Its magnetic field collapsed. Its once-fearsome volcanoes sputtered out.

Over subsequent eons, while the Earth stabilized, formed oceans, and developed a hospitable atmosphere, Mars changed very little. Because of this, scientists believe, Mars is the planetary equivalent of a time capsule. "Mars is a snapshot that shows us what terrestrial planets look like at an early age," said David Crisp, a senior research scientist at JPL.

Getting to Know Our Neighbors

In 2013, NASA will launch Terrestrial Planet Finder, a space telescope with revolutionary optics that will be able to detect and characterize small rocky planets around other stars. We might find another planet like Mars, or a planet like Earth. But finding either at exactly the same point in their evolution as our own Solar System is unlikely.

"With Terrestrial Planet Finder, you don't get to pick the age of the solar system you look at," Crisp said. "You only get to look at solar systems in various stages of their evolution. We may find planets that look like early Earth, or early Mars. So it would be nice to understand them."

For the time being, the best way scientists have to prepare is by understanding the history of our own terrestrial neighbors.

"Terrestrial planets in our Solar System are remarkably diverse," Meadows said, "and I don't think they span the range of what you might see [in other solar systems]. If you don't understand your nearest neighbors, there's no point in studying the distant ones."

Now answer Numbers 1 through 9. Base your answers on the article "Mars Mission Offers Clues in Hunt for New Worlds."

1 Why do scientists want to find other planets that are like Earth and Mars?

   A. They are the easiest to find.
   B. They are small and rocky.
   C. They are the most likely to have life.
   D. They are found in our solar system.

2 How are the planets Jupiter and Saturn ALIKE?

   F. They are both frozen solid.
   G. They are both small in mass.
   H. They are both gaseous planets.
   I. They are both able to harbor water.

3 Which of these is essential for life to exist on a planet?

   A. radiation
   B. solid rock
   C. volcanoes
   D. liquid water

4 What is the MAIN idea of the article?

F. Scientists can learn more about Earth by studying planets like Mars.
G. Scientists hope to find signs of life on planets beyond our solar system.
H. Scientists have discovered over one hundred planets outside of our solar system.
I. Scientists can identify planets that are like Earth and Mars by learning about Mars.

5 Read the sentence below.

The Viking mission, which placed two landers on Mars in the 1970s, told scientists that the planet has undergone massive alterations since its formation.

What does the word *alterations* mean?

A. changes
B. decaying
C. eruptions
D. explosion

6 What organization method does the author use in the first paragraph?

F. time order
G. spatial order
H. question/answer
I. comparison/contrast

7 Which detail supports the idea that Mars is a "time capsule"?

A. Mars is frozen solid.
B. Mars is smaller than Earth.
C. Mars once had a magnetic field.
D. Mars once had active volcanoes.

8 What is the MAIN idea of the paragraph that begins "In 2013, NASA will launch Terrestrial Planet Finder . . ."?

F. The Terrestrial Planet Finder will find planets like Mars.
G. The Terrestrial Planet Finder will find solar systems like ours.
H. The Terrestrial Planet Finder will find rocky planets the same size and age as Mars and Earth.
I. The Terrestrial Planet Finder will find small, rocky planets that are not the same age as Mars and Earth.

9 What prevented Mars from becoming another Earth?

A. It was too small.
B. It was too far from the sun.
C. It had too many volcanoes.
D. It had too strong of a gravity field.

Read the article "Tech-Trash Tragedy" before answering Numbers 1 through 9.

TECH-TRASH TRAGEDY

by Liam O'Donnell

In our wired world, technology moves at a laser-fast pace. Every day, a new gadget arrives and promises to bring us the future, today. In the race for faster computers and more powerful gadgets, it's easy to forget about yesterday's high-tech wonders.

Unfortunately, many times used computers and gadgets end up in landfills across the country. Each year, we throw away 12 million computers. By the end of 2004, we had junked 30 million cell phones, and that is not good news for the environment. To make our gadgets work, many of them use materials like lead and mercury. When mercury and lead end up in a landfill, they spread poisons into the earth, water, and air for miles around. This is called e-waste—and it's becoming a big pollution problem around the world.

Big problems call for big solutions, so adults and kids from dozens of countries are working hard to clean up our e-waste. And you can help, too.

Turning Old Into New

The trick to stopping e-waste is to catch it before it gets into the landfill. That's why the seventh-grade students at Cityside Middle School in Zeeland, Michigan organized a computer drop-off event. They put up posters and spread the word around the town, telling people to bring out their old computers.

And the people of Zeeland got the message. They dropped off dozens of old computers, monitors, and printers at the school.

With their school gym filled with old computers, the students were ready for the next step in cleaning up the high-tech trash: turning old computers into new ones.

That's where companies like RePC step in. The Seattle company takes e-waste and turns it into e-gold. "Almost all of the parts of a computer can be reused or recycled," says Mark Dabek, owner of RePC. Any computer parts that can't be reused or sold get recycled in a way that won't hurt the environment. "The circuit boards are sent to a circuit board recycler that chops them and sends them to a facility with a very, very hot furnace called 'the reactor,'" Dabek says. After the computer parts are safely crushed and burned, their raw materials can be reused to make everything from appliances to office buildings.

Sometimes you can make a new computer from the parts of an old computer. Called refurbishing, it's what the tech whizzes at RePC do best. Buying a refurbished computer is a lot cheaper than buying a new one. But who wants a computer made up of old parts?

A lot of people, actually. Places like schools and community centers are often short on cash, but need computers to help them get things done. Robert Sterling, a computer teacher at Estancia High School in California, uses computers donated from local businesses to motivate students and teach them about recycling. "If kids learn to recycle everything," says Sterling, "they will set a good example for some of the older people who are not in the habit yet of recycling everyday."

Computers aren't the only technology that can be reused. Last year, schools in New Mexico gave old cell phones a new lease on life while also helping to raise money for charity. The students collected 11 garbage bags of old cell phones, sold them to a cell phone refurbishing company, donated the money to charity, and helped keep the environment clean—all at the same time.

Building a Greener Future

Some computer makers are tackling tech trash by designing more environmentally responsible products. More new computers are made with recycled plastic and use less electricity. Many also have no lead in their circuits, which makes them less damaging to the environment. The same goes for those new flat monitors. Not only do they look cool, but they also use less-harmful chemicals.

Computers are an important part of our wired world. It's up to us to make sure that they don't pollute our planet. Talking to others about e-waste is a great way to start tackling the problem. Speak to your teacher about organizing a computer collection drive at your school. Next time your baseball team is raising money, try collecting old cell phones. By working together for a clean future, we can make e-waste a thing of the past.

Now answer Numbers 1 through 9. Base your answers on the article "Tech-Trash Tragedy."

1 What organization method does the author use in the article?

    A. question/answer
    B. problem/solution
    C. cause and effect
    D. compare and contrast

2 What is the MAIN idea of the article?

    F. Landfills are being filled up with used computers.
    G. Computers and cell phones are polluting the environment.
    H. People are taking action to clean up and prevent tech-trash.
    I. Technology is making our lives easier, but it is also causing problems.

3 What is the meaning of the word *refurbish*?

    A. fix up
    B. give away
    C. break down
    D. throw away

Getting the Point

4 What is the MAIN idea of the second paragraph of the article?

    F. High-tech trash can pollute the earth.

    G. Many high-tech gadgets are made with toxic substances.

    H. People throw away millions of high-tech gadgets each year.

    I. Mercury and lead in landfills can poison the earth, water, and air.

5 What can you infer from the information that kids who recycle will set an example for older people?

    A. Kids learn new habits faster than older people.

    B. Kids understand technology better than older people.

    C. Older people have less concern for the environment.

    D. Older people did not learn about recycling when they were kids.

6 How are new computers DIFFERENT from older computers?

    F. They are made to last longer.

    G. They use lead in their circuits.

    H. They are better for the environment.

    I. They take up more space in landfills.

7 Which detail supports the idea that cell phone technology changes very quickly?

    A. People threw away 30 million cell phones in 2004.

    B. Collecting cell phones is a good way to raise money.

    C. Cell phones can be taken to special recycling companies.

    D. Students in New Mexico collected cell phones to help a charity.

8 What is the author's message in the last paragraph?

    F. Computer collection drives can help schools.

    G. Computers are an important part of modern life.

    H. We need to stop relying so much on technology.

    I. We should all take action to prevent high-tech trash.

9 According to the author, who is responsible for making sure that computers do not pollute the earth?

    A. everyone

    B. computer makers

    C. computer recyclers

    D. computer instructors

MAKING SENSE OF IT

On the FCAT, you will often be asked to identify the main idea, supporting details, and organizational pattern of a reading selection. To do so effectively, you should use the strategies covered in this chapter.

- **Main Idea:** the most important point a writer makes; can be stated or implied
- **Details:** support the main idea; usually factual or sensory
- **Organization:** ways of ordering sentences and paragraphs; used to convey meaning; examples include

cause and effect	comparison and contrast
spatial order	time order
flashback	foreshadowing
bulleted lists	question/answer

Chapter Four

The Author's "Why"

Benchmark: L.A.E.2.3.2

The student identifies the author's purpose and/or point of view in a variety of texts and uses the information to construct meaning. (Includes **LA.A.2.2.2** Identifies the author's purpose in a simple text, and **LA.A.2.2.3** Recognizes when a text is primarily intended to persuade.)

"How long has she been up there?" Randi asked the police officer.

"Eight hours," the officer responded. Randi peered up into the oak tree for signs of Jocelyn.

"Do you think maybe you could talk her down?" he asked.

"I can try," Randi said. "Jocelyn! Can you hear me? You won! No one realized that this was the first tree planted by the city founders! They're not going to cut it down! They're going to make a special plaque for it and everything! C'mon, Jocelyn! Please come down!"

Way up in the tree, they saw the branches quiver, and then a blue-jean-clad leg appeared, along with a sneakered foot, searching for a branch. Another leg appeared, and an arm, and another arm. Randi held her breath as her friend made her way down the tree.

No one would sit for eight hours in a tree for no reason. Randi's friend Jocelyn did it because she wanted to stop people from cutting it down. That was Jocelyn's purpose for doing what she did (even though she could have taken safer actions to call attention to her cause!). Her point of view was that this tree was important historically and should be honored, not destroyed.

103

Like Jocelyn in her oak tree, writers have a purpose and a point of view when they write. Their purpose could be to persuade people not to do something, or to persuade them to do something. But writers also write for other purposes, such as to inform people about topics or just to entertain people. Their purpose for writing and their point of view determine what they write and how they write about their topic.

This chapter focuses on helping you identify an author's purpose and point of view, so that as a reader, you will understand what the author (like Jocelyn) is "up" to—and why.

Key Concepts

- **Author's Purpose:** All writing has a purpose. Usually it is to persuade, inform, entertain, or share an experience.
- **Author's Point of View:** A writer's experiences and beliefs influence the way he or she writes about a topic.
- **Root:** The *root* is the main part of the word, to which prefixes or suffixes may be added. Sometimes a root can stand alone as a word.

LESSON 1: Author's Purpose

Sometimes students think that a person would have to be a mind reader to know what an author's purpose might be. They ask, "How am *I* supposed to know what the author's purpose is?" or say, "I don't know the author. He probably just likes to write!" While many authors *do* write because they like to, all authors write for at least one other reason as well.

WHY STUDY THIS?

Authors do things in their writing for specific reasons. Recognizing why an author has written something is an important part of being a consumer, an informed citizen, and an active reader. There are four basic **reasons** people write: to persuade, to inform, to entertain, or to share a personal experience. A good way to remember these reasons is with the use of a "memory helper" called a mnemonic device, such as the one here.

The Author's "Why"

> **Reasons people write**
>
> P = to Persuade (Example: an newspaper editorial asking people to obey leash laws when they walk their dogs)
>
> I = to Inform (Example: an article explaining the causes of pollution in a local lake)
>
> E = to Entertain (Example: a mystery novel about a girl who solves a decades-old crime in her community)
>
> S = to Share a personal experience (Example: an autobiographical story about a boy and his relationship with his grandfather)
>
> To remember the reasons people write, think of **PIES**.

FCAT Fred Says:

You can practice figuring out the author's purpose no matter what you're reading, even this book! Go ahead! Give it a shot!

Why did the author of this book include the information about PIES in the last paragraph?

A. because the author would like some pie

B. because FCAT Fred would like some pie

C. because the author enjoys tormenting cats by talking about pie when there *is* no pie

D. because the memory trick PIES will help the reader remember the four basic reasons writers write

Writing That Persuades

Another word for *persuade* is *convince*. People who are writing to persuade—or convince—use language to try to make their readers *do* something. What they want readers to do could range from voting for a presidential candidate to volunteering at a school car wash to raise money for a field trip. A writer could be attempting to convince readers to try a new brand of cereal or to visit a theme park.

Persuasive writing can take many forms including, letters, speeches, advertisements, editorials, and essays.

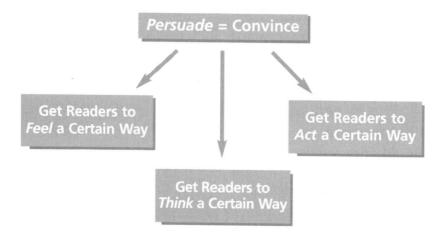

Writing That Informs

Writing meant to inform is everywhere. In fact, pieces written to persuade, entertain, or share personal experiences often have sections meant to inform as well. Informational writing tells you *about* something. It could be a textbook on reading skills, like this one, or an article about the life cycle of a butterfly in a nature magazine. Writing meant to inform wants to teach you about something. It does not try to persuade you to do anything.

So where else might we find writing that informs? It can be found in newspapers, pamphlets, and reference books (for example, encyclopedias, dictionaries, how-to manuals).

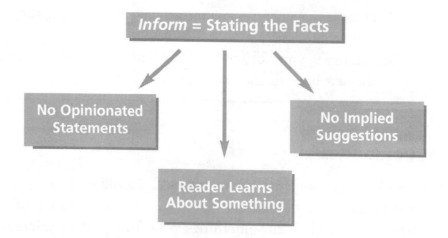

Writing That Entertains

Much of the reading people do is for fun. When we read a scary story, we enjoy the tingly feeling of being scared out of our wits. When we read a science-fiction book, we are interested in the characters and what happens to them, and we enjoy discovering the fantastic world created by the author. When we read a poem, we enjoy the rhythm, the sound, and the images created by the words. When authors write to entertain, their goal is to make us laugh, cry, scream, have fun, and enjoy the magic of the words themselves.

Writing That Shares a Personal Experience

Often, writers wish to share their special memories, interesting experiences, or hopes and dreams. This type of writing sometimes takes the form of letters, diary entries, essays, or articles.

When an author writes to share a personal experience, readers may feel strong emotions as they identify with the writer. For instance, you might be inspired by a teenager's composition about the moment he risked his own reputation to stand up for a friend.

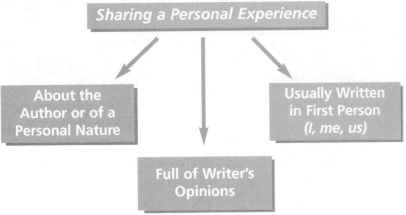

FCAT Fred Says:

Reading only the first or last few sentences of an article or a story might mislead you about the author's purpose. Titles can also be misleading. For this reason, you should always read the entire piece before deciding why an author wrote it. On the FCAT multiple-choice questions, you must read all possible answers. The answer you select should be the BEST of all options.

To give you an example, after I read this headline in the newspaper, I hid under the bed for two weeks!

"CAT BURGLAR STRIKES AGAIN!"

Finally, I read the rest of the article:

> For the third time in a month, a thief has managed, under the cloak of darkness, to sneak unnoticed into one of our city's finest homes and steal thousands of dollars worth of jewelry. No other valuables were touched. The sleeping residents and their highly valued purebred Persian cats were unharmed.
>
> Jewelry! All they took was jewelry! Nothing for me to worry about, although I did change the combination on the safe where I kept my faux-diamond-studded collar.

SEEING IT IN ACTION

Now that we have talked about the four basic reasons authors write, we can take a look at a few pieces of writing. As you read, pay attention to the author's choice of words. Notice the verbs and nouns used in each paragraph that help the author achieve his or her purpose.

Now read the following letter to the principal of the school, written by a woman in response to a local decision to end a summer concert series.

> October 22, 2005
>
> To the Editor:
>
> I have just learned that the outdoor summer concert series in Cooper's Park has been canceled due to complaints from nearby residents about the noise. Okay, then let's shut down the airport, too, so that we won't have to listen to those noisy jets taking off and landing! No one would think of closing the airport due to noise because it's important to our community. The summer concerts are important to our community, too. I can't think of a more enjoyable way to spend a lovely summer evening than by listening to great music in beautiful Cooper's Park with my friends and family. It is a tragedy that a few people have taken it upon themselves to rob our community of the gift of music. Today, the summer concert series—tomorrow, it could be the fireworks at our annual Fourth of July celebration. Where will it end?
>
> Sincerely,
>
> Sofia Brown

The Author's "Why"

The author's purpose is not stated outright in this letter, but the message is still clear. Although the author doesn't come right out and say "Bring back the summer concert series," that is clearly what she hopes will happen. She achieves her purpose by first suggesting that the airport be shut down, too, since airplanes are also noisy. She doesn't really want this to happen. She's just using sarcasm to make a point. Then she states that just as airports are important to the community, so are outdoor concerts. She uses the phrase "a lovely summer evening" to create a happy image of an enjoyable summer night in the mind of the reader. Then she uses strong words like "tragedy" and "rob" to show how wrong she thinks it is to have the concert series shut down. Then she warns that these same people might shut down the fireworks at the Fourth of July celebration. This example suggests that the people who complained about the noisy concerts might even be un-American!

An FCAT question about this reading might take on the following form:

What was Sophia Brown's main purpose for writing her letter to the editor?

   A. to show that music has many benefits to a community
   B. to persuade people to shut down the airport as well as the concerts
   C. to convince people that it was wrong to shut down the summer concerts
   D. to inform people about the future plans of the people who shut down the concerts

Which answer choice do you think is correct? The writer might have the viewpoint that music has many benefits, but this was not her main purpose. Therefore, choice A is incorrect. As noted above, she was just being sarcastic to make a point when she said the airport should be shut down, so choice B is also incorrect. As for choice D, she does talk about what might happen to the Fourth of July fireworks display, but that is just a detail to help support the real purpose of her letter, which is choice C, to convince people that it was wrong to shut down the summer concerts.

FCAT Fred Says:

When authors write to persuade, they use many methods. They may speak badly about other people or product names. They may describe emotionally upsetting or uplifting scenes to tug at readers' heartstrings. Sometimes they list only the facts that support their main points while ignoring facts that support the opposition.

In most instances, tactics are used to make you "think" with your emotions instead of with your mind.

Be aware: There are times when writers do not state their opinion directly. In these instances, the reader is expected to *infer* the author's purpose. That requires putting two and two together. The reader must become a detective, reading carefully for clues.

See if you can infer, or figure out, the purpose of this letter, which was written by my opponent a few years back when I was running for governor. As you read it, be aware of the tactics my opponent uses.

My Fellow Floridians,

Last week, I was enjoying time at the beach with my sweet husband and two beautiful children. FCAT Fred was there, too. Suddenly, a heart-wrenching cry came from far out in the bay, "Help! Jellyfish!" Some poor, helpless child had been attacked by one of those stinging monsters of the deep! We all sprang to our feet. But what did FCAT Fred do? He whipped out a fancy bib, took out a knife and fork, and yelled, "Where! Where's the jellied fish!"

"Not 'jellied fish,' you fool! 'Jellyfish'!" I yelled, running headlong into the pounding surf with no thought for my own safety. I swam out and rescued the child just as he was about to bob under the surface for the last time. When the ambulance arrived, that selfish, uncaring FCAT Fred felt no concern for the child, just a crushing disappointment that there was no "jellied fish" for dinner.

I thought the community would appreciate this glimpse into the real FCAT Fred.

Sincerely,

Polly Tishian

What was Polly Tishian's main purpose for writing her letter to the editor?

A. to show people her bravery in a life-threatening situation

B. to inform people of the danger that jellyfish pose to swimmers

C. to persuade people to keep a close watch over their children at the beach

D. to convince people that FCAT Fred lacks the personal qualities to be governor

The Author's "Why"

The answer was D. Well! What could I do but write a letter to the editor myself, explaining that I had planned to use the knife and fork to skewer that jellyfish and rescue the child. Unfortunately, the public believed Polly's letter because of her emotionally charged language, and I lost the election. But looking back, it's just as well. The duties of governor would have severely cut into my nap time.

If you were curious about eagles, you would probably look for information in a textbook or on the Internet. You wouldn't expect the information to encourage you to love or hate eagles, as you would in a letter to the editor about eagles. You would expect the text simply to state the facts. Then you would form your own opinion about these birds. This is what people who want to make informed decisions do: They read all the information they can find about a topic and form an opinion based on facts. Here is a passage about eagles that is written simply to inform:

Eagles of the World

Most, if not all, Americans are familiar with our national bird, the bald eagle, and in certain parts of the country, people are also familiar with our other North American eagle: the golden eagle. However, many people are unaware that, in addition to the bald eagle and the golden eagle, there are fifty-seven other species of eagles throughout the world, living on all continents except Antarctica.

The world's eagles share many features: They all have large, hooked beaks, powerful talons, and keen eyesight. These characteristics help them to hunt, catch, and eat their prey. But there are many differences as well. The largest eagles in the world can weigh more than twenty pounds and have an eight-foot wingspan, while one of the tiniest eagles is only the size of a pigeon.

Their prey varies as well. One of the largest eagles, the African harpy eagle, hunts deer. The crested serpent eagle, as its name suggests, hunts snakes. The main prey of the American bald eagle is fish, while in

Greece, golden eagles eat turtles by first hoisting them into the air and then dropping them on rocks to crack open their shells.

There is another thing, however, that the world's eagles have in common. Because of hunting, pollution, and destruction of their habitats, many species of eagles are seeing their populations dwindle.

Now read a passage written by another author on the same topic. This time you should be able to see how the writer puts a persuasive spin on the information. How does she accomplish this?

Eagles are the most magnificent creatures that ever walked, or rather, *flew* the earth. Throughout history, kings and emperors have worshipped the eagle and used it as a national symbol, taking strength and inspiration from the courage, power, and grace of these glorious birds of prey. But in spite of their magnificence, many of the fifty-nine species of eagles throughout the world are in peril due to hunting, habitat destruction, and the poisoning of their remaining habitats with pollution. We must continue to give our support to groups like S.O.A.R. (Save Our American Raptors), a group founded by Florida's "Eagle Lady," Doris Mager. Please help S.O.A.R. continue to bring its educational programs to our classrooms so that they can educate the next generation of Americans to protect and cherish the eagles in our country.

See the difference? While this writer presents facts, she also includes opinions and emotional appeals. She wants to persuade readers to support groups that are working to educate the public about eagles.

Now read the following poem and think about what its purpose might be.

The Author's "Why"

The Eagle
by Alfred, Lord Tennyson

He clasps the crag with crooked hands;

Close to the sun in lonely lands,

Ring'd with the azure world, he stands.

The wrinkled sea beneath him crawls;

He watches from his mountain walls,

And like a thunderbolt he falls.

What would you say the purpose of this poem is? Does it try to teach us something about eagles? Does it try to make us feel a certain way about this particular eagle? The author creatively uses vivid phrases like "crooked hands" and "azure world" to paint an image in the reader's mind of a perched eagle that suddenly dives off a mountain cliff like a "thunderbolt." The rhythm of the poem and the rhyming lines at the end of each stanza make the poem fun to read. The poem was meant to entertain by giving the reader the enjoyable experience of "seeing" the eagle through the poet's words.

Read the following letter and consider what the author's purpose for writing it might have been.

Dear Monique,

Well, Albert and I had an interesting weekend! The rivers were finally back to normal after the high waters of spring runoff, so we took the canoe down the Bitterroot for the first time this year. It was a beautiful morning. A soft fog curled up the pine trees along the banks, and there were little wisps of steam rising from the river. Within the first hour of the float, we saw a doe and her tiny spotted fawn, an otter, and some wild turkeys.

But the most amazing thing we saw appeared near the end of the trip, right before the take-out point. We came around a bend in the river and saw a bald eagle on a sand dune with a fish in its talons. As we got closer, we expected it to fly away, but it didn't. It just hopped back a few feet and then stared at us. We realized that it couldn't fly. Something had damaged its wing.

We beached the canoe and Albert grabbed our picnic blanket. Between the two of us, we managed to herd the eagle into the blanket. At first, it beat its wings like crazy, but it tired out quickly and then was more or less still. We got back in the canoe, and I paddled us the short distance to the take-out point while Albert held onto the eagle.

Fortunately, we still had the dog's crate in the car from the last time we took him to the vet, so we placed the eagle in the crate, drove home, and called the Raptors of the Rockies rehabilitation center. After they examined the eagle, they told us that its wing had been shot, but that its chances of recovery were good.

The author's main purpose for writing this letter is to *share* what happened to her. No attempt is made to persuade the reader to do anything. The author does not suggest that the reader, think, act, or feel any particular way. Neither does she attempt to teach her friend or share important information. Her story is interesting because it is written in such a way that the reader can see the events unfolding. Therefore, if an FCAT question asked, "What is MOST LIKELY the author's purpose for writing the above letter?" a reader should answer, "to share a personal experience."

The Author's "Why"

FCAT Fred Says:

An author may have more than one "fish to fry," so to speak! By this I mean that an author may have more than one reason for writing. Don't assume that every personal story was written merely because the writer wanted to share his or her experience. Sometimes authors write about personal experiences in order to teach lessons or persuade.

For example, when I was adopted, my owner suffered from the misconception that cats were supposed to sleep on a floor rug in the cold, dank basement. So I told him this story:

> Once upon a time, there was a kitten named, Fred—I mean, Franklin. His owner lived in a beautiful but very old house. In fact, it was a house about the same age as our house. His owner adored him so much that he let him sleep at the foot of his bed. One night, a terrible fire broke out, sparked by faulty wiring in the house, which, as I said, was a very old house, just like our house. Franklin's owner was a very sound sleeper, just like you, and he didn't wake up even as deadly smoke filled the bedroom. But Franklin woke up, realized there was a fire, and jumped up on his sleeping owner's chest and meowed and meowed until his owner woke up and got them both out of the burning house.

Did my owner pick up on the *real* reason I told him this story? Not exactly. Instead of letting me sleep on the bed, he installed a smoke detector in the bedroom!

Since an author may have more than one reason for writing, be sure to read FCAT passages all the way through to find the *main* reason the author is writing. Other reasons are secondary. And remember that you might have to do a little reading between the lines!

Try It Out — Read the poem "Stopping by Woods on a Snowy Evening." Then answer the questions that follow.

Stopping by Woods on a Snowy Evening
by Robert Frost

Whose woods these are I think I know.
His house is in the village, though;
He will not see me stopping here
To watch his woods fill up with snow.

My little horse must think it queer
To stop without a farmhouse near
Between the woods and frozen lake
The darkest evening of the year.

He gives his harness bells a shake
To ask if there is some mistake.
The only other sound's the sweep
Of easy wind and downy flake.

The woods are lovely, dark, and deep,
But I have promises to keep,
And miles to go before I sleep,
And miles to go before I sleep.

❶ What is the author's MAIN purpose for writing this poem?
- A. to persuade the reader to take the time to enjoy nature
- B. to express his frustration at having to keep all the promises he made
- C. to explain how much easier it is to enjoy nature when you are by yourself
- D. to share a moment when he was caught up by the beauty of the woods in winter

❷ Why does the author describe his horse's reaction to his stopping in the woods?
- F. to show the close bond between him and his horse
- G. to show how cold it was in the snowy woods that evening
- H. to show how horses are able to communicate their feelings to people
- I. to show that stopping there at that time of night was an unusual thing to do

The Author's "Why" 117

3. Why does the author repeat the last line, "And miles to go before I sleep"?
  A. to stress how far he still has to go on his journey
  B. to show that he is determined to make his destination that evening
  C. to suggest that he is falling asleep under the magic spell of the woods
  D. to reveal that he does not want to continue this journey

Now read how one student answered these questions.

1. The poem seems to be about an experience the poet had when he noticed how "lovely, dark, and deep" the woods were that evening. Therefore, choice D must be correct.

2. The horse seems puzzled by the author stopping in the woods in the middle of the night. Choice I must be the correct answer.

3. Repeating the line "And miles to go before I sleep" is almost like saying "I have miles and miles and miles to go." The repetition makes the journey seem like a very long one, so choice A must be correct.

FCAT Fred Says:

To be better prepared when taking the FCAT, you should practice as much as possible! One good way to practice is to find newspaper articles with interesting headlines and ask yourself, "What was the author's purpose for writing this?" You should find articles in the paper that cover each of the four basic reasons for writing.

Read the following headlines and write *P* if the writer will most likely try to persuade you to do something in his or her story, *I* if the writer wants to inform you, *E* if the writer wants to entertain you, or *S* if the writer wants to share a personal story with you

_____ 1. "The Legacy of Hurricane Andrew: One Florida Family Tells Its Story"

_____ 2. "Volunteers Needed for Fall Food Drive"

_____ 3. "Monarch Butterfly Migration Happens Early This Year"

_____ 4. "Take My Dog!—Please! Living with a Great Dane in a 'Chihuahua' House"

LESSON 2: Author's Point of View

Recognizing an author's point of view is very important in becoming an informed reader. Every author has a point of view, or opinion, that is formed by his or her life experiences. A point of view is the position or standpoint from which he or she considers a topic. Often the point of view includes beliefs and assumptions that the author makes about a topic.

WHY STUDY THIS?

Often, the author's point of view reflects biases, or personal judgments. For example, suppose an author is a teenager who likes to dress in a way that expresses her individuality. She is writing a letter to the school board about a plan to have students wear school uniforms. Writing from the point of view of a teenager who wants to express her own personal style, this author would most likely be against the idea. Her bias against school uniforms could keep her from seeing any positive effects uniforms might have at her school. She might also assume that most teenagers are against school uniforms and that most adults are for uniforms.

Imagine that the school board got another letter from a person who was strongly in favor of school uniforms. However, the author of this letter is the president of a company that makes school uniforms. His company would make a lot of money if the school board decided to have students wear uniforms. His bias for school uniforms would keep him from seeing the value of students expressing their own individuality through their clothing.

Recognizing an author's point of view—his or her attitude toward a subject—can help readers determine whether they want to consider seriously what the author has to say. It also helps readers understand and become more involved personally with a piece of text.

THINK OF IT THIS WAY

Examining any written work closely will help you gain insight into the author's point of view. Here are a few things to pay attention to when reading.

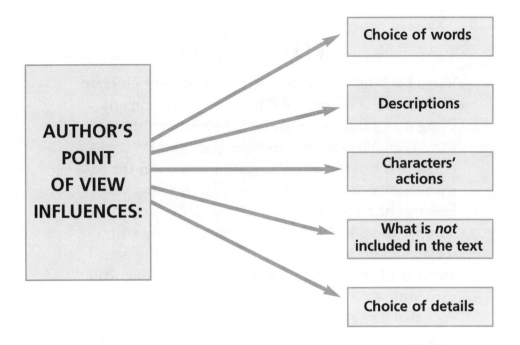

The table below shows how the letters written by the teenager and the president of the school-uniform company would have been influenced by their different points of view:

The Author's Point of View Influences . . .	Teenager's Letter	Uniform Company President's Letter
Choice of words	freedom, individuality, personal style, creativity	control, responsibility, work values, classroom management, school pride
Descriptions	description of teenagers acting like robots	description of orderly, well-behaved teenagers
What is not included in the text	positive effects of school uniforms	negative effects of school uniforms
Choice of details	description of the uniforms as ugly and boring	description of the uniforms as sharp and classy

SEEING IT IN ACTION

Read the following paragraph about parents using television as a babysitter for their kids.

DVD on Board

It's bad enough that many parents park their children in front of the television at home for hours on end, using it as a full-time electronic babysitter. But now parents are buying vehicles equipped with DVD players so that this intrusive babysitter can go on the road with them as well. I understand that traveling with kids can be a challenge. There's the endless chorus of "Are we there yet?" and "I'm hungry!" along with the inevitable turf wars between siblings over the prized territory of the back seat. But traveling on long road trips with your kids can also be a rewarding experience that can give your family the opportunity for meaningful conversation. Don't let video intrude on the quality time provided by a family car trip.

After reading this passage, do you know what the author's purpose is? He or she wants to persuade readers not to get DVD players in their cars.

What is his or her point of view? His or her point of view is that car trips give families the opportunity to get closer through conversation and that DVD players in cars can ruin this opportunity.

Now read the following passage on the same topic. Does the author have the same or a different point of view?

I Want My DVD

Recently, I overheard a couple discussing, with horror, the optional DVD players that are now available for cars. They swore they would never have one in their vehicle because it would destroy the wonderful opportunity long car trips provide for families to enjoy quality time together. Let me just say this: When I was a kid, we used to travel from Iowa to Kansas three times a year to visit my dad's brother in Junction City. These trips were the most excruciatingly boring experiences of my young life. Mile after mile of cornfield after cornfield, interrupted only by the occasional barn or silo. I would try to escape the tedium by reading, only to become carsick. My older sister did not get carsick and would have her face buried in a book for the whole trip. My dad was one of those always-in-a-hurry drivers, so he was too busy passing in and out of traffic to be much company, and my mom was just praying that we would survive the trip. So as far as I'm concerned, DVD players should be standard equipment in all vehicles.

Key Concepts

- An **author's purpose** is usually to persuade, to entertain, to inform, or to share an experience.
- Everybody—writers as well as readers—has a point of view.
- A **point of view** is a personal attitude that affects the way someone interprets the world.
- Point of view can influence the way an author writes, the words he or she chooses, the actions and descriptions of characters, the conclusions drawn, etc.

Read the article "Internet Safety: Safe Surfing Tips for Teens" before answering Numbers 1 through 9.

Internet Safety: Safe Surfing Tips for Teens

How could we exist without the Internet? That's how most of us keep in touch with friends, find homework support, research a cool place to visit, or find out the latest news. But just as there are millions of places to visit and things to do, there are also lots of places to waste time—and even get into trouble. And, just like the rest of the world, there are some people who can take advantage of you—financially or physically.

You've probably heard stories about people who get into trouble in chat rooms. Because users can easily remain anonymous, chat rooms often attract people who are interested in more than just chatting. These people will sometimes ask visitors for information about themselves, their families, or where they live—information that shouldn't be given away.

Usually, the people who request personal information like home addresses, phone numbers, and e-mail addresses use this information to fill mailboxes and answering machines with advertisements. In some cases, though, predators may use this information to begin illegal or indecent relationships or to harm a person's or family's well-being. It's rare, but it does happen.

Of course, the Internet is home to millions of places you can and should visit. Like a library, the Web can take you to the ends of the earth with the information it contains.

You can use it as an encyclopedia to do research for school. If you're interested in going to college, you can save gas and money by checking out university Web sites in advance. And finding employment or volunteer opportunities is easier online, too. Instead of being limited to one local newspaper or word of mouth, you can find out what's available all over your city, state, or country with a click of the mouse.

The key is to protect yourself while you surf.

Smart Surfing

First rule of smart surfing? Remain as anonymous as possible. That means keeping all private information private. Here are some examples of private information that you should never give out on the Internet:

- full name
- home address
- phone number
- social security numbers
- passwords
- names of family members
- credit card numbers

Most credible people and companies will never ask for this type of information online. So if someone does, it's a red flag that they may be up to no good.

Think carefully before you create an e-mail address or screen name. Web experts recommend that you use a combination of letters and numbers in both—and that you don't identify whether you're male or female.

In chat rooms, use a nickname that's different from your screen name. That way, if you ever find yourself in a conversation that makes you uncomfortable, you can exit without having to worry that someone knows your screen name and can track you down via e-mail. Some people who hang out with their friends online set up private chat rooms where only they and the people they invite can enter to chat. Check to see if your service provider (such as AOL, MSN, or Earthlink) offers this option.

Experts recommend that people keep online friendships in the virtual world. Meeting online friends face to face carries more risks than other types of friendships because it's so easy for people to pretend to be something they're not when you can't see them or talk in person.

If you ever get involved in a chat room conversation that makes you feel uncomfortable or in danger for **any** reason, exit and tell a parent or other adult right away so they can report the incident. You can also report it to the Web site of the National Center for Missing and Exploited Children as www.missingkids.com—they have a form for reporting this type of incident called CyberTipline. They will then see that the information is forwarded to law enforcement officials for investigation.

Cyberbullying

It's not just strangers who can make you feel uncomfortable online. Cyberbullying is a word that refers to cruel or bullying messages sent to you online. These might be from former friends or other people you know. They can be irritating and, in some cases, even frightening.

If you get these bullying messages online, it's often better to ignore them rather than answer them. Cyberbullies, just like other bullies, may be angry or disturbed people—and may be looking for attention or a reaction.

Fortunately, most people never experience cyberbullying. But if you're gettting cyberbullied and ignoring it doesn't make it go away, getting help from a parent, school counselor, or another trusted adult may be a good idea. That's especially true if the cyberbullying contains threats.

Online Annoyances

Although e-mail is relatively private, hackers can still access it. If you find that your mailbox is getting clogged with spam—e-mails you didn't ask for like advertisements or harassing or offensive notes—contact your service provider to let them know there's a problem and to find out about options that allow you to block certain senders and topics. Many service providers will help you block out or screen inappropriate e-mails if your parents agree to set up age-appropriate parental controls.

If you don't recognize the sender of a document or file that needs to be downloaded, delete it without opening it to avoid getting a virus on your machine. Virus protection software is a must for every computer. And you can also buy software that helps rid your computer of unwanted spyware programs that report what your computer is doing. There's even software out there to help block spam. Some service providers make software available to protect you from these online annoyances—such as blockers for those in-your-face pop-up ads.

If you do invest in protective software, you'll need to keep updating it to be sure it continues to do its job as new technologies evolve.

With all the problems you can face online, is it worth it? For most people, the answer is definitely yes. You just need to know where the pitfalls are, use some common sense and caution, and you'll be in control.

For more articles like this one, visit www.KidsHealth.org or www.Teens Health.org.

Now answer Numbers 1 through 9. Base your answers on the article "Internet Safety: Safe Surfing Tips for Teens."

1 What is the author's purpose for writing this article?

   A. to show how to use the Internet for research
   B. to explain the dangers of surfing the Internet
   C. to convince teenagers not to use the Internet
   D. to teach teenagers how to use the Internet safely

2 With which statement would the author MOST likely agree?

   F. We depend too much on the Internet.
   G. We should limit our use of the Internet.
   H. The Internet is an important part of modern life.
   I. The Internet is a dangerous threat to our families.

3 Why does the author compare the Internet to a library?

   A. to explain how the Internet is organized
   B. to show how useful the Internet is for research
   C. to reassure readers that the Internet is safe to surf
   D. to discuss the different kinds of information they have

The Author's "Why"

4 What does the word *anonymous* mean?

    F. unaware

    G. unnoticed

    H. unidentified

    I. uncomfortable

5 Why does the author mention the Web site for the National Center for Missing and Exploited Children?

    A. so that teens can visit the site for additional safety tips

    B. so that teens can report problems they have in chat rooms

    C. so that parents can post messages for their runaway teenagers

    D. so that parents can learn how to keep track of teens' Internet use

6 What is the author's opinion of parents in regards to the Internet?

    F. He thinks that parents are not very well informed about the Internet.

    G. He knows that parents are not as comfortable using the Internet as their children are.

    H. He believes that parents should be notified when a teen runs into problems on the Internet.

    I. He feels that parents should trust their teenagers to recognize unusual activity on the Internet.

7 Why are online friendships more risky than face-to-face friendships?

    A. People can hide who they really are online.

    B. People can get others to trust them more easily online.

    C. People can find out more personal information online.

    D. People can figure out your e-mail address from your online nickname.

8 Which e-mail address would the author think was BEST for a teenager named Sara Smith?

    F. sara@mvp.net

    G. 1sara2@mvp.net

    H. sarasmith@mvp.net

    I. 1s2smith3@mvp.net

9 Which of the following would the author MOST likely support?

    A. a law banning teenagers from surfing the Internet

    B. a required class for all teenagers on protecting one's identity online

    C. a way to prevent teenagers from using the Internet except for school research

    D. a law against teenagers visiting chat rooms without permission from their parents

Read the poems "The door" and "George Gray" before answering Numbers 1 through 9.

The door
by Miroslav Holub

Go and open the door.
    Maybe outside there's
    a tree, or a wood,
    a garden,
    or a magic city.

Go and open the door.
    Maybe a dog's rummaging.
    Maybe you'll see a face,
or an eye,
or the picture
      of a picture.

Go and open the door.
    If there's a fog
    it will clear.

Go and open the door.
    Even if there's only
    the darkness ticking,
    even if there's only the hollow wind,
    even if
        nothing
            is there,
go and open the door.

At least
there'll be
a draught.

George Gray
by Edgar Lee Masters

I have studied many times
The marble which was chiseled for me—
A boat with a furled sail at rest in a harbor.
In truth it pictures not my destination
But my life.
For love was offered me and I shrank from its disillusionment;
Sorrow knocked at my door, but I was afraid;
Ambition called to me, but I dreaded the chances.
Yet all the while I hungered for meaning in my life.
And now I know that we must lift the sail
And catch the winds of destiny
Wherever they drive the boat.
To put meaning in one's life may end in madness,
But life without meaning is the torture
Of restlessness and vague desire—
It is a boat longing for the sea and yet afraid.

Now answer Numbers 1 through 9. Base your answers on the poems "The door" and "George Gray."

1 What is the author's MAIN purpose in writing "The door"?

  A. to encourage others to get out and experience life
  B. to share an important experience from his own life
  C. to paint an image of a door opening out onto the world
  D. to warn people that they may not get what they want in life

2 Why does the author of "The door" repeat the line "Go and open the door" several times?

  F. to stress how important it is for people to open the door to life
  G. to demonstrate that there's always something new each time you open a door
  H. to show that a person can open a door repeatedly even if he or she doesn't like what's on the other side
  I. to convince the reader that it is not difficult to overcome obstacles in life

3. What does the author stress by writing the words "even if nothing is there" on three lines of the poem instead of one?

   A. that the reader will probably not find anything on the other side
   B. that the poet is tired of opening doors and finding nothing on the other side
   C. that it is disappointing not to find anything on the other side of the door
   D. that the act of opening the door is what matters, not what is on the other side

4. What does the author believe will definitely happen if the reader opens the door?

   F. The reader will see a magic city.
   G. The reader will find a fog outside.
   H. The reader will let in a draught of air.
   I. The reader will hear the noise of the wind.

5. In the poem "George Gray," what is "The marble which was chiseled for me"?

   A. a part of a ship
   B. a statue in a park
   C. a plaque on a wall
   D. a headstone for a grave

6. How does the speaker in "George Gray" feel about the life he led?

   F. He is thankful that he lived life to the fullest.
   G. He is proud that he achieved his life's goals.
   H. He is regretful that he turned away from life.
   I. He is sad that other people live in fear.

7. With which saying would the author of "George Gray" MOST likely agree?

   A. Better to be safe than to be sorry.
   B. All good things must come to an end.
   C. The grass is always greener on the other side of the fence.
   D. It is better to have loved and lost than never to have loved at all.

8. How are the author's purpose in "George Gray" and the author's purpose in "The door" ALIKE?

   F. Both want the reader to fulfill his or her destiny.
   G. Both want the reader to go after what life has to offer.
   H. Both want the reader to face life's problems with courage.
   I. Both want the reader to be unafraid to fill his or her life with love.

9 Which idea from the poem "George Gray" BEST supports the author's purpose?

A. Sorrow knocked at my door, but I was afraid
B. Ambition called to me, but I dreaded the chances.
C. In truth it pictures not my destination / But my life.
D. But life without meaning is the torture / Of restlessness and vague desire

---

Read the article "You're It!" before answering Numbers 1 through 9.

You're It! You're the Bull's-Eye
by Shari Graydon

Once upon a time, advertisers didn't pay much attention to kids. They aimed all their sales pitches at adults.

But things have certainly changed. Starting in the 1950s, advertisers began to realize that kids not only had money of their own to spend, but they also influenced a lot of their parents' shopping decisions.

Imagine a dartboard with a picture of you and your friends in the center of the board. You're now an important "target," and many advertisers think about your interests when designing their products and ads. In fact, advertisers in North America spend more than $2 billion a year trying to convince you to spend your money—or your parents' money!—on the stuff they're selling.

How can they afford to do this? Because the dollars they invest in advertising amount to a drop in the ocean compared to the dollars they get back when you respond to their sales pitches. In fact, some marketers estimate that kids in North America spend more than $100 billion every year on clothes, candy, games, videos, music, movies, and food.

And then there's what advertisers call the "nag factor": they deliberately try to dream up ads that will help you to convince your parents to buy one kind of pizza instead of another, or rent this movie over that one. They conduct research to find out what kinds of commercials are most effective—for example, which jingle or special meal deal is most likely to help you drag your mom or dad to the fast-food restaurant.

One roadside ice-cream stand in Pennsylvania took advantage of the "nag factor" by putting up a sign that said: "Scream Until Dad Stops."

They also know that kids influence adults' decisions about much more expensive items, like computer equipment and family vacations. Car manufacturers have a name for this: they refer to 8- to 14-year-olds as "back-seat customers," recognizing that kids may even cast the deciding vote about which car their parents should buy. In fact, one kids' magazine—meant to be read by people too young to have their own driver's license—carried ads for minivans!

Some marketers estimate that kids have a say in close to $300 billion worth of their parents' spending. So some advertisers target you in order to get to adults.

Research also tells advertisers that if they hook you when you're young, chances are better that you'll keep buying their products as you get older. This is called "brand loyalty." Shopping experts have figured out that a customer who regularly buys from the same store, from childhood until she dies, is worth as much as $100,000 to the store. So advertisers try to come up with what they call "cradle to grave" marketing strategies that will help them turn you into lifetime customers.

> *If you own this child at an early age, you can own this child for years to come.*
> —Mike Searles, president of the marketing company Kids 'R Us

---

Now answer Numbers 1 through 9. Base your answers on the article "You're It!"

1 How was advertising DIFFERENT in the past than it is today?

    A. Advertisers directed their ads only at adults.

    B. Parents would not let their kids be influenced by ads.

    C. Advertisers spent more money on ads that targeted kids.

    D. Kids were less likely to influence their parents' decisions.

2 What is the author's MAIN purpose in this article?

    F. to let kids know that they are important to the nation's economy

    G. to teach advertisers how to get kids to influence their parents' spending

    H. to let parents know that their kids influence the way they spend money

    I. to make kids aware that advertisers try to influence how they spend their money and their parents' money

3 Why does the author use the example of kids' pictures on a dartboard?

    A. to show how much money kids spend each year

    B. to explain that advertisers must follow certain rules

    C. to demonstrate that kids are the target of advertisers

    D. to prove that advertisers think of their job as a game

The Author's "Why"

4 Which word would the author MOST likely use to describe advertisers?

    F. loyal
    G. stingy
    H. honest
    I. sneaky

5 How much money do marketers think that North American kids spend each year?

    A. around $2 million
    B. around $2 billion
    C. less than $10 billion
    D. more than $100 billion

6 Why does the author explain advertising terms like "nag factor" and "back-seat customer"?

    F. to explain that special terms are created in every field, including advertising
    G. to demonstrate that you have to know special terms in order to understand advertising
    H. to prove that advertisers use a special language so that kids and parents won't suspect what they are up to
    I. to show that advertisers value kids so much that they've developed special terms to talk about them

7 What does the word *deliberately* mean?

    A. purposely
    B. accidentally
    C. carelessly
    D. thoughtlessly

8 What is the MAIN idea of the paragraph that begins "And then there's what advertisers call the 'nag factor'"?

    F. Advertisers test their ads to see which ones work best.
    G. Advertisers can't help it if their ads have a negative effect on a family.
    H. Advertisers should be more responsible when developing their ads.
    I. Advertisers try to find ways to get kids to push their parents into buying things.

9 In which publication would this article MOST likely appear?

    A. a daily newspaper for a major city
    B. a magazine for people who work in advertising
    C. a monthly newsletter published by a large shopping mall
    D. a consumer magazine that helps people make smart purchases

MAKING SENSE OF IT

In this chapter you have learned more about reading actively. The skills and main points of this chapter are summarized here.

- **Author's Purpose:** the reason an author writes something
- **Four Basic Purposes for Writing:** Persuade, Inform, Entertain, and Share a Personal Experience
  - **Persuade:** convince; change someone's mind; get someone to do something or to stop
  - **Inform:** writing that teaches, give facts, and shares information with the readers
  - **Entertain:** written for readers to enjoy
  - **Share Personal Experiences:** written for the main purpose of sharing an experience with readers
- **Author's Point of View:** an author's personal attitude about the subject he or she writes about
- **Finding the Author's Point of View:** evidence of an author's point of view can be found in word choice, character descriptions, character actions, direct or sarcastic statements, choice of details

Chapter Five

Looking It Up

Benchmark: L.A.A.2.3.5

The student locates, organizes, and interprets written information for a variety of purposes, including classroom research, collaborative decision making, and performing a school or real-world task. (Includes **LA.A.2.3.6** The student uses a variety of reference materials, including indexes, magazines, newspapers, journals, and tools including card catalogs and computer catalogs, to gather information for research topics, and **LA.A.2.3.7** The student synthesizes and separates collected information into useful components using a variety of techniques, such as source cards, note cards, spreadsheets, and outlines.)

Quentin sat in front of the TV set, transfixed. He couldn't believe that his best friend Brianna was actually a contestant on *Who Wants to Be a Kijillionaire?* AND that she had picked him to be her "Brain Buddy," the one she would call if she needed help with one of the quiz show's questions.

"Alright, Brianna, by answering the last question, 'How many legs does an octopus have?' correctly, you now have $10,000. Are you ready for the $20,000 question?"

Brianna squirmed excitedly in the contestant's chair. "I am, Bob!"

"Here it is, then: What is the capital of Lithuania?"

Brianna blinked. And gulped. *The capital of Lithuania?!*

"Is it: A. Telsai; B. Ukmerge; C. Alytus; or D. Vilnius?"

Brianna shook her head and said, "Bob, I'm going to have to call my Brain Buddy."

133

Almost immediately, Quentin's phone began to ring.

"Brain Buddy," said the game show host, "Are you there?"

"Yes, Bob! I'm here!"

"Brianna, please repeat the question for your Brain Buddy."

But Quentin wasted no time listening to the question again. Instead, he raced to the set of encyclopedias his parents kept in the living room, grabbed the volume marked "L," and began whipping through the pages, hunting for "Lithuania." The entry for Lithuania was about five inches long. He scanned it, but could find no mention of the capital. Then he saw the map that went with the entry. There was a big star beside the city of Vilnius. That had to be it! But just to make sure he read the list of facts about Lithuania beside the map. "Capital: Vilnius"! Bingo!

"Brain Buddy, we need your answer."

"The answer is D. Vilnius!"

"Are you sure, Quentin?" Brianna sounded trusting but scared at the same time.

"Positive!"

"I'll go with D. Vilnius, Bob!"

"Young lady, I'm afraid that . . . you're going to have to find a way to spend $20,000! You are correct! That's all the time we have left today, folks! Join us tomorrow for another game of *Who Wants to Be a Kijillionaire?*"

Brianna was lucky she had picked Quentin to be her Brain Buddy. Even though Quentin didn't know the answer to every question in the world, he knew how to *find out* the answer to just about every question in the world, through research.

Many students think research is always difficult or boring and that only scientists or people in school ever do research. But think about Quentin. He used a *resource* (the encyclopedia) to find the information they needed about a *topic* (Lithuania). It wasn't difficult or boring at all, in fact; it was very exciting to help his friend win $20,000 by answering one research question!

WHY STUDY THIS?

Maybe you've heard about the Stone Age or the Industrial Age, which are words that describe the kind of technology that human beings were using at different points in history. The age we are in today is called the Information Age because people have more access to more information than they have had at any other time in history.

This makes being a good researcher more important than ever. Whatever the task, an understanding of the research process will help you achieve your goal. The first step in this process involves knowing which resource to use.

For example, imagine discussing movies with your friends. If you want to know who won the first Academy Award for best picture, you could look it up in an almanac. Or maybe you have found out that your new teacher was born in Mauritius, a place you've never even heard of before. You could use an atlas to find out that Mauritius is an island country in the southwest Indian Ocean, east of Madagascar.

Think Of It This Way

Research can be frustrating if you don't know where to look for help. Different information is found in different places. The list on the left shows various kinds of information people might need. Can you match each one with the best resource for finding that information?

NEED	RESOURCE
1. library phone number	_____ dictionary
2. information on upcoming football game	_____ almanac
3. meaning of a word	_____ online sports Web site
4. map of Canada	_____ phone book
5. population growth of your city	_____ atlas

In the pages that follow, you will learn about some of the most important resources for conducting research.

Reference Materials

Dictionary

If someone asked you what information you could get from a dictionary, chances are you would answer that a dictionary gives you the definitions of words. But that's just the beginning of what a dictionary has to offer.

A dictionary can show you how to spell a word, how to pronounce it, and how to use it properly in a sentence. It can also tell you about the origin of a word.

Some of the features in most dictionaries include the following:

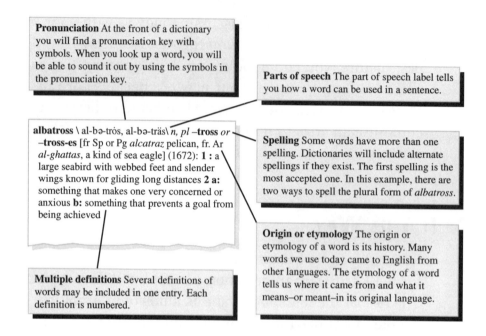

Encyclopedia

An encyclopedia contains information about almost everything. Some areas that might be researched in an encyclopedia include people (Nelson Mandela's life story), places (the South Pole), things (the Mississippi River), ideas (Einstein's theory of relativity), events (the Persian Gulf War), cultures (the Australian Aborigines), and history (the French Revolution). The items contained in an encyclopedia are arranged in alphabetical order by subject. Some encyclopedias are limited to one field, such as science or art.

Some encyclopedias are available on CD-ROM and include video and audio clips of speeches, people, or events in history.

Atlas

An atlas contains maps and other geographical information. It includes details about places, such as average rainfall, elevation (number of feet above sea level), population, agricultural patterns, transportation routes, and borders.

You would use an atlas if you wanted to find out information like the geographic location, population, or natural geographic features (mountains, lakes, rivers, and so forth) of a certain area.

Almanac

Published each year, almanacs contain facts, figures, graphs, tables, and other statistical information on many subjects.

You can refer to an almanac if you want to find out detailed information about weather, winning and losing records of sports teams, and even lists of Academy Award-winning actors and movies.

World Wide Web

The world is literally at your fingertips when you use the World Wide Web. Are you looking for a Quiche Lorraine recipe to cook for your French club? Just log on to a search engine and type *Quiche Lorraine* in the search box to find hundreds of recipes for this dish, including recipes in French. For other kinds of research, you can find online versions of dictionaries, encyclopedias, and other traditional research sources. However, when you use the Web for research, be sure to get your information from credible Web sites. For example, a biography of Enrique Iglesias that came from an online encyclopedia would be more reliable than one that came from a Web page created by a twelve-year-old fan of Enrique's!

Libraries

Libraries contain information on every topic under the sun. In fact, there is so much information available that it can seem overwhelming. However, if you know how to get the information you need, you won't have trouble finding what you are looking for. The following pages will provide resources to help you use the library for research.

The Card Catalog

The card catalog with wooden, pull-out drawers filled with cards on every item in the library is quickly becoming outdated. These days, most libraries have computer stations with electronic card catalogs. However, you still may find card catalogs in school libraries and libraries in smaller cities, so it is a good idea to learn how to use them. The card catalog helps you find information by means of three types of cards.

Author card. The author card is the primary card. It tells you which books by a certain author are in the library.

Subject card. The subject card tells you what books the library has on a particular subject.

Title card. The title card lists the books in the library by title. By using these different cards in the card catalog, you can look up the title of any book, video, or audio resource that is in the library.

If you need information on a specific subject but don't know the titles of any books to refer to, look under the subject cards. You will find the names of books pertaining to your topic.

You can also search for books by using the author cards. For example, suppose you have just read *The Hobbit* and would like to read a book about J. R. R. Tolkien, you would see what books about him were available in the library.

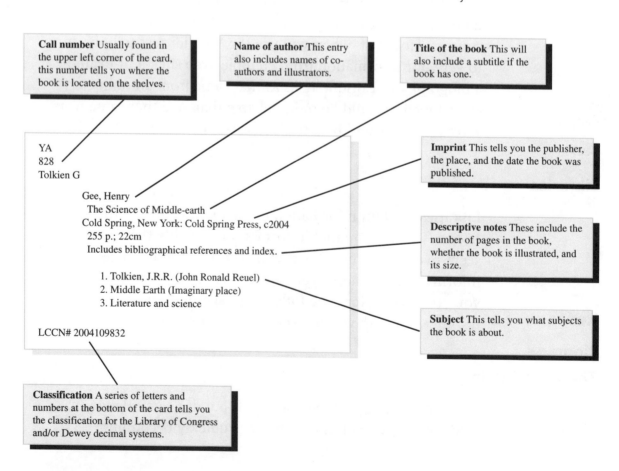

Looking It Up

The card catalog contains a great deal of information that may be useful to you. The previous illustration shows what you would typically find on these cards.

Computer Catalogs

Although the information on the computer is the same as in the card catalog, you have to access it electronically. There are many advantages to a computer catalog. The search is easier, quicker, cleaner, and more fun. Also, you can do *keyword searches*. These searches will usually provide you with good information. But remember: Be specific in your requests. If your request is too general, the keyword result will bring up useless information that will not only frustrate you but also waste your time.

Let's say you want to find out if any whales beached themselves in Florida in 2005. Write *TG* beside the keyword phrase that is too general. Write *TS* beside the keyword phrase that is too specific. Write *JR* for the keyword phrase that is just right.

_____ beached hump-backed whales Miami Florida 2005
_____ Florida beached whales 2005
_____ Florida whales

FCAT Fred Says:

FCAT questions will not directly ask you, "What reference would you use to find out where the Catskill Mountains are?" (an unfortunate name for a mountain range, I might add!). Rather, the test will require you to show how well you can use information from different types of materials. For example, you might be asked to evaluate graphs, tables, illustrations, maps, and other visuals. Usually, you will be asked to base your inferences on both a visual and a written text.

Reference Sources in the Library

Biographical Reference Books

Some of the most often used reference sources in a library are biographies of well-known people, either living or dead. You will find some of the following sources helpful.

Who's Who and Who's Who in America

Both of these reference works include facts about living persons only, for example, current governors, the current president, and other politicians.

Webster's Biographical Dictionary

Webster's Biographical Dictionary contains very short biographies of famous persons, both people from modern times, like astronauts, and famous people from history, such as ancient kings and queens.

Current Biography

Current Biography contains information about people currently in the news, such as professional athletes. It is published monthly.

Other Important Reference Sources

Guide to Reference Books is a basic guide to reference books. Reference books are grouped by general headings with many subdivisions.

Book Review Digest includes book reviews that appear in journals and magazines. If you were writing a book report on *To Kill a Mockingbird*, you could look in the 1960 volume of *Book Review Digest* to see what reviewers thought of the book.

Education Index will help you find interesting articles about school and educational issues.

Periodicals

Materials printed on a regular daily, weekly, or monthly basis are referred to as *periodicals*. Newspapers and magazines are periodicals. To find information on articles printed in a periodical, the following sources will be useful.

Looking It Up

Readers' Guide to Periodic Literature

One of the most popular reference sources in the library, *Readers' Guide to Periodic Literature* includes references to magazine articles on any subject, taken from many magazines. *Readers' Guide* is a useful tool in helping you research a specific topic. This guide lists the source by subject and author and then lists the date of publication and the name of the magazine. At the front of *Readers' Guide* is a very comprehensive list of the magazines it references.

Suppose that you are writing a paper on the director Steven Spielberg. You could find the most recent magazine articles about him by choosing the most recent volume of the *Readers' Guide* and looking under *Spielberg*. Choose the article you would like to read and write down the name of the article, the name of the magazine, and the month and year the article appeared in the magazine. Take this information to the librarian, who will find the magazine for you in the library's collection of back issues.

Periodic Index

The *Periodic Index* directs you to the latest information on any subject and provides summaries of the information.

Newspaper Indexes

Newspaper indexes tell you where to find recent information on most subjects in a more detailed way.

After the Library

Visiting the library is the first step in doing research. After a research visit to the library, you should have gathered information in the form of books, magazines, pamphlets, and other resources. Now you need to sort through those materials and pick out the most useful information for the project you are working on or the questions you are trying to answer.

When doing formal research for school, it is important to keep good notes. Note cards provide a helpful way of organizing your ideas. Use note cards to single out each important point, fact, or statistic you find in your resources.

As you proceed, the note cards will help you organize the information. They will also help you keep track of the sources you used to find that information.

THINK OF IT THIS WAY

You can think of each note card as a summary. Write one sentence that sums up a whole paragraph. That is the main idea. After you get the main idea, think about one or two ways the author explains it. Jot those down in your own words. This will help you understand what you have read. It will also help you avoid using the author's exact words without giving him or her credit. If you come across an important quotation that would be useful to you, write it on a separate note card, with quotation marks to remind yourself that it is a word-for-word quotation. When you are done, your project starts to take form.

Read the following paragraph on German shepherds and see how one student took notes on the paragraph.

> Have you ever wondered why German shepherds are the breed of choice for so many police departments? It isn't because they're the fastest dog. The slowest greyhound could outrun the fastest German shepherd. And it isn't because they have the best "nose" in the business for tracking people. That honor would go to the bloodhound, whose deep wrinkles trap smells like an air filter. And they aren't the most battle-ready dogs on the block, either. Dogs bred for fighting, such as the pit bull, hold this (dubious) distinction. But although German shepherds aren't the number-one dog at any of these things, they are the only dog that is second best at everything. Add to this their keen intelligence, their intense loyalty, and their utter devotion to their work, and you have the ultimate police dog.

Looking It Up

Main idea → German shepherds are the most popular dogs for police work even though they aren't the "best" dog at many police-dog-related skills

Details →
1. They are second-best at many skills
2. They have other important qualities

Second best at many skills:
- German shepherds not the best dog at anything
- Greyhounds are faster
- Bloodhounds better at tracking people
- Pit bulls are better fighters
- But German shepherds are "second best" at everything

Other qualities:
- smart
- loyal
- travel in schools
- devoted to their work

Note cards are like tiny parts of a research paper. When you finish making note cards, your report is all but finished. If you take good, clear notes, you will find it easy to complete the paper or project you are working on.

Documenting Your Sources

For a formal research paper, you may be asked to turn in a list of all the sources you used. This is called a *bibliography*. For this reason, it is a good idea to write on the other side of your note card where you got that particular information. Write down the author's name, the name of the book, magazine, Web site, or other source, the city and state where the source was published, the name of the publisher, and the year it was published. (The publisher information can be found on one of the first few pages of the source.) A bibliographic entry for the paragraph above might look like this:

Henricks, Stella. *The German Shepherd Dog*. Dayton, OH: Dog Star Publishing, 2003.

The author's last name comes first, followed by his or her first name. The entries are arranged alphabetically.

SEEING IT IN ACTION

Whether your task is to write a paper, present an oral project, or build a Web page, you must know how to combine information from different sources to make inferences and draw conclusions. For example, you might find out from an article that a sunken ship has been discovered off the Hawaiian Islands. Using the information from article and the map that goes with it, you can pinpoint the location of the sunken ship.

On the FCAT, you must demonstrate your ability to combine information from tables, maps, and graphs with written information. Here is a step-by-step approach to combining information from two sources:

> **1.** Read the first source carefully. Try to state the main idea of the source in one sentence.
>
> **2.** Read the second source and try to state its main idea in one sentence. If it is a table, graph, or map, you might mention the information that stands out the most. For example, on a table showing the growth rate of cities in the United States, you might note that Austin, Texas, is

one of the fastest-growing cities, while Detroit, Michigan, is one of the slowest-growing cities.

3. Next, read the FCAT question to see what information it is asking you to find.

4. Here's the tricky part! Now you must find the information in BOTH sources that have to do with the FCAT question.

5. Use the inferencing skills you learned in Chapter 1 to draw a conclusion based on the information you located in both sources.

6. Test each possible answer against the conclusion you have drawn to see which answer is correct.

Read the following to see an example.

Charlotte looked up from the magazine she was reading to see her mother pushing her mountain bike up the driveway toward the garage. The look on her mother's face told her that it had been another difficult bike trip.

"Hi, Mom! How'd it go this time?" Charlotte said.

"Don't ask!" Her mother said, as she wheeled the bike into the garage. Then she climbed the porch steps and sat down next to her daughter on the porch swing. She took off her bike helmet and shook out her tangled hair. "But if you must know, I was almost hit by the ice-cream truck on Maple Street, then the Dickersons' poodle chased me for two blocks, and finally, I got a flat tire! I don't know if getting in shape is worth the trouble!"

"Hm," said Charlotte. "Maybe you could try walking instead. Then you could take Duke with you. No poodle would mess with you then! And no flat tires."

"Yes, honey, that's true, but biking is better exercise than just walking."

"Not according to this magazine I'm reading. How much do you weigh?"

"That is top secret information!" Her mother smiled.

"Okay, well, it doesn't really matter. Look at this table: No matter what you weigh, you burn more calories walking than you do biking."

"Hey! I would burn 7.5 calories per minute walking compared to 6.5 biking. And even playing golf I would burn almost as much as biking!"

The next afternoon, Charlotte was watching TV in the living room when she heard the kitchen door open.

"Hello," her mom called, "Charlotte?"

"Yeah, Mom?"

"Your magazine article was wrong! I'm not burning more calories walking, I'm gaining more calories!"

Charlotte clicked off the TV and walked to the kitchen. There was her mother with a half-eaten ice-cream cone in one hand and another cone in the other hand, being eaten in big gulps by an ecstatic Duke.

"Ice-cream truck?"

"Ice-cream truck."

CALORIES BURNED PER MINUTE

Activity	Your Weight			
	120 lb	140 lb	160 lb	180 lb
Cycling (10 mph)	5.4	6.5	7.2	8.1
Golf (pull or carry clubs)	4.5	5.5	6.3	7.0
Golf (power cart)	2.0	2.6	2.9	3.3
Tennis	6.0	6.8	7.9	8.8
Walking (4.5 mph)	6.4	7.5	8.8	9.6

Looking It Up

Now look at some sample FCAT questions that might accompany this story and table.

1. About how much does Charlotte's mother weigh?

   A. 120 lb
   B. 140 lb
   C. 160 lb
   D. 180 lb

2. What conclusion can be drawn about how Charlotte's mother usually plays golf?

   F. She normally uses a golf cart rather than walk.
   G. She prefers to walk rather than use a golf cart.
   H. She enjoys playing golf at least three times a week.
   I. She usually plays for more than 90 minutes each time she plays.

To answer both these questions, you must use information from the table and the text.

Even though Charlotte's mother says her weight is "top secret information," she gives it away when she says that she would burn 7.5 calories per minute by walking and 6.5 calories by biking. Looking at the table, you can see that these are the calories per minute for people who weigh 140 pounds. Therefore the answer is B.

Charlotte's mother also reveals how she usually plays golf. She states that by playing golf she would burn almost as many calories per minute as when she bikes. The table shows that golf burns 5.5 calories if you pull or carry your clubs, which suggests that the golfer is walking, not using a cart. That is only 1 calorie less than biking. But when a golfer uses a golf cart, he or she burns only 2.6 calories per minute. Choice F must be incorrect. Neither the article nor the table mentions how often a player should play or how long a player should play, so H and I are incorrect. The correct answer must be G.

Read the article "The Big Dipper" and song lyrics from "The Drinking Gourd." Then answer the questions that follow.

Big Dipper

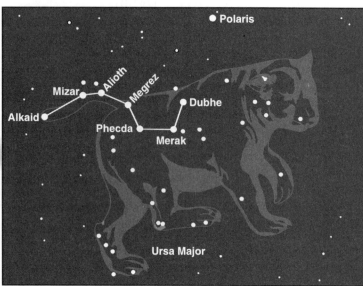

The Big Dipper is the most recognizable pattern of stars in the night sky. Most people think the Big Dipper is a constellation, but it is actually an *asterism*, or unofficial formation of bright stars, that makes up part of the constellation Ursa Major, the Great Bear. What we think of as the Big Dipper's handle is the bear's tail. The cup of the Big Dipper is the bear's flank.

In addition to helping you identify the Ursa Major constellation, the Big Dipper can also help you find important stars. Just follow two of the stars in the Big Dipper's cup and you will find the North Star (Polaris). Follow the line, or arc, formed by the Big Dipper's handle and it will lead you to Arcturus, a very large, bright star.

Different cultures around the world think the Big Dipper resembles other things and therefore call it different names, such as the "cart" or the "bull's thigh." In England, it is known as the "Plow." In fact, early Americans who were originally British or descendants of British citizens also referred to the Big Dipper as the "Plow." The name "Big Dipper" evolved in America from African-American slaves who called the formation the "Drinking Gourd," which is how these stars were referred to in their homelands in West Africa. The slaves' masters changed it to the "Big Dipper," after the utensil they themselves used for dipping and pouring liquids.

But the Big Dipper's most significant connection to African-American history is the role it played prior to the Civil War as part of a coded song used by the Underground Railroad. The song urged slaves to "follow the drinking gourd." This meant that escaped slaves should use the Big Dipper to help guide them north to freedom. Other lines in the song gave instructions on when they should travel so that the rivers would be iced over and therefore crossable, and information on landmarks to follow on their journey.

Looking It Up

from The Drinking Gourd

When the sun comes back and the first quail calls,
Follow the drinking gourd,
For the old man is awaiting for to carry you to freedom
If you follow the drinking gourd.

The riverbank makes a very good road,
The dead trees will show you the way,
Left foot, peg foot traveling on,
Follow the drinking gourd.

1. Using information from both the article and the star map, what are the names of the stars that you can use to find the North Star?

    A. Mizar and Alkaid
    B. Merak and Dubhe
    C. Phecda and Alioth
    D. Polaris and Arcturus

2. Based on information from both the article and the song lyrics, what does the first line of the song refer to?

    F. the stars that will guide them north
    G. the best time of year to make the trip north
    H. the person who will help them on their journey
    I. the landmarks they should follow along the way

Now read how one student answered these questions.

1. The article says to use two of the stars that are in the Big Dipper's cup to find the North Star. Mizar and Alkaid are in the handle, so A is incorrect. A line drawn through Phecda and Alioth would point away from the North Star, so C is wrong. Polaris is another name for the North Star and Arcturus is not a star in the Big Dipper, so D is incorrect. Therefore, B: Merak and Dubhe is the answer.

2. The stars that guided them north were called the "Drinking Gourd," and the drinking gourd is not talked about in the first line of the poem, so choice F is incorrect. Choice H is incorrect, because the guide is talked about in a different line. Choice I is also wrong because the landmarks are talked about in the second verse. G is the correct answer choice.

Read the article "History and Geography of the Olympic Games in Ancient Greece" before answering Numbers 1 through 9.

HISTORY AND GEOGRAPHY OF THE OLYMPIC GAMES IN ANCIENT GREECE

by Rick Price

The Olympics came to us as one of the oldest institutions of Classical Greece. Although the first written record of the games dates to 776 B.C., their origins go back at least five hundred years earlier and are linked to religious events well before that. The games honored Zeus, supreme god of all the Greeks and ruler of the sky (Zeus's brothers Poseidon and Hades ruled the sea and the Underworld respectively). The Olympic Games were officially abolished by the Roman emperor in 394 A.D. after a run of 1170 years!

As god of all kings and of all humans, Zeus ruled from lofty Mt. Olympus north of Athens. His primary role was to keep the peace among those same gods and "men" on earth. In his honor a universal truce applied during the Olympic Games every four years, and even though the truce was broken on several occasions, the games were never interrupted as a result of war.

The reasons for the location of the games in "Olympia" near the west coast of the Peloponnesian peninsula are lost in history. The site was never a major city or permanent settlement except during the games themselves when tens of thousands of spectators and participants camped on the grounds. Evidence suggests that the site of Olympia was once the location of a religious festival honoring Gaia, the Earth Mother. Indeed, the site must have had strong historic and religious roots as it is located on the western edge of Classical Greece far from the Greek heartland, as this map shows.

The games were held every four years, and records show that the games in 776 B.C. consisted of only one footrace held on one day. The ensuing century must have seen a revival of earlier games, since a variety of other events were added during that first century, including longer races (likely the predecessors of our 400 meter, 1,500 and

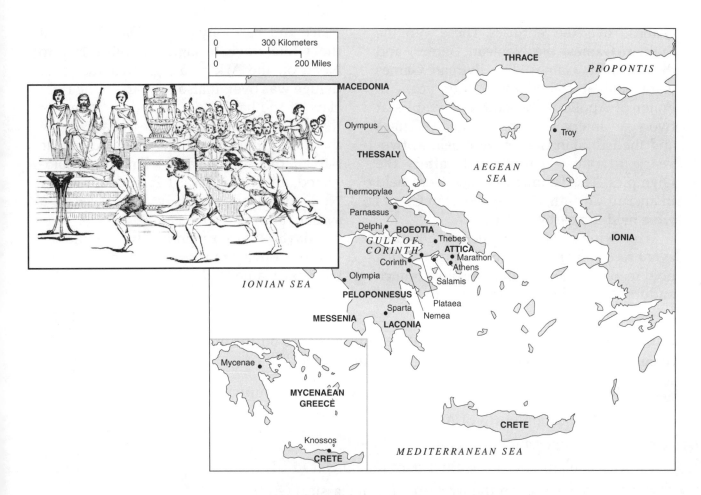

5,000 meter races.) Wrestling was added as was the pentathlon and horse races, including the chariot race. All competitions derived from and honored the skills valued among warriors.

Although the games attracted participants from throughout the Classical Greek world and Magna Grecia (see map), the games themselves were not lengthened beyond one day until 472 B.C., when they were extended to four days and, later, to five.

One of the running events practiced in the ancient games that we no longer practice required competitors to run two to four "stade" (the length of the stadium, approximately equivalent to 200 or 400 meters) in full battle gear! The marathon, which is so popular today, was not included in the ancient Olympics. Introduced in the modern Olympics in Athens in 1896, the marathon commemorates the victory of the Athenians over the Persians on the plains of Marathon about twenty-five miles north of Athens. The messenger Pheidippides ran to Athens with the news of the victory, becoming a hero in the process and giving us an athletic tradition that lives on today. (Most famous, perhaps, among Marathons is the Boston Marathon, an event which began in 1897, the year after the first modern Olympics began).

The "modern Olympics" were revived in Athens in 1896 through the efforts of a young Frenchman, Baron Pierre de Coubertin. De Coubertin was optimistic and persistent in reviving the Games, which were attended by participants from thirteen countries who participated in forty-three events divided among nine sports: cycling, fencing, gymnastics, lawn tennis, shooting, swimming, track and field, weight lifting and wrestling.

The Olympics were so popular that they gave rise to a set of three other "Panhellenic

Games," over the centuries. These were the Pythian Games, the Nemean Games, and the Isthmian Games. The Pythian Games were held at Delphi every four years in honor of Apollo (between the Olympics at two-year intervals). The Nemean Games and the Isthmian Games were held at two-year intervals before and after the Olympics. The Isthmian Games were held in ancient Corinth, and the Nemean Games were held in nearby Nemea.

The winner of each ancient Olympic event received an olive branch rather than a gold medal in recognition. The olive branch endures to this day as a symbol of universal peace and harmony. In the Old Testament the white dove brought an olive leaf to Noah on the Ark as a sign that the great deluge was over. It also appears in the right claw of the bald eagle on the great seal of the United States (also on the dollar bill), on the flag of the United Nations, and on the flag of the Arab League. Finally, a gold-plated olive branch was left on the moon by Neil Armstrong on July 29, 1969, as a symbol of universal peace.

Maybe, as a reminder, we should be offering olive branches to winners at the Olympic Games today.

Now answer Numbers 1 through 9. Base your answers on the article "The History and Geography of the Olympic Games in Ancient Greece."

1 What information from the article about Olympus is supported by the map?

    A. its location north of Athens

    B. its importance as the home of Zeus

    C. its historic value as the site of religious festivals

    D. its position on the western edge of classical Greece

2 Using the information from the article, what does the triangle symbol on the map represent?

    F. a city

    G. a mountain

    H. the capital of Greece

    I. the site of the first Olympic Games

3 Based on the information in the article and the map, for which Panhellenic Games would you have to stop and ask directions to find the city in which it was held?

    A. the Olympics

    B. the Pythian Games

    C. the Nemean Games

    D. the Isthmian Games

4 You can find out the distance in miles between which two cities based on information from both the article and the map?

    F. Delphi and Nemea

    G. Olympia and Sparta

    H. Olympia and Corinth

    I. Athens and Marathon

Looking It Up

5 What can you infer from the information about the Roman emperor who banned the Olympics?

   A. The Romans were in control of Greece around the year 394 A.D.
   B. The Romans were poor athletes and never did well at the Olympics.
   C. The Romans were planning to start their own athletic games in Rome.
   D. The Romans were concerned with keeping the peace between nations.

6 What did all the events of the ancient Olympics have in common?

   F. They were held over a five-day period.
   G. They were created as part of a religious festival.
   H. They were conducted wearing full suits of armor.
   I. They were related to skills used by soldiers in times of war.

7 What information about the Olympics does the discussion of olive branches support?

   A. The Olympics began in ancient Greece.
   B. The Olympics honored peace among nations.
   C. The Olympics attracted athletes from throughout Greece.
   D. The Olympics grew both in number of events and number of countries.

8 When did the marathon event become part of the Olympics?

   F. when the first Olympics were held
   G. when the other Panhellenic Games were created
   H. when the Olympics were started up again in 1897
   I. when the Athenians defeated the Persians at Marathon

9 Read the sentence below.

   The ensuing century must have seen a revival of earlier games, since a variety of other events were added during that first century, including longer races.

   The origin of the word *revival* is from the Latin *vivere*, meaning "to live." What does *revival* mean?

   A. to live again
   B. to live before
   C. to live on forever
   D. to live a long time

Read the article "Florida Panther" before answering Numbers 1 through 9.

Florida Panther

The Florida panther is a subspecies of cougar, also known as puma, mountain lion, or catamount. Cougars were historically found throughout the United States, but are now extinct east of the Mississippi. This particular subspecies, *Felis concolor coryi*, is now found only in the southern tip of Florida. The population numbers approximately 87 animals.

Panthers utilize a variety of habitats, from forested uplands to cypress swamps. A critical factor in their habitat is adequate cover, necessary for hiding and stalking their prey. As solitary hunters, they make kills by stealth, rather than through cooperative packs.

The most critical threat to the Florida panther is the devastating loss of habitat. Pushed out by urban, agricultural, and industrial development, they remain only in large protected areas and in isolated pockets of degraded habitat, fragmented by roads and highways that pose an additional threat to the wide-ranging panther.

Vehicle collisions are a major cause of death for the panther; an indirect effect of the loss of habitat. Since 1972, 78 panther deaths were documented from collisions with cars and trucks.

To alleviate the problem, underpasses were constructed when Alligator Alley was converted to I-75 in 1993, to aid the crossing of panthers and other wildlife. A smaller design, more suited for two-lane highways, was developed and installed on State Road 29 north of I-75. Crossings in these zones have eliminated accidents.

Wildlife crossings can be extremely beneficial in expanding habitat, and they have aided the efforts to save the Florida panther. However, this situation makes the case that crossings are not a panacea. Even with crossings, continued development and degradation of the panther's habitat will certainly drive the species closer to extinction.

STEER CLEAR

How to Avoid Wildlife-Vehicle Collisions (*ROADKILL*)

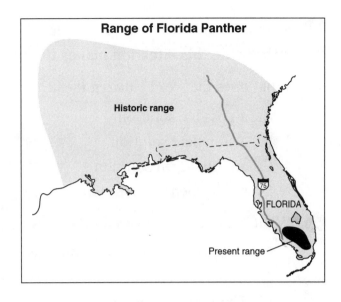

1. **Heed wildlife crossing signs.**
   Drive with increased awareness and caution when traveling in wildlife areas.
2. **Limit driving at night.**
   Between dusk and dawn a driver's visibility is lowest and wildlife traffic is highest.
3. **Reduce your speed in wildlife areas.**
   This will increase your response time to avoid colliding with a crossing animal.
4. **In the event you are involved in a wildlife-vehicle collision, report it to the local police.**
   Once alerted, wildlife agents can treat injured animals, examine dead ones, and search for any young left behind. If you hit an endangered or threatened species, immediately report it to the state department of natural resources and the U.S. Fish & Wildlife Service.
5. **Don't litter.**
   Some species enjoy "human" food just as much as we do and will be attracted to roadsides if they smell fast-food containers, apple cores, candy wrappers, soda bottles, etc.
6. **Get involved in your local government.**
   Attend county-commission, zoning, or metropolitan-planning organization meetings. Vocalize your concern about loss of wildlife habitat in favor of new road construction and urban expansion.
7. **Write to your state department of transportation.**
   Encourage officials to incorporate wildlife considerations into future transportation planning. Inquire about their current efforts to reduce the impact of transportation on wildlife.

Now answer Numbers 1 through 9. Base your answers on the article "Florida Panther."

1 If the main article needed a new title, which of these would be BEST?

  A. Habitats, Highways, and the Florida Panther
  B. Why Did the Florida Panther Cross the Road?
  C. Wildlife Crossings Help Florida Wildlife Survive
  D. The Incredible Shrinking Range of the Florida Panther

2 What does the author think about the future of the Florida panther?

  F. The panther will become extinct if it keeps losing habitat.
  G. The panther is out of danger thanks to efforts to protect its habitat.
  H. The panther will become extinct if people keep having collisions with them.
  I. The panther will be safe when more wildlife crossings are constructed.

3 Read this sentence from the article.

However, this situation makes the case that crossings are not a panacea.

What does the word *panacea* mean?

    A. a possible solution

    B. a complete solution

    C. an intelligent solution

    D. an inexpensive solution

4 What idea from the main article does the map support?

    F. Cougars are now found only west of the Mississippi.

    G. Cougars were once found everywhere in the United States.

    H. The Florida panther's habitat has shrunk over the years.

    I. The Florida panther's range is crisscrossed by highways.

5 What will people who read the sidebar article mainly learn about?

    A. how to spot wildlife at night to help prevent accidents

    B. ways to prevent and reduce collisions with wild animals

    C. methods of restoring wildlife habitat lost to development

    D. ways to get your neighbors involved in protecting habitat

6 According to the sidebar article, why should people avoid driving at night?

    F. Animals are more active at night.

    G. Cars are more difficult to see at night.

    H. Drivers have a slower response time at night.

    I. Panthers do not use wildlife crossings at night.

7 Which topic do both the main article and the sidebar article discuss?

    A. getting involved in city and zoning planning

    B. preventing animals from eating human food

    C. writing officials to show your concern for animals

    D. building roads that take animals' needs into account

8 Which sections of the sidebar article BEST support information in the main article?

    F. 1 and 2

    G. 2 and 5

    H. 4 and 6

    I. 6 and 7

9 How is the sidebar article DIFFERENT from the main article?

A. The sidebar article gives only information, while the main article gives helpful tips.

B. The sidebar article talks about all wildlife, while the main article talks only about the panther.

C. The sidebar article discusses successful wildlife crossing projects, while the main article discusses only the dangers of habitat loss.

D. The sidebar article deals only with fixing existing highways, while the main article deals with building new highways with wildlife crossings.

Read the article "Be a Nutrition Detective" before answering Numbers 1 through 9.

Be a Nutrition Detective

by Jeanne Miller

The best way to make sure that the food you put into your mouth has no hidden—and unhealthy—surprises is to read the ingredient list and the Nutrition Facts label, printed on almost all packaged food. The ingredients are listed in order of quantity, with the most plentiful being first. The Nutrition Facts label includes the number of calories and the amount of fat, carbohydrate, and protein per serving of the product. Here you'll also find out how much of the fat is saturated and how much of the carbohydrate is in the form of sugars (including naturally occurring sugars like those in fruit and milk). Beginning in 2006, the label will also state the amount of trans-fat. Be careful to make sure that the serving size listed matches the amount you actually eat.

A good procedure for identifying the substances you want to eat regularly or in moderation is to:

☞ Search the ingredient list for evidence of trans-fat (which is hydrogenated fats). Forty percent of the average supermarket's food products contain trans-fat. You'll find it in microwave popcorn, cookies, cakes, doughnuts, fried snacks, whipped toppings, and dozens of other products-even in frozen foods like potpies, fish sticks, and French fries. If the ingredient list includes "shortening" or "hydrogenated" or "partially hydrogenated" oil, the product has trans-fat, and you should avoid it. The safe level for trans-fat in your diet has not been determined.

☞ Next, search the ingredient list for added sugars. A seemingly healthy beverage like "fruit juice drink" or "fruit punch" can have as little as 10 percent actual fruit juice and may have high-fructose corn syrup as its first or second ingredient. A one-cup serving could easily have the equivalent of six teaspoons of sugar in it. Commonly added sugars include white and brown sugar, honey, molasses, corn syrup, maple syrup, and dried or crystallized cane juice. Keep your consumption of these added sugars as low as possible, since they are digested quickly and can cause abrupt changes in blood-sugar level. They also add calories to your diet without adding nutrients.

☞ Look for whole grains in the ingredient list. Whole-grain products should list whole wheat, whole oats, whole rye, or other whole grains in their contents. If the label says "wheat flour," the manufacturer may just be trying to trick you into think it's whole wheat. If it says "enriched" flour or "unbleached" flour, you can be sure that it's made from highly refined grains. The more often you eat whole grains, the better.

☞ Find out how much saturated fat is in the product. For this, you need to check the Nutrition Facts label. Keep the amount of saturated fat you consume as low as possible, but even healthy sources of unsaturated fats, such as peanut oil and salmon, usually have a little saturated fat in them, too. Just make sure that, if it's listed, the unsaturated fat is greater than the saturated fat.

Now you're ready to do a little sleuthing around the supermarket or kitchen or school cafeteria to make the healthiest food choices possible.

Sample Label for Macaroni and Cheese

Nutrition Facts
Serving Size 1 cup (228g)
Servings Per Container 2

Amount Per Serving
Calories 250   Calories from Fat 110

	% Daily Value*
Total Fat 12g	18%
Saturated Fat 3g	15%
Trans Fat 1.5g	
Cholesterol 30g	10%
Sodium 470mg	20%
Total Carbohydrate 31g	10%
Dietary Fiber 0g	0%
Sugars 5g	
Protein 5g	
Vitamin A	4%
Vitamin C	2%
Calcium	20%
Iron	4%

*Percent Daily Values are based on a 2,000 calorie diet. Your Daily Values may be higher or lower depending on your caloric needs:

	Calories	2,000	2,500
Total Fat	Less than	65g	80g
Sat Fat	Less than	20g	25g
Cholesterol	Less than	300mg	300mg
Sodium	Less than	2,400mg	2,400mg
Total Carbohydrate		300mg	375mg
Dietary Fiber		25mg	30mg

Start Here

Limit these Nutrients

Get Enough of these Nutrients

Footnote

Quick Guide to % DV

5% or less is low

20% or more is high

Looking It Up

Now answer Numbers 1 through 9. Base your answers on the article "Be a Nutrition Detective."

1 According to both the article and the Nutrition Facts label, how much saturated fat should people eat?

- A. none at all
- B. a small amount
- C. a medium amount
- D. a large amount

2 What information in the article explains the "Start Here" suggestion on the Nutrition Facts label?

- F. the information on looking for whole grains on the ingredient list
- G. the information on searching the ingredient list for evidence of trans-fat
- H. the information on matching the serving size to how much you really eat
- I. the information on making sure that the unsaturated fat is greater than the saturated fat

3 Which topic is discussed in both the article and the Nutrition Facts label?

- A. the nutrients that you should limit in your diet
- B. the vitamins that you should include in your diet
- C. the number of calories you should consume each day
- D. the whole-grain products you should consume each day

4 With which statement would the author MOST likely agree?

- F. Food manufacturers are often dishonest in their Nutrition Facts labels.
- G. Food manufacturers are sometimes dishonest in their ingredient lists.
- H. People can get all the information they need from the ingredient list.
- I. People should read only the Nutrition Facts label to learn about their food.

5 According to the article, which nutrient will be added to the Nutrition Facts label?

- A. trans-fats
- B. saturated fats
- C. hydrogenated oil
- D. partially hydrogenated oil

6 What information can you find in the Nutrition Facts label's footnote section?

- F. the total amount of iron to include in your diet
- G. the number of calories everyone should eat each day
- H. the total daily recommended amounts of certain nutrients
- I. the percentage of cholesterol found in that particular food

7 What can you tell about a fruit juice that has high-fructose corn syrup as the first item on its ingredient list?

    A. There is a small amount of corn syrup in the product.
    B. There is a healthy amount of corn syrup in the product.
    C. There is as much corn syrup as there is fruit juice in the product.
    D. There is more corn syrup than any other ingredient in the product.

8 If you are on a 2,000-calorie diet, how much total cholesterol should you have in your daily diet?

    F. less than 30 mg
    G. less than 300 mg
    H. at least 10 percent
    I. at least 20 percent

9 According to the Nutrition Facts label, macaroni and cheese has a high percentage of which two nutrients?

    A. sugars and protein
    B. vitamin A and iron
    C. sodium and calcium
    D. saturated fat and cholesterol

MAKING SENSE OF IT

On the FCAT, you will be asked to interpret materials that could be used for research and to synthesize, or bring together, information from more than one source. The strategies covered in this chapter will help you to do these tasks.

Here is a review of how to combine information from two sources:

> 1. Read the first source carefully and state its main idea.
> 2. Read the second source and state its main idea.
> 3. Next, read the FCAT question.
> 4. Find information in BOTH sources that have to do with the FCAT question.
> 5. Use inferencing skills to draw a conclusion based on information from both sources.
> 6. Test each possible answer to see which choice is correct.

Chapter Six

Looking Into It

Benchmark: L.A.A.2.3.8

The student checks the validity and accuracy of information obtained from research, in such ways as differentiating fact and opinion, identifying strong vs. weak arguments, and recognizing that personal values influence the conclusions an author draws.

The latest TV commercial for XS Sneakers: The scene is an outdoor basketball court in a suburban neighborhood. Six boys are strolling importantly toward the court, one of them dribbling a basketball. The camera zooms in on the boys' feet to show that all of them are wearing orange and black sneakers with the brand name "XS Sneakers," except for one boy who is wearing plain, white, no-brand sneakers.

They begin to play a three-on-three game, and all the boys are making miraculous lay-ups, rebounds, and jump shots. Except for the boy in no-brand sneakers. Every time he gets the ball, he drops it, or shoots and misses the net by a mile. Finally, he gets the ball again and trips over his own feet while trying to do a lay-up. Another boy (wearing XS Sneakers) takes his place in the game.

The boy limps off the court, ashamed, and goes to sit on a bench behind a fence by the basketball court. He looks very unhappy. Suddenly a tiny, bright light appears in the sky. It gets bigger and bigger until POOF! A giant, professional basketball player appears. The basketball player touches the boy's feet with a magic wand, and his plain sneakers are transformed into a pair of XS Sneakers.

The boy bounds out on the court, steals the basketball, and makes a phenomenal game-winning shot. The other boys cheer and pat him on the back. A cute girl from the sidelines with a dazzling smile runs up and links her arm through his. The camera zooms in on the boy's XS Sneakers, and the words "Be Somebody!" flash across the screen.

Many commercials, like this one for XS Sneakers, suggest that their products will make people more successful, more popular, more beautiful, and so forth, without giving any solid evidence to support these big promises. To be a smart consumer and to make good decisions, it's important that you know how to analyze the arguments being presented in what you see, hear, and read. You need to decide whether the message you are receiving is a strong argument supported with facts, or a weak argument filled with opinions that may be trying to influence you by appealing to your emotions.

Why Study This?

As you learned in Chapter 5, knowing where to find the information you need is an important skill. However, once you have that information there is still one more step: You need to decide if the information is accurate. This applies to everything you read—books, Web sites, articles, and advertisements.

There are three ways to analyze information. Mastering these techniques will help you

- tell the difference between fact and opinion
- identify strong and weak arguments
- see how personal values influence an author's arguments and conclusions

Key Concepts

- **Fact:** information that can be proved or disproved
- **Opinion:** a statement that cannot be proved or disproved
- **Strong arguments:** thoughtful opinions that are supported by relevant reasons, facts, and examples
- **Weak arguments:** personal opinions that are not supported by facts and examples
- **Personal values:** beliefs that influence a writer's arguments and conclusions about a topic

Distinguishing Fact From Opinion

Written materials often contain facts *and* opinions. Being able to tell them apart will help you judge the accuracy of a writer's ideas. It will also help you choose good sources with reliable information when doing research.

Facts are pieces of information that you can verify, or prove to be true, by checking other sources. Here are some examples of facts:

- The rapper Queen Latifah's real name is Dana Owens.
- Wolves have been reintroduced into many Western states.
- Some school districts are eliminating their music departments.

An opinion, on the other hand, cannot be verified. Here are some examples of opinions:

- Queen Latifah is the best female rapper of all time.
- Wolves are beautiful and noble animals.
- Music education is an important part of each child's school experience.

Can you tell which of the following are facts and which are opinions? Which one has both a fact *and* an opinion?

_____ The capital of Montana is Helena.

_____ Autumn is the best time of year.

_____ Fourteen-year-olds are too young to drive.

_____ Many of Stephen King's books have been made into movies.

_____ Soccer is more dangerous than football because soccer players do not wear helmets.

Identifying Strong and Weak Arguments

A second way to check the validity of information is to decide if a writer has presented a *strong* or *weak* argument. A strong argument usually begins with an opinion that is related to the topic. This opinion is supported by facts and reasons. The argument is clearly and logically organized. A weak argument, on the other hand, often has unrelated opinions that are not supported by facts or reasons.

Read the following example of a strong argument.

> Dear Editor:
>
> Many adults are against the plan to create a teen center out of Fillmore Elementary School, which was recently closed due to low enrollment. As a teenager, I believe a teen center would be a great addition to the community. As it is right now, there is nowhere for people my age to go to hang out with their friends, especially in the winter. This means that we usually end up at the mall, which is great for the

mall, since we end up spending our money there. However, I think it would be much better if there were a place where we could go to play sports, take fun classes, or maybe even do theatrical productions. I learned in my French class that in French-speaking countries there are teen centers called *maisons des jeunes*. These centers offer a variety of activities for young people and are very popular. Finally, there has been talk of getting rid of many after-school programs in the middle schools and high schools because of lack of money. If this happens, it will be even more important for teenagers to have a place like the planned teen center.

   Sincerely,

   Liza Thompson

   The writer clearly states her opinion in the second sentence: A teen center would be a great addition to the community. Her opinion is clearly related to the topic of whether or not a former school should be turned into a teen center. Then she supports her opinion with relevant facts, such as the fact that she and her friends spend all their time, and money, at the mall. She also describes the kinds of activities that could be offered at the teen center. Then she talks about popular teen centers in French-speaking countries. Finally, she points out the fact that many after-school programs might be cut, which would make a teen center even more useful.

   Liza's letter presents a strong argument for the teen center that will likely convince many people that it is a good idea. Now read another letter that is an example of a weak argument.

Dear Editor:

First they closed Fillmore Elementary School. That school had been around for 100 years! I went to Fillmore, my parents went to Fillmore, and my grandparents went to Fillmore! Why did they have to close it? And now they want to turn it into a teen center! There's a brilliant idea! Teenagers are spoiled rotten these days. They have every advantage. I didn't have a teen center growing up! If we wanted fun and excitement after school, we played volleyball at Fillmore. And suppose we did make a teen center out of Fillmore. They would just wreck it. There would be graffiti all over the walls and soda cans thrown everywhere! Teenagers are nothing but trouble.

Sincerely,

Pat Crane

This writer starts by complaining about the school being closed, which may be unfortunate but is not relevant to the topic of what to do with the school now that it is closed. Her opinion that it should not be turned into a teen center is not stated clearly. Then she doesn't use any facts to support her belief that it should not be a teen center. Instead, she uses her opinion that teenagers are "spoiled rotten" as an argument against the center. Next she weakens her argument by stating that she herself went to Fillmore to play sports after school when she was a teenager. This would seem to support the idea that it should be a teen center! She ends her letter with more negative opinions about teenagers.

Pat's letter presents a weak argument against the teen center. Her negative opinions will probably not go far in persuading people to accept her opinion.

Recognizing the Influence of Personal Values

The third way to check the validity and accuracy of information involves recognizing how personal values influence an author's conclusions.

Looking Into It

The following two paragraphs illustrate this point. Although each author discusses the same subject, they do so in very different ways.

> There is a growing feral cat population that is overrunning our neighborhood. Last week I was relaxing on my deck, enjoying the amazing aerial acrobatics of a ruby-throated hummingbird that was visiting one of the feeders I put up in my backyard. Suddenly, from out of the shrubbery slunk a mangy orange cat, headed straight for the hummingbird feeder. Before I had time to react, the beast had leapt from the ground and snatched the tiny bird in midair. It was a horrifying scene to witness. These wild cats are survivors. Rejected by the human race, they have managed to earn a cruel living by preying on birds.

> I set the three bowls of canned cat food on the ground and retreated back to my car. Once I shut the car door, it was as if some kind of kitty corral had been opened up. Cats of all sizes and colors, some of them fuzzy little kittens, came stampeding out of the woods toward the bowls of food. I hated to think what would happen to them if I didn't make the daily trip to feed them. This area had become a dumping ground for unwanted cats and kittens. I knew people who wanted to see these cats hunted down and killed because of their impact on the wild bird population. But I don't think being a hungry, abandoned kitty is a crime worthy of a death sentence, especially when people are the ones responsible for their situation in the first place.

Can you see how personal values affect the way each author feels about feral cats? The first author values the lives of birds more than the lives of wild cats. The author says mainly negative things about cats. The author does say that the wild cats are "survivors" but puts a negative "spin" on this, too, by saying that they are earning a "cruel living."

In the second paragraph, the author values the lives of the feral cats much more than the author of the first paragraph does. The author also believes there is a problem with too many cats being out in the wild. However, the author writes about the cats in a sympathetic way. The author describes some of the cats as "fuzzy little kittens." The author admits that the cats eat birds but puts the blame on people for putting the cats in a position where they have to kill birds to survive.

SEEING IT IN ACTION

The following paragraph is loaded with opinions. See if you can find them.

> "Rap *music*"? Isn't that a little like "jumbo shrimp"? The horrible phenomenon known as rap "music" is not music at all. Music is music only when people sing lyrics or play a musical instrument or both, and untalented rappers neither sing nor play musical instruments, unless you consider the irritating racket of DJs "scratching" a needle on a record album to be the same thing as playing a musical instrument. I mean, how much talent could it possibly take to string together a few sentences that rhyme? I think that all people who enjoy rap are uncultured and simply cannot understand or appreciate real music.

Which words or phrases express a judgment by the writer? List the words and phrases you find.

_____

_____

_____

Did you include the words *horrible, irritating, idiotic, uncultured, real music*? These are just a few of the words and phrases that reflect the writer's opinions.

Some opinions are more valid than others. A record producer might have a good idea of what kinds of music are most popular at any given moment. However, everyone has different tastes, especially when it comes to musical preferences. Even a record producer would not be credible if he or she claimed that people who enjoy rap are "uncultured."

FCAT Fred Says:

Whenever you read or hear words such as *all, nothing, everyone*, or *no one*, you should beware. There are almost always exceptions that prove that what is being said is not a fact but an opinion. Once I overheard one of my owner's friends say, "All cats are aloof." I looked up the word in the dictionary and found out that *aloof* means "unfriendly and standoffish." From that point on, I made a special point to hop up on his lap at every opportunity. How was I supposed to know he was allergic to cats? Nevertheless, I made my point: Not *all* cats are aloof.

Be on the lookout for signal words when you read the selections on the test.

Now read the passage that follows. It contains both facts and opinions. As you read, underline the facts.

Rap music is a unique and expressive form of rhythmic, urban poetry. This fascinating music style began in the late 1960s when DJ Kool Herc moved to New York City from the island nation of Jamaica. Kool Herc introduced to America the Jamaican practice of calling out rhymes during the instrumental sections of reggae records. He would also chant instructions to the crowd to get them involved in the action. This kind of interaction with the audience became known as "rapping."

The first rap album was released in 1979. By the mid-1980s, rap became more and more controversial as artists used rap to express the realities of the black experience in America's urban communities. Many people outside of this urban culture saw the music as angry ranting with a violent message. They chose to ignore the many artists who performed raps with a positive and constructive message, for example, the early female rappers who championed women's rights in their music.

By now, rap music has been around long enough that mainstream America does not feel quite as threatened as it originally did by this powerful and vibrant art form. However, there are still critics who believe that rap music is simplistic and requires little or no talent. However, nothing could be farther from the truth. It takes a great deal of talent and imagination to develop the elaborate lyrics characteristic of today's rap music.

Do you notice the difference between the two passages? While both selections express judgments, the second one also includes facts. These statements are factual because they can be checked in outside sources.

- Rap music began in the late 1960s.
- DJ Kool Herc from Jamaica introduced adding rhymes to music.
- The first rap album was released in 1979.
- Rap music became controversial by the mid-1980s.

Try It Out

Read the editorial "Insurance Rates Are Unfair to Teenagers." Then answer the questions that follow. As you read, table the facts, opinions, and strong and weak arguments.

Insurance Rates Are Unfair to Teenagers

I am a seventeen-year-old high school student. When I got my driver's license at age sixteen, I went right out and found a part-time job and started saving up for a car. It took me a whole year, but I finally saved up enough money to buy a nice used car. I thought it was a dream come true, that is, until I found out how much insurance I would have to pay! My monthly insurance rate is double what my twenty-six-year-old sister pays. I have never received a speeding ticket and I have never been in a car accident. My only crime is that I am a teenager and therefore must be a reckless, inexperienced, and irresponsible driver. I think working toward a goal shows a lot of responsibility. And no way am I going to drive recklessly and get in a wreck in the car that I worked so hard to get. This is so unfair. Teenage drivers are the best drivers out there. We have much better reflexes and eyesight than adults. Plus, it's because I'm a guy, not a girl. If the insurance companies think I'm a worse driver than my sister, they should just see how well she drives with her cell phone plastered to her ear! Besides, everyone knows men are naturally better drivers.

1. What conclusion can be drawn from the author's statement "Teenage drivers are the best drivers out there"?

   A. The statement is an opinion.
   B. The statement is a fact.
   C. The author's personal beliefs are unclear.
   D. The author values being treated as an individual.

2. How well does the author present his case?

   F. The author presents a mostly strong argument.
   G. The author presents a mostly weak argument.
   H. The author does not take a stand.
   I. The author presents a completely strong argument.

Now read how one student answered these questions by using a table to organize his or her ideas.

ARGUMENTS

Strong (Facts/Examples)	Weak (Personal Feelings/Irrelevant Details)
Working toward a goal shows responsibility.	This is so unfair.
He will not drive recklessly and risk wrecking his car.	Teenagers are the best drivers out there.
Teenagers have better reflexes and eyesight than adults.	His sister is a bad driver because she talks a lot on her cell phone. Men are naturally better drivers than women.

1. What conclusion can be drawn from the author's statement "Teenage drivers are the best drivers out there"?

    A. The statement is an opinion.
    B. The statement is a fact.
    C. The author's personal beliefs are unclear.
    D. The author values being treated as an individual.

Although the author presents some evidence to support the idea that teenage drivers are better than adults, many people would still disagree, making this statement a matter of opinion. Therefore, B is incorrect. The author makes it very clear how he feels about higher rates for teenagers and teenaged drivers; therefore, C is incorrect. Choice D is also incorrect, since the author claims that "teenage drivers are the best drivers out there." He never states that teenage drivers should be judged individually. By process of elimination it becomes clear that A is the correct answer.

2. How well does the author present his case?

    F. The author presents a mostly strong argument.
    G. The author presents a mostly weak argument.
    H. The author does not take a stand.
    I. The author presents a totally strong argument.

By looking at the table, you can see that much of the argument presented by the author is weak. Even though the author uses some statements that are strong, he doesn't include enough facts to prove that it is unfair for insurance companies to charge teenagers more for insurance. The best answer is choice G.

Read the article "Night Siege: The Hudson Valley UFO Sightings" before answering Numbers 1 through 9.

Night Siege: The Hudson Valley UFO Sightings

by Dr. J. Allen Hynek, Philip J. Imbrogno, and Bob Pratt

Something truly extraordinary happened not long ago in the Hudson River Valley just a few miles north of New York City. Hundreds, and probably thousands, of astonished people looked up in the sky and saw something they had never seen before.

It was enormous, awesome, and spectacular.

It was seen not just once but many times over a period of more than three years.

No one knew what it was. No one yet knows.

Many people believe it was a spaceship from another world. Whatever it was, it was described by many competent, professional people as a startling series of brilliant lights, generally in the form of a V or a boomerang.

It moved slowly and silently and was easily as big as a football field; some witnesses said as big as three football fields. That would make it anywhere from 300 to 900 feet long, far larger than any aircraft manufactured in the United States or any other country.

One witness said: This was a flying city. It was not a small craft. It was huge.

This mysterious unidentified flying object, or UFO, was also very close to the ground, often no more than a few hundred feet in the air, and many people were able to get a good, long look at it.

It quickly became known as the Westchester Boomerang because so many early sightings of it took place in Westchester County. The sightings, however, soon spread to several nearby counties in New York State and Connecticut. Even so, many people still have never heard about it.

The American media has remained largely silent about this spectacular phenomenon, either from ignorance or, more likely, on purpose. Area newspapers, radio, and television stations did carry stories, but there was little in the way of national coverage.

The United States has the most extensive, sophisticated, and freest mass communications system in the world. Trivial events are often flashed everywhere. Yet, news of this utterly astounding happening was carried on only one network.

Could it possibly be that the whole thing never happened? Absolutely not.

Hundreds of people, many of them highly educated professionals, have gone on record as saying that the Boomerang was undeniably very real to them. The great majority of people we interviewed had no previous interest in UFOs; they were taken completely by surprise. Many witnesses were separated geographically and were unknown to each other at the time of the sightings. Police records show that countless residents phoned their local police stations in concern, and police officers themselves witnessed this strange spectacle.

Something truly astonishing was happening, but those who are responsible for protecting us—the law enforcement agencies, state and federal governments, and the military—ignored it.

Hundreds of people living in the affluent suburbs within commuting distance of one of the world's largest and most cosmopolitan cities were astonished, awestruck, and frightened by what they could only regard as a very bizarre event, yet the Federal Aviation Administration (FAA), which monitors the air lanes through which the boomerang-shaped object flew repeatedly, persisted in denying its existence.

From the nation's scientists, to whom these events should have been of breathtaking concern, nothing was heard. We find that shocking.

Scientists generally are straightforward, plain-thinking men and women who deal in facts and calculations. Their day-to-day business is to make observations and conduct experiments, thereby learning about our world and universe. They are, or should be, imaginative and curious.

But no scientists showed any curiosity about the strange events in the Hudson Valley. Throughout the forty or more years that the world has been aware of UFOs, most scientists have dismissed them out of hand. Just as they turn a deaf ear to the wild, fanciful stories of people who claim they have been taken to Venus and Mars, scientists also have failed to heed the serious reports of the hundreds of thousands of people who have seen inexplicable things in our skies.

It has been said that the most heinous offense a scientist can commit as a scientist is to declare to be true that which is not true. The Nobel Prize-winning scientist who said this was referring to falsifying or inventing evidence, but he probably would agree that it is also a heinous offense for a scientist to declare that something does not exist when, in fact, it may, especially if he or she has not attempted to determine its validity.

There are, fortunately, a few hundred scientists around the world who do take the UFO phenomenon seriously. Some became interested when they experienced sightings of their own, and others simply were curious.

It may be that UFOs pose a question that science cannot answer. However, we don't believe this is the case. We—two scientists and an investigative reporter—believe there is an answer. But we will never know what it is until scientists accept the phenomenon of UFOs as something fascinating and bizarre, but very real, and begin to study it.

Now answer Numbers 1 through 9. Base your answers on the article "Night Siege: The Hudson Valley UFO Sightings."

1 What is the BEST evidence that the authors give that the witnesses were not working together to trick people into thinking there was a UFO?

   A. The witnesses did not know each other.
   B. The witnesses all described the UFO as a large boomerang.
   C. Many of the sightings happened in Westchester County.
   D. Many of the witnesses reported their sightings to the police.

2 Which fact from the article supports the idea that scientists should be curious about UFOs?

   F. A scientist works with facts and calculations.
   G. Some scientists have had their own UFO sightings.
   H. Most scientists pay no attention to UFO sightings.
   I. A scientist's job is to learn more about the universe.

3 Which sentence from the article weakens the authors' argument that scientists should admit that UFOs may be real?

   A. "They are, or they should be, imaginative and curious."
   B. "But no scientists showed any curiosity about the strange events in the Hudson Valley."
   C. "There are, fortunately, a few hundred scientists who do take the UFO phenomenon seriously."
   D. "It has been said that the most heinous offense a scientist can commit as a scientist is to declare to be true that which is not true."

4 What personal belief explains why the authors were angry at the government's reaction to the UFO sightings?

    F. the belief that government should concentrate on political issues
    G. the belief that the government should put more faith in its citizens
    H. the belief that the government should not interfere in the work of scientists
    I. the belief that the government should defend its citizens from possible harm

5 An eyewitness account from which of these people would BEST strengthen the authors' argument that the sightings were real?

    A. an eight-year-old child
    B. a Federal Aviation Administration spokesperson
    C. a respected scientist who had actually seen a UFO
    D. a person who claimed to have been taken aboard the UFO

6 What fact about the authors supports their argument that the Hudson Valley sightings should be taken seriously?

    F. Two of the authors are scientists.
    G. Two of the authors witnessed the UFO.
    H. One of the authors won the Nobel Prize.
    I. One of the authors is an investigative reporter.

7 How do the authors support their opinion that most news media did not report the Hudson Valley UFO sightings on purpose?

    A. by stating that one network did report the sightings
    B. by describing the ignorance of the American news media
    C. by pointing out that even small and unimportant stories get reported
    D. by stating that the UFO sightings occurred in both New York and Connecticut

8 What did the authors want to prove by describing the witnesses as "professional" people?

    F. that the witnesses were reporters
    G. that the witnesses were scientists
    H. that the witnesses were believable
    I. that the witnesses were intelligent

9 Why do the authors discuss people who claim they were taken to Venus and Mars?

    A. to show that most reports of UFO sightings should not be believed
    B. to show that scientists treat all UFO sightings as true until proved to be false
    C. to show that scientists have already studied many UFO sightings and found them all to be false.
    D. to show that scientists consider all UFO sightings to be stories that come from people who cannot be believed

Read the article "Evidence Supporting Continental Drift" before answering Numbers 1 through 9.

Evidence Supporting Continental Drift

The Earth's crust is constantly moving, both vertically and horizontally, at rates of up to several inches a year. A widely held theory that explains these movements is called "plate tectonics." It was developed in the mid 1960s by geophysicists. The term "plate" refers to large rigid blocks of the Earth's surface that appear to move as a unit. These plates may include both oceans and continents. When the plates move, the continents and ocean floor above them move as well. Continental drift occurs when the continents change position in relation to each other.

While plate tectonics is a relatively new idea, scientists have been gathering data in support of the continental drift theory for a very long time. In 1912, Alfred Wegener and Frank Taylor first proposed the theory that 200 million years ago the Earth had only one giant continent, from which today's continents broke apart and drifted into their current locations. Wegener used the fit of the continents, the distribution of fossils, a similar sequence of rocks at numerous locations, ancient climates, and the apparent wandering of the Earth's polar regions to support his idea.

The Shapes Match

The continents look as if they were pieces of a giant jigsaw puzzle that could fit together to make one giant super-continent.

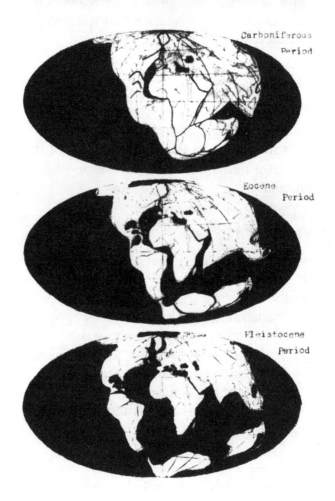

The bulge of Africa fits the shape of the coast of North America while Brazil fits along the coast of Africa beneath the bulge.

The Plants and Animals Match

Wegener noted that plant fossils of late Paleozoic age found on several different continents were quite similar. This suggests that they evolved together on a single large land mass. He was intrigued by the occurrences of plant and animal fossils found on the matching coastlines of South America and Africa, which are now widely separated by the Atlantic Ocean. He reasoned that it was physically impossible for most of these organisms to have traveled or have been transported across the vast ocean. To him, the presence of identical fossil species along the coastal parts of Africa and South America was the most compelling evidence that the two continents were once joined.

The Rocks Match

Broad belts of rocks in Africa and South America are the same type. These broad belts match when you fit the shapes of the two continents together, like pieces of a puzzle.

The Ice Matches

Wegener was aware that a continental ice sheet covered parts of South America, southern Africa, India, and southern Australia about 300 million years ago. Glacial striations on rocks show that glaciers moved from Africa toward South America. Such continuous glaciation suggests that the continents were once joined and there was no Atlantic Ocean.

The Positions Don't Match

If the continents were cold enough so that ice covered the southern continents, why is no evidence found for ice in the northern continents? Simple! The present northern continents were at the equator 300 million years ago. The discovery of fossils of tropical plants (in the form of coal deposits) in Antarctica led to the conclusion that this frozen land previously must have been situated closer to the equator, in a more temperate climate where lush, swampy vegetation could grow.

Why Few People Believed

Wegener's continental drift theory was not readily accepted by the science community of his day. It was difficult to conceive of large continents plowing through the sea floor to move to new locations. What kind of forces could be strong enough to move such large masses of solid rock over such great distances? Wegener suggested that the continents simply plowed through the ocean floor, but Harold Jeffreys, a noted English geophysicist, argued correctly that it was physically impossible for a large mass of solid rock to plow through the ocean floor without breaking up. Recent evidence from ocean floor exploration and other studies has rekindled interest in Wegener's theory, and led to the development of the theory of plate tectonics.

Now answer Numbers 1 through 9. Base your answers on the article "Evidence Supporting Continental Drift."

1 How far does Earth's crust move in a year?

    A. about a mile

    B. about an inch

    C. several miles

    D. several inches

Looking Into It

2 What can you infer from the article about the position of the continents in the future?

- F. They will be spaced farther apart.
- G. They will be joined together again.
- H. They will be in different positions.
- I. They will be in the same positions.

3 How does the shape of Africa support the idea that in the past there was just one giant continent?

- A. It is the same shape as South America.
- B. It shows how the land wore away over time.
- C. It fits into the coasts of North and South America.
- D. It reveals how rocks formed in Africa millions of years ago.

4 What fact did Wegener use to support the idea that plant fossils found in South America and Africa prove that the two continents were once together?

- F. The plants could be found only in the form of fossils.
- G. The plants could not have traveled across the Atlantic Ocean.
- H. The plant fossils Wegener found were all from the late Paleozoic age.
- I. The plant fossils in South America were very different from those in Africa.

5 What can you infer from the section "The Ice Matches"?

- A. Glaciers always move from east to west.
- B. Glaciers always destroy rocks in their path.
- C. Glaciers most often travel across solid land.
- D. Glaciers may leave marks on rocks in their path.

6 What fact from the article supports the idea that the Antarctic was once at the equator?

- F. Tropical plant fossils can be found in the Antarctic.
- G. Proof of ice is not found in the northern continents.
- H. Rocks in the Antarctic match rocks found at the equator.
- I. Glacier evidence shows that there was no Atlantic Ocean.

7 What kept many scientists from believing Wegener's theory of continental drift?

- A. the theory that continents could move
- B. the notion that oceans could change location
- C. the suggestion that continents could break apart
- D. the idea that continents could cut through the ocean floor

8 What does the author believe about Wegener's continental drift theory?

    F. It was confusing because it left a lot of questions unanswered.

    G. It was damaging because it made scientists believe an impossible theory.

    H. It was important because it led to the discovery that Earth's plates move.

    I. It was valuable because it showed how continents cut through the ocean floor.

9 Read this sentence from the article.

Recent evidence from ocean floor exploration and other studies has rekindled interest in Wegener's theory . . .

What does *rekindled interest* mean?

    A. made people interested again

    B. made people less interested in

    C. made people completely lose interest in

    D. made people interested for the first time

Read the article "Are Computers a Benefit or a Risk to Children?" before answering Numbers 1 through 9.

Are Computers a Benefit or a Risk to Children?

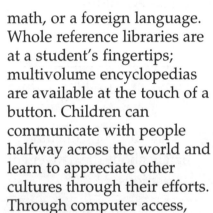

Letter One:
Computers Are an Important Part of Children's Education

Dear Editor:

Much has been written lately about the dangers of exposing young children to computers, and all of it is ridiculous. Children have everything to gain from early exposure to computers. Computers have become an absolutely integral part of our lifestyles at home, at school, and at work. It makes about as much sense to keep children away from computers now as it would have made to keep them away from telephones a hundred years ago. Progress is here to stay, and children must be part of it if they are to be able to function in a technologically advanced society.

The importance of computers in the adult world, however, is not the only reason to allow children to use them. Children benefit tremendously from playing on the computer. They are exposed to a learning tool that is unrivaled by anything previously known to educators or parents. Through the computer, children can receive individualized tutorials on everything from reading skills to biology, math, or a foreign language. Whole reference libraries are at a student's fingertips; multivolume encyclopedias are available at the touch of a button. Children can communicate with people halfway across the world and learn to appreciate other cultures through their efforts. Through computer access, children can participate in world activities in a way that has been previously impossible. Because children are our future, it is crucial to allow them to be part of our present.

Letter Two:
Computers Will Not Benefit Children in the Classroom

Dear Editor:

Supporters of computer-enhanced education argue that computers benefit students, and this may be true. We cannot deny that the World Wide Web has enabled many people to access new information and experiences. However, there is a dark side to this new technology that is frequently overlooked. Children who spend hours in front of a computer monitor sacrifice other skills that are learned in the early years of life. Among these are the power of imaginative play and the ability to socialize, compromise, and interact with other children. Without these skills, they will become part of a generation of technically skilled but emotionally lacking humanoids.

A loss of these skills is not the only reason to be cautious about exposing children to computers. Through computers, children can be exposed to concepts that they may be too young to handle. There is material on the Internet that is offensive to mature adults let alone young children. Even in what appear to be wholesome, child-oriented websites, children are exposed to advertising disguised as games. A child visits the website of a breakfast-cereal company and is greeted by the cartoon characters used to advertise that cereal. These commercial websites are used as marketing tools to generate information about the children and their families that can later be used to sell more products. Children should not be used as pawns in an unregulated marketer's game. They should not be exploring worlds that even many adults find unacceptable. They should not spend hours sacrificing their imagination or their socialization to a machine. Children should be encouraged to go out and play.

Now answer Numbers 1 through 9. Base your answers on the article "Are Computers a Benefit or a Risk to Children?"

1 What can you conclude from the first sentence of Letter One: "Much has been written lately about the dangers of exposing young children to computers, and all of it is ridiculous"?

    A. It is a fact.

    B. It is an opinion.

    C. The author is an open-minded person.

    D. The author knows a lot about computers.

2 Which fact would weaken the Letter One author's argument that computers are as safe as telephones for children?

    F. Computers are a more recent invention than telephones.

    G. Computers are a sign of a technologically advanced society.

    H. Computers allow children to communicate in writing instead of by talking.

    I. Computers allow children to access much more information than telephones do.

3 What evidence BEST supports the Letter One author's argument that computers are a learning tool?

    A. Children are the future of our society.

    B. Children are able to participate in world activities.

    C. Children can take online classes on many school subjects.

    D. Children can communicate with people around the world.

4 What is the Letter One author's opinion of children communicating with people around the world?

    F. It is an excellent way to learn about other cultures.

    G. It is a convenient way for children to learn a foreign language.

    H. It is the only way for children to find out about other countries.

    I. It is a dangerous way for children to meet people from other countries.

5 What is one way Letter Two is DIFFERENT from Letter One?

    A. It shows that the author cares about children.

    B. It admits that the opposing viewpoint has some truth in it.

    C. It supports its argument with more than one concrete example.

    D. It supports its argument with strong words and emotional appeals.

6 Which of the following would strengthen the Letter Two author's argument that children who spend too much time at the computer become "humanoids"?

    F. a quotation from a teacher about the value of computer tutorials

    G. an interview with a computer science teacher about advances in computer science

    H. a table showing the amount of time children of different ages spend on computers

    I. a study showing that students who spend a great deal of time on computers have few friends

7 What evidence does the Letter Two author give to support her opinion that children might see offensive materials on the Internet?

    A. Children may spend several hours every day on the Internet.

    B. Children may find child-oriented websites on the Internet.

    C. Adults sometimes get offended by what they find on the Internet.

    D. Adults sometimes target children on commercial websites on the Internet.

8 What evidence does the author of Letter Two give to prove that advertisers target children on their product Web sites?

    F. Children are greeted by cartoon characters.

    G. Children are used as pawns by unregulated marketers.

    H. Children are asked to give out information about their families.

    I. Children are asked to fill out questionnaires to find out more about them.

9 What conclusion can be drawn from the Letter Two author's statement "Children should be encouraged to go out and play"?

   A. The author values the benefits children get from play.
   B. The author believes children are expected to grow up too fast.
   C. The author thinks that children are much too serious these days.
   D. The author cares about the stress and pressure children experience.

MAKING SENSE OF IT

While going to the library is an important first step in conducting research, your job doesn't end there. Being able to analyze, sort through, and make sense of information is important—whether you are researching or reading an article in your favorite magazine.

- **Fact:** information that you can verify by checking other reference sources such as encyclopedias, dictionaries, nonfiction books, and Web sites
- **Opinion:** a statement of a writer's feelings about something or someone
- **Strong argument:** supported by facts, reasons, and examples that are relevant to the topic
- **Weak argument:** consists of opinions unrelated to the topic and the writer's personal feelings; usually not supported by facts and examples
- **Personal values:** what a person believes is important, unimportant, good, bad, right, or wrong
- **Personal values:** affect the conclusions an author draws about a topic; identifying them can help you better analyze the content of research materials

Chapter Seven

Why Did That Happen?

Benchmark: L.A.E.2.2.1

The student recognizes cause-and-effect relationships in literary texts.

Trey pulled open the door to the movie theater and cast one more glance down the street for LaTasha. And there she was, walking hurriedly up the sidewalk and waving to him.

"Trey! I am so sorry! I can explain!" she said as he held open the door for her.

"You can explain during the previews," he said, in a not-too-happy voice.

They bought their tickets and rushed inside. The only seats left were in the very front row. They craned their necks at a painful angle to watch the preview of *Slime*, a new horror movie. They both jumped when it looked like a slimy, green, three-headed monster was about to leap through the screen and land in their laps.

"Okay," said Trey when the preview was over, "why were you late?"

"Because the moon was full last night," LaTasha said.

"Let me get this straight: You were late today because the moon was full last night. What, did you turn into a werewolf?"

"No, I didn't turn into a werewolf! The moon was full and the light from the moon made it so bright in my bedroom that I woke up and couldn't get back to sleep."

185

"And . . . ?"

"And I went downstairs to get a glass of milk because that's supposed to help you sleep."

"It's warm milk that's supposed to help you sleep."

"Warm milk? Yuck! Anyway, when I was in the kitchen, I heard the cat meowing in the backyard. I opened the door to let him in, but he wouldn't come when I called. So I went outside to hunt for him and the door closed and locked behind me."

"You don't have a key hidden under a planter or anything?"

"No key. And my parents were visiting my aunt in Springfield, so I was all alone."

"What did you do?"

"I sat on the porch until my parents got home this morning. When they finally came home, I went to bed and crashed! I didn't wake up until half an hour ago! So that's why I was late."

"Because the moon was full last night."

"Yup."

The direct cause of LaTasha's lateness was that she had taken a long nap and overslept. But why did she take such a long nap? Because she had been out on the porch all night. Why was she out on the porch all night? Because the door locked behind her when she went outside. Why did she go outside? Because she was in the kitchen and she heard the cat meow. Why was she in the kitchen? Because she was getting a glass of milk. Why was she getting a glass of milk? Because she couldn't sleep. Why couldn't she sleep? Because of the light in her bedroom. Why was there light in her bedroom? Because the moon was full! Whew!

When you think about it, you can trace the causes for many things that happen. Some things that happen have a single cause. Other events are the end result of a chain of causes and events, like the series of events that caused LaTasha to be late.

Understanding how events unfold and are related is an important skill that will help you be a successful and savvy reader.

Why Study This?

If you open up the washing machine and find that all your white gym socks have turned pink, you don't have to be Sherlock Holmes to figure out what happened. After investigating the situation, you might discover that a red sock was accidentally mixed up with all the white ones; it is no mystery connecting the two events and seeing that the dye in the red sock **caused** the white socks to turn pink.

On the other hand, if you are learning to scuba dive and want to avoid decompression sickness, also known as the "bends," you will want to read an article on the subject very carefully to find out the causes of this painful condition so that you can take steps to avoid it happening to you.

Key Concepts

- **Cause:** A cause is an event or an action that makes something else happen.
- **Effect:** An effect is a result. It is what happens because of, or as the result of, another event or action.

Active readers analyze cause-and-effect relationships to help them get information from what they are reading. For instance, a student might read an article in a health magazine about the benefits of resistance training. The student reads that by increasing muscle mass through resistance training, a person can boost his or her metabolic rate, which causes him or her to burn more calories and therefore lose weight. Other benefits include a stronger heart, lower pulse rate, and lower blood pressure. In other words, the writer explains the results or, *effects*, which resulted from a *cause*-resistance training.

Troubleshooting means figuring out what happened when something mechanical breaks down—in other words, looking for the *cause* of an *effect* (the malfunction). In the following exercise, see if you can match the problems (effects) on the left with the reasons (causes) on the right.

1. The TV remote control will not work. _____ The battery is getting low.

2. The numbers on your clock radio are flashing. _____ There is a scratch on it.

3. The smoke alarm beeps, but there is no smoke. _____ There was a power outage.

4. A music CD begins to skip. _____ The batteries are dead.

Think Of It This Way

Writers of short stories, novels, poetry, and other types of literature use cause and effect in their writing. In fact, readers often remember a story as simply a list of cause-and-effect relationships. Just think about the classic movie, *The Wizard of Oz*.

In the movie, Dorothy runs away from home because a mean-spirited woman in the neighborhood threatens to take away her dog, Toto. She changes her mind about running away and hurries home, only to be swept away, house and all, by a tornado. The house lands in Oz, right on top of the Wicked Witch of the East. Because of this, Dorothy acquires the magical ruby slippers. The story continues with one event happening because of another until Dorothy is finally back home in Kansas.

It is a good example of cause-and-effect relationships.

Seeing It In Action

Now read the following dialogue.

"Jake, where is your lab journal?" Mr. Jensen asked.

"Um, my dog ate it." Jake pulled a tattered spiral-bound notebook from his backpack.

"Your dog ate it?" Mr. Jensen said skeptically.

Why Did That Happen?

> "Okay, maybe I *accidentally* dipped it in peanut butter first," Jake said.
>
> "Accidentally, Jake? Or were you deliberately trying to conceal the fact that you haven't been keeping up with your lab journal this semester? Let's open it up and see if you have indeed written *anything* in your lab journal this *entire* semester!"
>
> Mr. Jensen opened the notebook to the first page and read the words scribbled there in large letters: APRIL FOOL'S!
>
> Jake handed his real lab journal to Mr. Jensen and said, "Gotcha, Mr. J.!"

Figuring out the causes and effects in this dialogue is a little tricky because you don't discover what kicks off the chain of events until the end of the dialogue. But no matter where the first cause is, you can find it by reading the whole passage and asking yourself, "What happened first?" What happened first is the cause.

In this dialogue, what happened first was that Jake wanted to pull an April Fool's Day prank on his teacher, Mr. Jensen. So he put some peanut butter on a fake lab journal to make his dog chew on it. Then he pretended that the chewed-up journal was his real lab journal and made a big show of turning in the mangled journal that smelled of peanut butter. This caused Mr. Jensen to get angry and accuse Jake of not writing in his lab journal at all. His suspicions made him open up the journal and therefore become Jake's April Fool's Day victim. Becoming the target of Jake's prank was the effect, or what happened last, as a result of Jake's elaborate joke.

Read the following short passage and see if you can identify which event happened first. Label that the *cause*. Then find and label the *effect* of that action.

The Suitcase

Samantha and Alyssa exited the terminal and waited for Alyssa's dad to bring the car around. As they drove to the Gordons' house in downtown Missoula, Samantha was awestruck by the beautiful mountains that encircled the town. At the house, Alyssa showed her where she'd be staying, and Samantha began to unpack. But when she opened the suitcase and saw a pair of cowboy boots lying on top, she realized that she had made a terrible mistake. She looked at the tag on the suitcase. It read: Tom Hall, Lone Pine Ranch, Lolo, Montana, plus a phone number.

"Alyssa! This isn't my suitcase! Can I borrow your phone?" Samantha said.

"Yeah, sure! Here! I'll go tell my dad we have to go back to the airport to find your suitcase."

Alyssa came back and asked, "How'd it go?"

Samantha grinned and said, "Great! I talked to Tom Hall, and you're not going to believe this, but we're going to help him and his family brand cattle at their ranch tomorrow!"

Alyssa laughed and said, "No, I don't believe it. You're in Montana for less than an hour and you're already a ranch hand!"

What happened first? How did Samantha get invited to brand cattle at a ranch? She got invited by calling and talking to Tom Hall on the phone. So the invitation was the effect, and the cause was telephoning Tom Hall.

But there are other causes and effects in this story. What happened first that made it necessary for Samantha to phone Tom Hall? She grabbed his suitcase by mistake at the airport.

But what made her grab the wrong suitcase? She was excited about meeting her friend Alyssa and beginning her vacation. So the cause of Samantha being invited to brand cattle was that she was in such a hurry that she didn't check to make sure she had the right suitcase.

Why Did That Happen?

Notice that we asked ourselves, "What happened first?" or "Why did this happen?" Asking questions is a great way to guide your own discovery of cause-and-effect relationships in what you read. Reading actively means asking questions as you read.

FCAT Fred Says:

Sometimes it is not easy to find the reason that events unfold. Sometimes events are described out of order, or the writer doesn't tell us what caused the events at all. In these instances we have to read carefully to find the cause, or to infer what likely would have led to the events that took place.

For example, I am in the process of writing a mystery called *The Mousetrap*. It's about a town where, for some unknown reason, all the mice have disappeared. In the end, the clever cat detective, Furlock Holmes, solves the mystery by piecing together the clues scattered throughout the story. The clues are the causes that lead to the effect of the disappearing mice.

Now practice finding cause-and-effect relationships in a passage that doesn't ever use the words *cause* and *effect*. Read the story "The Wedding Cake." Then answer the questions that follow.

The Wedding Cake

Mark carefully placed the last rose at the bottom of the cascade of frosting roses that spilled down the side of the wedding cake. "Why did I say I'd make Janelle's wedding cake? I only started culinary school two weeks ago and here I am decorating the most important cake in my sister's life! But this looks good. I pulled it off!"

Then he looked around for the bride and groom figurines to be placed on top. Where *were* they? He searched the empty grocery bags lying discarded on the kitchen floor. Not there. He ran out to his car and hunted under the driver's side, the passenger's side, the back seat, and even the trunk. Not there. He had missed the wedding on purpose to finish the cake, and he knew the ceremony was almost over. Guests would be arriving back at the house for the reception in no time.

He raced upstairs to his sister's bedroom and stood in the doorway, hunting the room for an idea, any idea, to save the day. His eyes fell on the shelf full of trophies from his sister's high school softball days. He grabbed one of them and ran to his own room and found a similar trophy of his own, and ran back downstairs to the kitchen. He pried the male and female figures off the tops of the trophies and placed them side by side on top of the cake. It would have to do.

The wedding guests began arriving and filled the house with happy conversation. After everyone had visited the buffet and eaten their fill, it was time to bring out the wedding cake. Mark backed out of the kitchen carrying the heavy cake. Then he wheeled around and said, "Ta-da!"

The entire room, including his sister Janelle, burst out laughing. Later, she took Mark aside and said, "You could have at least had them aiming their bats *away* from each other, not *at* each other!"

1. What was the cause of Mark's concern?

   A. He was going to be late for the wedding.

   B. He was not going to finish frosting the cake in time.

   C. He had done a poor job of decorating the wedding cake.

   D. He had lost the bride and groom figures for the top of the cake.

2. What was the effect of the wedding cake's appearance?

   F. It made everyone laugh.

   G. It made his sister angry.

   H. It showed Mark's talent for baking.

   I. It showed Mark's attention to detail.

To answer both of these questions, the reader has to do a little thinking. The passage doesn't state, "Mark was concerned because . . ." Nor does it state, "The wedding cake caused . . ." or "The effects of the wedding cake were . . ." Remember, the FCAT requires the reader to understand what he or she reads. Most of the time, you will not be able to simply seek and find the answers. You must read the entire passage to figure things out.

Why Did That Happen?

For number 1, choice D is the correct answer. Let's review why the other choices are incorrect. Choice A is incorrect because the story states that he had missed the wedding on purpose to finish working on the cake. He had finished frosting the cake and just needed to put the bride and groom figures on top. That means that choice B is incorrect. Mark tells himself that the cake looked good and that he had "pulled it off," so choice C is incorrect. Therefore, D is the best answer for number 1.

For the second question, the correct answer is F. Choice G is incorrect because although his sister wishes the figures had been aiming their bats in a different direction, she is more amused than angry. The cake may have shown Mark's talent for baking and his attention to detail, but that wasn't the main effect of its appearance, so choices H and I are incorrect. The answer must be F.

Read the article "Ten Things You Can Do to Help Curb Global Warming" before answering Numbers 1 through 9.

Ten Things You Can Do to Help Curb Global Warming

Responsible Choices

The choices we make and the products we buy test our commitment to maintain a healthy planet. When we burn fossil fuels—such as oil, coal, and natural gas—to run our cars and light our homes, we pump carbon dioxide (CO_2) into the air. This thickens the heat-trapping blanket that surrounds the planet, causing global warming. Choosing modern technology can reduce our use of fossil fuels and help protect the planet. These ten steps will help curb global warming, save you money, and create a safer environment for the future.

1. Drive Smart!

A well-tuned car with properly inflated tires burns less gasoline—cutting pollution and saving you money at the pump. If you have two cars, drive the one with better gas mileage whenever possible. Better yet, skip the drive and take public transit, walk, or bicycle when you can.

2. Write to your leaders now. Urge them to raise fuel economy standards to 40 miles per gallon.

Modern technology can make our cars and trucks go farther on a gallon of gas. It's the biggest single step we can take to curb global warming. The less gasoline we burn, the less CO_2 we put into the air. Taking this step would also save nearly 4 million barrels of oil a day— more oil than we currently import from the Persian Gulf and could ever extract from the Arctic National Wildlife Refuge combined. And by saving gas, you save nearly $2,000 at the pump over the life of your car.

3. Support clean, renewable energy.

Renewable energy solutions, such as wind and solar power, can reduce our reliance on coal-burning power plants, the largest source of global warming pollution in the United States. Call your local utility and sign up for renewable energy. If they don't offer it, ask them why not?

4. Replace incandescent light bulbs with compact fluorescent bulbs.

Especially those that burn the longest each day. Compact fluorescents produce the same amount of light as normal bulbs, but use about a quarter of the electricity and last ten times as long. Each switch you make helps clean the air today, curb global warming, and save you money on your electricity bill.

5. Saving energy at home is good for the environment and for your wallet.

Start with caulking and weather-stripping on doorways and windows. Then adjust your thermostat and start saving. For each degree you lower your thermostat in the winter, you can cut your energy bills by 3 percent. Finally, ask your utility company to do a free energy audit of your home to show you how to save even more money.

6. Become a smart water consumer.

Install low-flow showerheads and faucets and you'll use half the water without decreasing performance. Then turn your hot water heater down to 120°F and see hot-water costs go down by as much as 50 percent.

7. Buy energy-efficient electronics and appliances.

Replacing an old refrigerator or an air conditioner with an energy-efficient model will save you money on your electricity bill and cut global warming pollution. Look for the Energy Star label on new appliances or visit their website at www.energystar.gov to find the most energy-efficient products.

8. Plant a tree, protect a forest.

Protecting forests is a big step on the road to curbing global warming. Trees "breathe in" carbon dioxide, but slash-and-burn farming practices, intensive livestock production, and logging have destroyed 90 percent of the native forests in the United States. And you can take action in your own backyard—planting shade trees around your house will absorb CO_2 and slash your summer air-conditioning bills.

9. Reduce! Reuse! Recycle!

Producing new paper, glass, and metal products from recycled materials saves 70 to 90 percent of the energy and pollution, including CO_2 that would result if the product came from virgin materials. Recycling a stack of newspapers only 4 feet high will save a good-sized tree. Please . . . buy recycled products!

10. Mount a local campaign against global warming.

Educate your community about how it can cut global warming pollution.

Support measures at the national, state, and local level that:

- Make automobiles go further on a gallon of gas;
- Accelerate the use of clean, renewable energy sources, such as solar and wind;
- Increase energy efficiency and conservation; and
- Preserve forests around the world.

Now answer Numbers 1 through 9. Base your answers on the article "Ten Things You Can Do to Help Curb Global Warming."

1 What is the cause of increased carbon dioxide in the air?

    A. burning fossil fuels

    B. using modern technology

    C. creating renewable energy

    D. raising fuel economy standards

2 What effect does increased carbon dioxide have on the "blanket" that surrounds Earth?

    F. It makes it thinner.

    G. It makes it thicker.

    H. It makes it trap less heat.

    I. It makes it absorb more pollution.

3 How can keeping a well-tuned car help curb global warming?

    A. by helping your car burn less gas

    B. by helping your car last much longer

    C. by helping your car's tires stay properly inflated

    D. by helping your car meet fuel economy standards

4 What is one result of raising fuel economy standards to 40 miles per gallon?

    F. We would need to buy cleaner-burning gas.

    G. We would need to spend more money on gas.

    H. We would import a lot more oil from the Persian Gulf.

    I. We would avoid drilling for oil in the Arctic National Wildlife Refuge.

5 How are compact fluorescent lightbulbs DIFFERENT from incandescent bulbs?

    A. They last longer.

    B. They are brighter.

    C. They cost less to buy.

    D. They need to be changed more often.

6 How can homeowners reduce their heating bill in the winter by 3 percent?

    F. by turning the hot water heater down to 120°F

    H. by buying appliances with the Energy Star label

    G. by lowering the thermostat 1 degree

    I. by removing caulking from doorways and windows

Why Did That Happen?

7 What is one effect of installing low-flow showerhead?

  A. Less water is used.
  B. More water is recycled.
  C. There is less water pressure.
  D. There is more water pressure.

8 How do trees help curb global warming?

  F. They help livestock production.
  G. They absorb carbon dioxide.
  H. They keep areas from being logged.
  I. They prevent slash-and-burn farming.

9 What is the MAIN idea of the tenth suggestion?

  A. to list four additional ways people can curb global warming
  B. to summarize all the suggestions from the first nine suggestions
  C. to show the reader that one individual can make a big difference
  D. to encourage the reader to get other people and the government involved

Read the article "Yao Ming: Gentle Giant of Basketball" before answering Numbers 1 through 9.

Yao Ming: Gentle Giant of Basketball

by Richard Krawiec

Most Americans still hold the stereotyped notion that Chinese people are short. But there are areas in China where the people grow just as tall as people in the United States. Yao Ming comes from Shanghai, where the people do tend to be taller. His parents were also tall, and not just by Chinese standards. Even if they lived in the United States, Yao Ming's father and mother would tower over most of their peers.

So it was no surprise that their child, born on Sept. 12, 1980, at an early age towered over his playmates. When Yao was only four, he was as tall as most children who were eight. By the time he reached the age of six, he had grown to the height of 4'9". Before he completed elementary school, he rose above nearly all of his teachers.

Given his height advantage, and the fact that his parents were skilled basketball players, it would seem natural that Yao would also excel at the sport. But at first that wasn't the case.

As a nine-year-old, Yao was more interested in science, in book learning, than in running around on a basketball court.

His parents didn't want to force Yao to play basketball. They wanted him to make the decision for himself. Still, they enrolled him at the Youth Sports School.

At first, Yao's height advantage made no difference. He was in such bad physical shape, that running up and down the court a mere two times left him exhausted. Despite his height, he wasn't a muscular person. In fact, he was extremely skinny, weak, and uncoordinated. Smaller children regularly knocked Yao around, and beat him out of rebounds. They laughed at his slight frame, his thin arms, and called him "chopsticks."

Yao's parents encouraged their son not to get discouraged, not to give up. His coach explained that it took time to learn how to play basketball, to be patient with himself. Work at small improvements, his coach counseled. Get better one step at a time.

His father took the time to explain the intricacies, the subtleties of the sport; a team game where individual skills meshed in a collective effort. Soon Yao Ming began to understand the beauty and grace of basketball. The more he understood, the more Ming learned to love the game.

When he was ten, and playing in his first organized children's league, Yao Ming's mother cooked him special treats before the game, so that he would look forward to game day. His father bought him small presents for every basket he made as a way to encourage his effort. His coach continued to tell Yao Ming to be patient, to look for improvement one step at a time.

This combination of encouragement and teaching had a positive effect on Yao. It helped him learn how to persevere. It taught him not to give up on himself. Soon, Yao began to develop more confidence.

In the long run, Yao's early failure probably helped him build character, too. He learned to be humble about his accomplishments, to appreciate whatever small successes he achieved.

For three years, Yao was trained and nurtured. By the time he turned twelve, he really loved basketball. There was no question that he was now serious about wanting to develop as a player. He was sent to a Shanghai sports academy, a preparatory school for young athletes. It is a place where children who are serious about developing their athletic skills would live away from home, sharing dorm rooms with other young children, and spend their days alternately attending classes and learning how to play their chosen sport.

The experience of being at a sports academy was a good one for Yao Ming. When he turned fourteen, he was selected to be a member of the Shanghai Oriental Sharks, a youth team similar to an AAU (Amateur Athletic Union) team in the United States.

Yao Ming was developing into a good, young Chinese basketball player. Maybe one day he would achieve the same success on China's National team as his mother had.

But he soon learned there was more to basketball than what he'd seen in his homeland. Yao Ming's basketball knowledge, and his personal horizons, were expanded by what he witnessed on TV.

Now answer Numbers 1 through 9. Base your answers on the article "Yao Ming: Gentle Giant of Basketball."

1 What reason does the author give for Yao Ming being so tall?

    A. Both his parents were tall.

    B. All Chinese people are tall.

    C. Both his parents were from Shanghai.

    D. Both his parents were basketball players.

2 Why were smaller children able to knock Yao Ming around?

    F. Yao Ming was thin and not very strong.

    G. Yao Ming was shy and easily frightened.

    H. Yao Ming was better at science than at sports.

    I. Yao Ming was not very good at basketball at first.

3 What made Yao Ming begin to understand and love basketball?

    A. His parents encouraged him not to give up.

    B. His coach told him to be patient with himself.

    C. His father taught him the finer points of basketball.

    D. His team showed him the ebb and flow of basketball.

4 Why did Yao Ming's mother make him special treats?

    F. so he would look forward to games

    G. so he would be motivated to practice

    H. to reward him for winning basketball games

    I. to reward him for each basket he made during a game

5 What made Yao Ming begin to develop more confidence?

    A. his increased knowledge of the game

    B. his success in winning basketball games

    C. his improved strength and physical condition

    D. his parents' and coach's support and instruction

6 How did Yao Ming's early failure affect him?

    F. He learned to appreciate his small improvements.

    G. He realized that he needed to attend a sports school.

    H. He became somewhat discouraged about his progress.

    I. He became more determined to become a great player.

7 Read this sentence from the article.

Most Americans still hold the stereotyped notion that Chinese people are short.

What is another example of a "stereotyped notion"?

    A. All drivers must get a driver's license.

    B. All people who wear glasses are smart.

    C. Most teachers are experts in their subject.

    D. Some people are better at sports than others.

Why Did That Happen?

8 Why was Yao Ming sent to a Shanghai sports academy?

    F. because he was not making any progress at home

    G. because he had become serious about playing basketball

    H. because most students in China attend sports academies

    I. because all students at the academy become players for the Sharks

9 What evidence does the author give to show that the sports academy was good for Yao Ming?

    A. He became a player on China's National team.

    B. He became a member of a youth basketball team.

    C. He became interested in basketball outside of China.

    D. He became fascinated with watching basketball on TV.

Read "Paul Laurence Dunbar" and the poem "Sympathy" before answering Numbers 1 through 8.

Paul Laurence Dunbar

Paul Laurence Dunbar was one of the first African-American poets to gain national recognition. He was born in Dayton, Ohio, on June 27, 1872, to Joshua and Matilda Murphy Dunbar, freed slaves from Kentucky. His parents separated shortly after his birth, but Dunbar would draw on their stories of plantation life throughout his writing career. By the age of fourteen, Dunbar had poems published in the *Dayton Herald*. While in high school, he edited the *Dayton Tattler*, a short-lived black newspaper published by classmate Orville Wright.

Despite being a fine student, Dunbar was financially unable to attend college and took a job as an elevator operator. In 1892, a former teacher invited him to read his poems at a meeting of the Western Association of Writers; his work impressed his audience to such a degree that the popular poet James Whitcomb Riley wrote him a letter of encouragement. In 1893, Dunbar self-published a collection called *Oak and Ivy*. To help pay the publishing costs, he sold the book for a dollar to people riding in his elevator.

Sympathy
by Paul Laurence Dunbar

I know what the caged bird feels, alas!
  When the sun is bright on the upland slopes;
When the wind stirs soft through the springing grass,
And the river flows like a stream of glass;
  When the first bird sings and the first bud opes,
And the faint perfume from its chalice steals—
I know what the caged bird feels!

I know why the caged bird beats its wing
  Till its blood is red on the cruel bars;
For he must fly back to his perch and cling
When he fain would be on the bough a-swing;
  And a pain still throbs in the old, old scars
And they pulse again with a keener sting—
I know why he beats his wing!

I know why the caged bird sings, ah me,
  When his wing is bruised and his bosom sore,—
When he beats his bars and he would be free;
It is not a carol of joy or glee,
  But a prayer that he sends from his heart's deep core,
But a plea, that upward to Heaven he flings—
I know why the caged bird sings!

Now answer Numbers 1 through 8. Base your answers on "Paul Laurence Dunbar" and the poem "Sympathy."

1 How did Dunbar pay for the cost of publishing his first book of poems?

    A. by selling the book to his elevator passengers

    B. by publishing his poems in the *Dayton Herald*

    C. by reading his poems to people on the elevator

    D. by giving poetry readings for a writers association

2 Which pair of words BEST describes Dunbar?

    F. talented and hardworking

    G. unsuccessful and struggling

    H. educated and sophisticated

    I. unappreciated and misunderstood

3 What time of year is described in the first stanza of the poem?

    A. winter

    B. spring

    C. summer

    D. fall

4 Read the following lines from the poem.

> I know why the caged bird beats its wing
>   Till its blood is red on the cruel bars;
> For he must fly back to his perch and cling
> When he fain would be on the bough a-swing;

What internal conflict do these lines show?

    F. The bird wants to sit in a tree and not on a perch in the cage.

    G. The bird wants to land on the perch, but it feels like it might faint.

    H. The bird wants to perch in the cage, but it has hurt its wings on the cage bars.

    I. The bird wants to get out of the cage, but it is too weak to break the cage bars.

5 According to the speaker of the poem, why does the caged bird sing?

    A. It feels happy.

    B. It wants to be free.

    C. It wants attention.

    D. It is celebrating the arrival of spring.

6 Which word BEST describes what the poet feels for the caged bird?

- F. envy
- G. happiness
- H. gratefulness
- I. understanding

7 What was the poet's MAIN purpose in writing this poem?

- A. to prove that it is wrong to keep birds in cages
- B. to show that all living creatures want to be free
- C. to demonstrate that even birds in cages still sing
- D. to show that some people live like birds in cages

8 What fact from Dunbar's biography MOST likely inspired him to write a poem on this topic?

- F. His parents were once slaves.
- G. His parents separated after he was born.
- H. He was unable to find money to go to college.
- I. He was encouraged by a former teacher and a poet.

MAKING SENSE OF IT

In this chapter you learned all about cause-and-effect relationships. Events unfold a certain way for a reason. Now you have a strategy for identifying these relationships. Remember: Active readers ask questions and sometimes have to do a little detective work to find answers.

- **Cause:** an event or an action that makes something else happen
- **Effect:** a result; it is what happens because of, or as the result of, another event or action
- **Cause-and-effect relationships:** interdependent—one cannot happen without the other
- **Ask questions:** "What happened first?" "Why did this happen?"; questions like these help you to figure out what caused an event to take place.

Chapter Eight

The Plot Thickens

Benchmark: L.A.E.2.3.1

The student understands how character and plot development, point of view, and tone are used in various selections to support a central conflict or a storyline. **(Includes LA.E.1.3.2** The student recognizes complex elements of plot including setting, character development, conflicts and resolutions.)

"Getting Mom a book for her birthday was *my* idea. That means *you* have to find the book!" Dan said to Jamie as they entered the bookstore.

"Do you really think that's a good idea?" The last book that Jamie had read willingly was *The Cat in the Hat* by Dr. Seuss.

"Okay, I'll find a book, but you make the decision. I'm tired of being the one responsible for choosing the perfect gift every year. Here's a good one: *A Pirate's Story*."

"What's it about?"

"There's this guy who becomes a pirate."

"So what happens?"

"I don't remember, but it was really good.

"Where does it take place?"

"On the ocean, I guess, but I can't remember which ocean. All I know is that it was a really good book."

"You might read a lot, but you don't remember much! I can't tell if Mom would like this book from what you say about it."

"So do you have a better idea of what to get her?"

"Yeah, I do! A gift certificate! That way she can pick out the book she really wants."

205

As you can see, Jamie didn't learn very much about the book from Dan. He had expected Dan to tell him about the book's plot. He also expected to hear about the main characters and the *setting*, or where the story took place. But Dan didn't give any of these details. Although he tried to tell Jamie about the books, he was not able to use words that clearly communicated his ideas.

If only Dan had had a knowledge of story elements. Then he would have been able to tell Jamie what the book was about (its *plot*), whom it was about (the *characters*), and what ended up happening to them (the *climax*). He also could have explained the story's major *conflict* and how the *protagonists* dealt with the forces of *antagonism*.

Knowing the parts that make up a story—whether it's in the form of a movie, a novel, or a TV show—will help you evaluate and talk about it with others. It will also help you get good grades on English papers and a high score on the FCAT.

Why Study This?

Understanding story elements will help you enjoy reading stories, novels, and autobiographical essays. It will make watching movies more fun, too. Or maybe you have an idea for a novel, short story, or movie that you'd like to write. Understanding story elements will help you include in your writing all the features that readers expect when they read a novel or short story, or see a movie.

Key Concepts: Story Elements

- **Setting:** *where* and *when* the story takes place
- **Characters:** the people who carry on the action in a story; characters are sometimes animals
- **Plot:** what happens in a story; the events that make up the action; includes *conflict* and *resolution*
- **Conflict:** a problem that must be solved; obstacle preventing the character getting what she or he wants
- **Resolution:** how the character solves the problem

- **Point of View:** the storyteller as a person taking part in the action (first-person point of view); the storyteller outside of the action (third-person point of view)
- **Tone:** manner of expression or style the author uses to reveal attitudes about characters, places, or events
- **Mood:** the overall feeling the reader gets when reading the story; the feeling or atmosphere suggested by the setting of the story
- **Theme:** the central message about life expressed in story

SEEING IT IN ACTION
Point of View

Who is the storyteller? In **first-person point of view**, the author uses the words *I* and *me*, and the story is told as though the author were taking part in the events.

> As I hunkered down in my sleeping bag by the campfire, I heard a low growl from the direction of the woods.

In **third-person point of view**, the pronouns used are *he, she, they*, and the author is a storyteller who is outside of the events.

> Kirsten took the guitar from its case and walked to the stage. She sat down on the chair, lowered the mike, and began strumming a chord.

The third-person storyteller may be **omniscient**, that is, know what all characters think and feel.

> Starla had no faith in Bridget's integrity. And Starla was right not to trust her, for Bridget had no intention of giving up the role of student president, even though she had won the election unfairly.

Or point of view may be **third-person limited**—the events are limited to what one character thinks and experiences.

> Starla wondered if Bridget would give up the role of student president, but she realized she would have to wait and see if Bridget's integrity could be trusted.

Tone

Tone is the author's attitude, style, or manner that is expressed mostly by word choice. The characters' actions may also give readers a sense of tone. Compare the following two sentences:

> It seemed as if all sense of time had disappeared, as the students worked quietly and studiously on their assignment in the slanting rays of sunlight falling across the classroom.

> It seemed as if time had slowed to a halt, as the students stifled yawns and nodded, trying helplessly to stay awake in the hot and stuffy classroom.

In the first sentence, the tone is one of peacefulness; in the second sentence, the tone is one of boredom and sleepiness.

Setting

Setting is the "when and where" of a story. It involves the time and place of the story.

Time

Some authors tell you exactly the day, the month, the year, and even the hour that the action begins. In other stories, the reader must figure out the time period by clues in the characters' clothing styles, modes of transportation, or way of speaking.

> Henry Culpepper swung down from his horse, removed his cowboy hat, and wiped his brow with a dirty bandanna. Then he tossed the reins to a boy standing by the hitching post and said, "Pardner, where can a hungry cowpoke find some good vittles in this town?"

Place

Stories always take place somewhere, and that somewhere is often very important to the story line itself.

> When Virginia woke up, she was lying facedown on a sandy beach. She looked around. The lifeboat was nowhere to be seen, and neither were the four strangers who had joined her and helped her paddle the boat away from the sinking cruise ship. The frightful realization came to her that she was shipwrecked alone on a desert island.

Mood

Mood is the feeling that the author tries to convey throughout the story. Does the author want the reader to be frightened or sad, or does the story make the reader laugh and enjoy happy thoughts? To figure out mood, examine how you feel while reading the story. Mood is often conveyed by the story's setting.

> It was a dark and stormy night.

Characters

A story cannot happen without characters. Sometimes, the words *protagonist* and *antagonist* are used to describe characters. The protagonist is the main character, or the hero while the antagonist is the villain

In many western movies, the main protagonist is often the sheriff (wearing a white cowboy hat), while the main antagonist is a stagecoach bandit, bank robber, or other outlaw (wearing a black cowboy hat). All the characters who work with the sheriff are also protagonists, while those riding with the head outlaw are all antagonists.

Conflict and Resolution

A story always has a problem that must be resolved. The problem, or struggle between two forces, is called the conflict. The way the problem is resolved or turns out is called the resolution.

Conflicts usually fall into one of the following types:

Character vs. Character

In this common conflict, what one character wants conflicts with what another character wants. Example: a play about a young, up-and-coming heavyweight boxer who challenges the reigning heavyweight champion.

Character vs. Society

The main character is someone who does not fit in with society—who goes against what society wants or expects. Example: a story about a young woman who completes medical school and decides to work as a doctor in a small, impoverished village in South America rather than accepting a high-paying position at a hospital in the United States.

Character vs. Nature

The characters in stories fight against natural forces such as storms, cold, or extreme heat. The natural force is called an antagonistic force. Example: a movie about a man and his dogs competing in the Iditarod sled-dog race in Alaska.

Character vs. Self

This conflict involves an internal struggle. A character must overcome problems within himself or herself. The character may wish to do one thing but be tempted to do another. Example: a short story in which a teenager learns that her friend is about to run away from home and debates whether or not to tell her parents.

The Plot Thickens

> To decide the type of conflict in a story, ask yourself:
> - Is the conflict between two main characters?
> - Is the conflict between a character and society?
> - Is the conflict between a character and some outside natural force?
> - Is a character struggling with his or her thoughts or emotions?

FCAT Fred Says:

On the FCAT you will find questions on conflict like "What is the MAIN conflict of the story?" or "What is the MAIN problem Bob faces in the story?" The reason they put the word *main* in big letters is that they want to make it clear that the story might have more than one conflict or problem. It's your job to decide which conflict or problem is the most important one.

Here, try it out. Read this excerpt from my autobiography and see if you can figure out the main conflict. Then try to identify two additional problems I'm facing.

> I clutched the microphone nervously. In less than five minutes it would be my turn to audition for *American Rock Star*. My heart was beating like crazy, and I fought the urge to run out the backstage door. I wondered how I would pay back the money I'd borrowed from my owner for the trip to the auditions in Palm Beach. He had reluctantly loaned me the money after a terrible argument in which he made it clear that he didn't think I could carry a tune in a backpack. "I've heard you yowling in the alley with those long-haired degenerates you call friends, and believe me, you're no Frank Sinatra!" Maybe he was right, I thought; maybe I should just leave right now. Suddenly I heard the MC's booming voice announce: "And now, from Miami, Florida, it's FCAT Fred, singing "I Can See Clearly Meow!"

The main problem I'm facing is that I'm supposed to go out and audition for a talent show, but I'm having a moment of self-doubt, and I must decide whether to go through with the audition or run out the back door.

The other two problems I face are:

1. I don't know how I will repay the money I borrowed.
2. My owner doesn't support my singing ambitions.

You can also count on seeing FCAT questions about conflict resolution. These will typically be worded like this: "How is the main conflict resolved?" or "How does FCAT Fred solve the main problem he faces in the story?" Read the rest of the excerpt about my *American Rock Star* audition and see if you can figure out how my main conflict is resolved.

> Panic flashed through me like a lightning bolt! I whirled around and raced to the backstage door, still clutching the microphone. Just as I was about to bolt through the door, an older man in coveralls and pushing a mop called to me. "Hey, you! Where are you going? You're not giving up your big chance, are you?" I halted uncertainly and confessed, "I can't do it. I can't!"
>
> The old man mopped his way over to me and said, "Son, I was cleaning up this same theater forty years ago on the night of a big Frank Sinatra-Sammy Davis Jr. concert. Well, Frank was rehearsing at the piano, that same piano out there right now, when he got the news that Sammy Davis was sick and couldn't make it. Frank was hot, I tell you! 'Now what'll I do?' he said. And I wanted to say, 'Frank! Let me go on with you! I can sing! I really can!' but you know what? I was too scared. So here I am forty years later, pushing a mop backstage when I could be singing center stage!"
>
> I shook the old man's hand wordlessly and walked back toward the stage. I could do this, I *would* do this, and, barring any unexpected fur balls, I would knock 'em dead!

How was my conflict resolved? By the kindly intervention of an older man who gave me courage by telling me his story. In this short excerpt, you don't find out how the audition went (I *rocked*!), but you do find out how my struggle between auditioning and fleeing the audition turned out.

Plot

Conflicts and resolutions, characters doing this and that throughout a story—all are part of the *plot* of the story. Some people use the term *story line* when referring to plot.

Basically, the plot is made up of the events that lead to the resolution of the conflict. For example, the basic plot of "The Ugly Duckling" traces the story of a duckling that looks nothing like his brothers or sisters. They call him an ugly duckling and tease him relentlessly until he runs away. Months go by, and the ugly duckling, convinced that he looks hideous, lives a lonely and miserable life. Then one day he sees some swans flying overhead. Looking into the water, he notices his own reflection and realizes that he is no longer an ugly duckling but a beautiful swan.

When you tell your friends about a great story you've read or an exciting movie you've seen, and they ask, "What happened next?" and "Then what happened?" your answers describe the events of the plot.

Plot Structure

Step 1: Exposition

The *exposition* introduces readers to characters and explains the setting. It gives background information that is necessary to fully understand the story. The exposition also helps readers identify the characters' relationships to each other.

Here's an example of the exposition from the story "Persephone":

Persephone

Long, long, ago, in ancient Greece, there was a beautiful young goddess named Persephone. Her father was none other than Zeus, the supreme ruler of all the gods. Her mother was Demeter, the earth goddess. Demeter was a loving and generous goddess who made everything on Earth grow. At that time, Earth was young and bursting with life, and both humans and gods enjoyed the warmth of summer all year long. Flowers, trees, fruits, vegetables, wheat, rice, and so forth, grew in abundance throughout the year because of Demeter's loving attention. In fact, the only thing Demeter loved more than making things grow was spending time with her beloved daughter, Persephone, who was as beautiful as she was ditzy.

In the exposition of this story, the reader learns about Persephone and her mother Demeter, and about the setting—Earth when it was young and new, with a never-ending summer.

Step 2: Inciting Incident

> One day, Persephone was alone in a beautiful meadow. All of a sudden, the earth split open, and a black chariot, pulled by two black horses, burst out of the ground. It was Hades, god of the Underworld. He leaned down from the chariot and whispered in Persephone's ear, "Beautiful Persephone, will you be my bride?"
>
> Persephone wrinkled her nose and said, "I don't *think* so! And quite frankly, you could really use a breath mint!"
>
> "How dare you speak so impudently to me! You *shall* be my bride!"
>
> Hades reached down and swept Persephone into the chariot. With a thunder of hooves, the chariot began its dark descent to the Underworld.
>
> When the cloud of dust settled, all that remained was Persephone's belt lying on the ground.
>
> When Persephone failed to come home, her mother Demeter was distraught with worry. She began to search for Persephone but could find no trace of her daughter. The search continued for weeks. During this time, Demeter was too upset to make anything grow, and Earth endured its first long, cold winter.

What is the problem, or conflict, in this story? Persephone is kidnapped by Hades, and her mother is so upset by her disappearance that she fails to make anything grow, and Earth is plunged into winter. The *inciting incident* occurs when Hades kidnaps Persephone. We wonder what will happen next. Will Persephone find her way home? Will summer come back to Earth? How will this conflict be resolved?

The Plot Thickens

Step 3: Rising Action

The *rising action* is the sequence of events during which the conflict develops or builds. In a good movie, you are on the edge of your seat watching to see what will happen next. In a good book, you can't stop reading because you've got to know what will happen next. Here's more of "Persephone":

> One day, a shepherd happened upon Persephone's belt. He returned the belt to Demeter, who guessed what had happened. She raced to Zeus and begged him to order Hades to release her daughter. She threatened never to bring an end to winter unless Persephone was allowed to come home.
>
> Zeus agreed to command Hades to give up Persephone, but told Demeter that if Persephone had eaten anything in the Underworld, then she must remain. Demeter joyfully began her journey to the Underworld, confident that she had taught Persephone never to accept food or candy from strangers, especially if the stranger were Hades.

The part of the story you just read represents the rising action. You want to know what happens next. Will Hades give up Persephone, or will he refuse?

Think of the rising action as the part that builds up your excitement as you read. It's like riding a ski lift for the first time. As you slowly ride up the ski slope, you wonder, "What's going to happen when we reach the top? Will I survive?" You won't know the answers to your questions until you reach the next part of the story.

Step 4: Climax

The action keeps building until it reaches a *climax*. The climax is the highest point of interest or suspense. This is the part where you get off the ski lift and begin hurtling down the ski slope. In a story about a boy learning karate, the climax might occur when the boy gets to fight a neighborhood bully in a martial arts competition.

Here's the climax of "Persephone":

> Demeter reached the Underworld and began pounding on the gate. "Hades, I know you have Persephone! Zeus commands you to release her!"
>
> Hades himself opened the gate and waved her in.
>
> "Where is she?" Demeter cried.
>
> "Mother! Here I am! Get me out of this place! It's so *gross* here!"
>
> "Not so fast," Hades said. "Persephone has eaten food here, and so here she must remain."
>
> "Persephone! Is this true?" Demeter asked.
>
> "No! I ate nothing!"
>
> Hades grinned cruelly. "Except for some pomegranate seeds—four seeds, to be exact!"
>
> "Oh, Persephone, what have you done?" Demeter sank heavily against the gatepost.
>
> "What? Seeds aren't food!" cried Persephone. "Seeds are seeds!"
>
> "Look, Hades," Demeter bargained, "if I can't get my daughter back, it will be winter on Earth forever. Think how angry Zeus will be with you!"
>
> "I suppose you're right," Hades said. "You can have her for eight months, but for those four seeds, she must become my bride and stay with me for four months of the year."
>
> And so Demeter and Persephone returned home. Summer returned, and Earth became warm and green. But when Persephone had to go back to Hades for four months, winter also returned, as Demeter mourned for her daughter held captive in the Underworld.

The climax is the moment when Demeter learns that Persephone has eaten four pomegranate seeds.

Let's examine the last two steps of plot development.

Step 5: **Falling Action**

Step 6: **Resolution**

After the climax, good stories end quickly. In a very short story such as "Persephone," there may be only a sentence or even a part of a sentence after the climax. In this story, the *falling action* occurs when Demeter tells Hades that winter will never end unless she gets her daughter back. This falling action leads the reader to the *resolution*. Hades suggests a compromise, and Demeter and Persephone return home.

In the resolution, the author explains anything that might have confused the reader along the way and may tell what happens to the characters in the future. In a fairy tale, this is the "And they lived happily ever after" moment. In a detective show on TV, the main characters talk about the clues that helped them solve the case. On a ski slope, the falling action and resolution are when the skier reaches the bottom of the slope and slows to a stop.

Some writers like to end the story abruptly at the climax, and the reader is left to fill in what probably happened next. Writer Frank Stockton does this in his short story "The Lady, or the Tiger?" The reader never finds out how the story ends, or whether the hero chooses the door behind which a beautiful woman awaits or the door that hides a ferocious tiger. Stories like this keep readers wondering.

THINK OF IT THIS WAY

Plot development often follows a basic structure similar to a pyramid. You can identify six important points on the pyramid, which move the story forward.

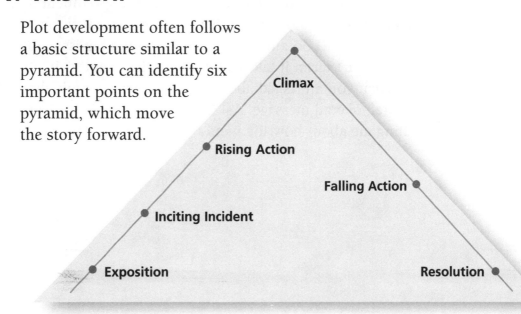

FCAT Fred Says:

On the FCAT you may be asked about the order in which events occur in a story. You may be asked a question such as "How did the character move the plot along?" or "How was the setting important to the plot?" or "What was the conflict in the story and how was it resolved?"

Theme

The last element of a story, but certainly not the least important to the author, is *theme*. Theme is similar to the main idea of the story. It is a general statement about life or people. To discover the theme of a story, think big. What big message is the author trying to say about the world in which we live? The theme of "Persephone" is that powers of good and evil are sometimes forced to compromise. Another example of a theme is the idea that love conquers all.

Notice how all these examples are statements about life, also known as "universal truths," or answers to universal questions. The word *universal* here means that everyone suffers or experiences this truth or asks this question. In other words, to be human is to wonder about things like good and evil, the meaning of life, and so on.

For instance, in "Beauty and the Beast," a story in which a young woman falls in love with a hulking, hairy beast because of his charming personality, the theme is that love conquers all. It is not "a young woman falls in love with a hulking, hairy beast." Theme is not about individuals; it doesn't mention names. In many stories, the theme can be stated simply in a few words. Just because the theme is about a big issue, like love, doesn't mean it takes a lot of words to express it.

When you are asked about a story's theme, think about its general, overall message. Ask yourself, "What is this story telling me about how life works, or how people behave?"

Remembering It

Point of View: Is the author outside the action (third person), or does the author take part in the action (first person)?

Setting: Where and when do events happen, and how does the author want the reader to feel while reading the story?

Characters: Who is the story about? How do they affect the events?

Tone: What manner of expression or style does the author use to suggest attitudes about characters, places, or events?

Mood: What overall feeling does the reader get when reading the story? What is the feeling or atmosphere suggested by the setting of the story?

Plot: What happens in the story? What major events take place?

Conflict: What is the problem? Against whom or what is the character struggling? Is it character vs. character, character vs. nature, character vs. society, or character vs. self?

Resolution: How does the main character solve the problem?

Theme: What is the big message about life in the story?

Read the story "The Night Crawler." Then answer the questions that follow.

The Night Crawler

Joseph dug his feet in sideways as he went down the steep, sandy bank to the edge of the river. The last thing he wanted was to take a header into the river, lose his fishing pole and night crawlers, and end up going back home without fish and sopping wet.

Life had been hard since his mom had lost her job as a waitress at Joe Bob's Barbecue. Even though the money wasn't that great, she had been able to bring home leftover brisket or barbecue chicken and baked beans every night. They qualified for free groceries at the Food Bank in town, but his mother refused even to consider accepting charity. So either he caught some fish this afternoon, or it'd be macaroni and cheese for the sixth straight night in a row. Plus, he wanted to see his mom's face light up as it did whenever she was proud of him.

He placed his small tackle box and night crawlers down and unfastened the hook from the cork handle of his fishing pole. He pried open the can of crawlers and dug out a fat, squirmy one. He had barely touched the worm's midsection with the point of the hook when he heard a voice say, "Ow! That hurt! What do you think you're doing?"

"Who said that?" Joseph said, looking all around him.

"I did!" said the night crawler, coiling into an S-shape in Joseph's hand. "And I want to know what business you have poking me with that sharp, pointy thing."

Joseph stammered, "I, I just . . . I have to catch some fish . . . for my mom . . . she lost her job . . . we've been living on macaroni and cheese . . . I *have* to catch some fish!" He pinched the worm between his thumb and forefinger and prepared to drive the hook into its soft, pink belly . . . but he couldn't do it.

"What am I going to do now?" Joseph said in despair.

The night crawler climbed up on the hook and swung on it as if it were a porch swing. "Listen," the crawler said in a kindly voice, "maybe there's some way I can help you."

The Plot Thickens

1. What is the MAIN problem that Joseph must solve?

   A. He must find a way to make his mother proud of him.
   B. He must find a way to catch fish without using night crawlers.
   C. He must find a way to avoid eating macaroni and cheese again.
   D. He must find a way to get down to the river's edge without falling.

2. Which pair of words BEST describes Joseph's mother?

   F. stingy and mean
   G. loving and proud
   H. anxious and worried
   I. uncaring and unappreciative

Now read how one student answered these questions.

1. What is the main problem that Joseph must solve? He wants to make his mother proud of him, but that isn't the main problem, so choice A is incorrect. He also wants to avoid eating macaroni and cheese and falling down the riverbank, but again, those aren't the main problem he faces. Therefore, choices C and D are not right. That means that choice B must be correct.

2. Which pair of words best describes Joseph's mother? Joseph's mother seems nice and not at all stingy, so choice F cannot be right. She might be anxious and worried because she lost her job, but the excerpt doesn't tell us that, so choice H is probably not the best choice. She brings home food for Joseph, so she must be a caring mother, and her face lights up when Joseph does things to make her proud, which means she appreciates him. Therefore, choice I is incorrect, making the correct answer G.

FCAT Fred Says:

The FCAT will not ask readers to simply identify main characters. Instead, the FCAT may ask questions about how characters change from the beginning of the story to the end, or ask readers to identify character traits, such as honesty or bravery. The previous question about Joseph's mother, is an example. If the FCAT test writers used the excerpt from my autobiography, they might ask a question like "How did FCAT Fred change after talking with the old man backstage?"

Read the story "Airborne" before answering Numbers 1 through 8.

Airborne
by Jesse Davidson

My early interest in the air mail began when, as a youngster growing up at the Hebrew National Orphan Home in lower Westchester County, New York, a group of us boys would fling open the windows of our dormitory at the sound of an approaching airplane that flew over our "Home" several nights a week at around nine o'clock. Our best judgment then was that the plane, outlined by red, white, and green navigation lights, was less than a thousand feet high. The fact that it appeared so regularly and so business-like in its singular purpose made us more curious as to where it came from and what its destination was.

About this time, because of our apparent interest in "aeroplanes," one of our guidance counselors, Jack Patent (my mentor), formed an aviation club to spur on our interests and to learn more through building and flying model airplanes. It was the greatest thing that happened to a group that shared the same interest, and it offered an escape from the boring sameness of daily institutional life.

In a short time, our club activities were funded by generous contributions from well-heeled members of the Board of Directors. We soon had a growing aeronautical library with subscriptions to aviation magazines, and we were on the mailing list of publicity releases from budding airlines. It was in one of the releases from Pitcairn Aviation News that we read about the Pitcairn Mailwing that made its nightly journey from Newark to Boston. And our "Home" was right on course!

These were exciting times, and we devoured everything on the subject. It was evident that the familiar biplane was giving way to the monoplane, which carried both passengers and mail. We marveled at the phenomenal progress of aviation as a result of Lindbergh's famous solo trans-Atlantic flight and its social effects that would influence most of our lives.

But none of us youngsters had ever seen a REAL airplane on the ground. We had visions that a plane must be very big—because it looked so small when it was high up. And like the rest of the club members, I had that feverish desire to see

one, touch it, admire it, and even sit in the cockpit. It became an obsession, and if I had to do something to realize this ambition, then I would do it and take the consequences.

One midsummer Sunday, a regular visiting day for those lucky youngsters who had at least one parent or members of their family coming to see them, and when there was considerable activity on the grounds, I felt my presence wouldn't be missed for several hours. With another chap, whose attitude was even more cavalier than mine on such matters, I "sneaked" off the premises and hiked from Yonkers to New Rochelle where, we had learned a bit earlier, there was a "landing field."

Kids can walk for miles when filled with such enthusiasm. Every turn on an unfamiliar road is an adventure, and miles don't seem to matter. As we neared a large open area, we heard a whirring sound, looked up and saw a large silver and blue biplane swooping low as if to land. We had arrived!

There, in a fairly large open field, sat a solitary airplane. Nearby was a small shack with OFFICE painted on the door. We approached it to ask permission to look at the airplane. No one was there, nor was anyone on the field. Since the plane had just recently arrived, it was a matter of time before someone would return.

At first, we stood in silent awe at a respectful distance, but always casting an over-the-shoulder look, expecting someone yelling at us to get off the field, or away from that airplane—or worse.

Then, like a couple of restrained watchdogs, we broke loose and ran up to the plane, circled around it, touched the smoothly painted fabric of the wings and tail surfaces. The engine cowling was still warm. The propeller had stopped in a horizontal position. Just great for a picture of ourselves: hands resting on the prop—like so many dashing aviators had posed. We made the most of the opportunity.

Another look around the deserted field and I climbed into the cockpit—and then I was in a world of my own. The instruments, the switch, the throttle, the control stick, and rudder pedals! Wow! With my head barely visible in the deep cockpit, I moved the control stick right and left, forward and back, and watched the ailerons and rudder and elevators respond to my gingerly touch.

In the shadows of the leather cockpit padding, I peered closer to read a nameplate that identified the airplane as an Eaglerock, manufactured by Alexander Aircraft Industries of Denver, Colorado. Its engine was a 90-horsepower Curtiss OX-5.

I sat there taking in all the sights and smells of the leather padding, the freshly doped and painted surfaces of a newly manufactured aircraft. A child never forgets.

Hours passed. No one had yet appeared. We began to take more pictures "for the boys back home" and were preparing to leave when I looked up and noticed that despite a mild breeze, the windsock attached to a post support atop the highest pine tree was hanging limply. We debated whether or not we should leave at this point or unfurl the windsock.

I won out, climbed up, and got it unstuck. It immediately billowed out with the breeze coming from an easterly direction.

On the way down, despite my extreme care, my trouser leg got hooked on a short, broken limb and resulted in a noticeably long rip right up to the knee. Now, not only were we in for possible disciplinary action, but I was bringing home evidence of our escape.

But I took comfort in the fact that at least I had made my small contribution to safety in aerial navigation. It was worth it.

We got home just as darkness fell. We were missed alright. Our empty seats in the dining room were obvious enough. When a supervisor asked the other boys at the table of our whereabouts, they just shrugged in ignorance. I think they really knew. But oh, were we hungry!

The punishment? Restriction to the grounds, loss of certain privileges, and work with the "farm gang" the very next morning. Early!

But that, too, was worth it.

If you ever walked through a field of growing celery and ripening tomatoes fresh with dew, it's another sight and smell you'll never forget.

After our tour of duty with the farm gang was over, our Club Director asked me about the location of the "flying field." No problem. That place left an indelible impression in my mind, and the following week, with the blessings of the supervisory staff, the whole club, thirty strong, plus a few soon-to-be-members, hiked to the field where another thrill awaited us. The Alexander Eaglerock was landing and taking off with sightseeing passengers at five dollars a head. What a time to be a penniless orphan!

Now answer Numbers 1 through 8. Base your answers on the story "Airborne."

1 What first sparked the narrator's interest in airplanes?

- A. joining an aviation club at the orphanage
- B. getting a subscription to aviation magazines
- C. seeing an airplane on the ground for the first time
- D. watching an airplane fly regularly over the orphanage

2 What fact made airplanes even more fascinating for the boys at the orphanage?

- F. Airplanes were a fairly new invention.
- G. Airplanes were being used in combat for the first time.
- H. Airplanes were flying passengers from Newark to Boston.
- I. Airplanes were carrying mail on regular routes in New York.

The Plot Thickens

3 How did the fact that the narrator lived in an orphanage affect his interest in airplanes?

A. He was unable to get any information about airplanes.
B. He had no one around who shared his interest in airplanes.
C. He could not leave to go see an airplane without risking punishment.
D. He was discouraged from believing he would some day fly airplanes.

4 How did the narrator fulfill his dream of seeing an airplane on the ground?

F. by taking flying lessons from a World War I pilot
G. by getting a scholarship to an aviation ground school
H. by leaving the orphanage when he thought no one would notice
I. by convincing the club director to take the aviation club to a landing field

5 Read the sentence below.

With another chap, whose attitude was even more cavalier than mine on such matters, I "sneaked" off the premises and hiked from Yonkers to New Rochelle where, we had learned a bit earlier, there was a "landing field."

What does *cavalier* mean?

A. worried
B. humorous
C. respectful
D. unconcerned

6 As the narrator and his friend approach the grounded airplane, what tone is conveyed by the phrase "like a couple of restrained watchdogs"?

F. fear
G. excitement
H. nervousness
I. determination

7 What can you infer about the narrator by his efforts to free the windsock?

A. He was brave.
B. He was careless.
C. He was thoughtful.
D. He was irresponsible.

8 What is the MAIN reason the author wrote this story?

F. to encourage readers to become pilots themselves
G. to persuade readers to follow their dreams no matter what happens
H. to share how he became interested in airplanes and learned more about them
I. to show how he achieved his dream even though he grew up in an orphanage

THE PINCHING MAN
by Joseph Lemasolai Lekuton

*My camp is full of fearless warriors,
The warriors of my generation.*

Some people might say our society is primitive, but I think it is the best, fairest system that I know. Our system is based not only on the family, but also on the village itself. No one goes hungry. We take care of each other. We watch out for one another. Children respect their elders. If children do wrong, any adult can correct him. That means everyone in the village is equal.

In almost every village there is a disciplinarian called the "pinching man." He punishes disobedient kids by pinching them. He pinches you really hard on the legs, and let me tell you, once you are pinched you remember it! Parents who want their children to obey will tell them, "If you don't behave, I will call the pinching man." That usually does the trick. Kids are so scared of the pinching man.

The pinching man in each village is a scary person. Sometimes he has long, pointy fingernails, or hair on his face. He chews tobacco and looks mean. Our pinching man was the worst one of all. You never wanted to be on his bad side, because then he would watch for you, and he would tell the pinching men in the other villages to watch for you, too. And parents rarely protect their kids from the pinching man because that is how discipline is enforced in the community.

A rule I often broke was the one against going to other villages by myself. We nomads live in an area with dangerous animals and poisonous snakes. Our villages are usually miles apart from each other—two, three, four—so kids are not encouraged to go to other villages to play. It is simply too dangerous. But I always liked to play with friends in the different villages.

One day when I was little, about six or seven years old, I was sent out with the calves as usual, but I told one of my friends, "Watch my cows for me a little while, because I want to go play with one of my friends in the next village." I always returned the favor by taking care of other kids' calves if they wanted to go somewhere.

The village I wanted to visit that day was two or three miles away. A narrow,

winding path through the woods led there. I took off running, but I had not gotten very far when I turned a corner in the path and came face to face with the pinching man. As soon as he saw me, he crouched down and put out his hands toward me. His fingernails were long and dirty and sharp. Tobacco juice was dripping from the hair on his chin. He was waving his hands, ready to pinch.

When the pinching man gets you like that you cannot run away because he will remember you. The next time he sees you, he will grab you when you are not looking and pinch you even harder.

"Where are you going?"

I had to think fast. "My mother asked me to get some sugar for tea at the next village, also some tea leaves if they have them," I said.

"This time of day?"

I said, "Oh, yes, yes, she wants the sugar right away, and she told me to run."

He looked at me and said, "Well, I was just going to your house, so I will ask her."

"Fine," I said, and I walked past him, but as soon as he couldn't see me anymore, I left the path and cut through the woods as fast as I could to get to my mother's hut before he did. I didn't care if elephants or rhinos killed me. I was more scared of him than of any wild animal.

When I got home, I told my mother the truth, the whole story— "Mom, I made a mistake today. I left my cows with the other kids, and the pinching man caught me. Mom, I wanted to play with my friend so much. I haven't seen him in such a long time. I really had to do something with him. Nothing bad was going to happen."

My mom was shocked. "You left our cows with someone else? What kind of a son are you?

"Please, Mom. Only protect me today. I will never do it again. This is the only time I'll ask you to protect me from the pinching man. Please, Mom. When he comes, just tell him you sent me to get sugar."

"Go!" she said, and I took off to look after my cows.

Sure enough, a little while later, the pinching man showed up at our hut. "Hey, Nkaririe Lekuton, are you home?" he called.

"Yes."

"Can I have some tea?"

"Yes, I am just cooking some. Come in and rest."

While sipping his tea, he said, "Oh, by the way, I just saw your son on the path leaving the village."

"Oh, yes, I sent him to the next village for sugar."

My mom loves me so much. She supported me. That was it, but if I hadn't told my mom, I would have been in trouble twice—with the pinching man and with her.

But I was an active boy, and my mom didn't always protect me. One time I got a whipping from a warrior right outside our hut, and my mom did nothing to interfere. That day, when my friends and I were watching our little cows, I pretended to be one of the village warriors. A little boy would often pretend to be a warrior, someone he admired and wanted to be like, but this was different. I was imitating this particular warrior to make fun of him. I was saying, "Who's this? Who's the ugly warrior? See how he struts?" The kids loved it. They were laughing and laughing, so I did it the whole day. But that night one of the kids told the warrior what I had done. I had been disrespectful of an elder, and that is very bad in our society.

At that time I loved doing things for older people. I liked running to do someone a favor, to get some sugar or tea, or to carry a message. Run, run, I loved to run. When that warrior came to our hut that night and asked for me, that's what I thought he wanted.

"*Ngoto* Lemasolai, Lemasolai's mother," he called.

"Yeah," she answered.

"Where is Lemasolai today?"

"I'm here," I yelled. I knew his voice and figured he wanted me to go to the next village or hut to get some tobacco for him or something like that.

"Come," he said, "I need to send you." So I came out of that hut quickly, and just as I did, he grabbed me. Before coming to our hut he had gone into the forest and cut a long, thin branch. It was like a whip. As soon as he grabbed me, he took the stick and cut the air with it just like a sword. *Swoosh.*

When I heard that sound, I thought, "Oh my!" I did not know if I was going to die or what.

"So, you have been making fun of me all day?"

"No, no, not me," I said.

"Tell me! What did you say! Tell me everything!"

Then he took that stick and, Phoom! Phoom! Phoom! He whacked me on my knees, my thighs, my calves, where it would leave no marks. Then he said, "Go."

I took off running, and I went to look for my friends. Who could possibly have told on me? We suspected one of the girls we had played with that day. We decided that if she didn't come back the next day with her little cows, she was the one who had told on me. She did not come back for a week.

My mom heard that warrior whip me, but she never said a thing about it. That is part of the discipline, part of the culture. We don't have many disrespectful kids in our villages. I can vouch for that.

Now answer Numbers 1 through 9. Base your answers on the story "The Pinching Man."

1 How is the village setting of the story important to the plot?

  A. Only in a village would there be a pinching man.

  B. Only in a village would it be dangerous for a child to travel alone.

  C. Only in a village would there be a community that looked out for each other.

  D. Only in a village would children be punished by people other than their parents.

2 Which pair of words BEST describes the pinching man in the narrator's village?

  F. cruel and selfish

  G. caring and protective

  H. creepy and threatening

  I. kind and understanding

3 What did the narrator do immediately after he spoke with the pinching man?

  A. He raced off to get his cows.

  B. He continued on to the other village.

  C. He ran to his mother and told her the truth.

  D. He went home and pretended he had never left the village.

The Plot Thickens

4 What is the MAIN conflict in the story?

    F. The narrator disrespects a warrior and is punished for doing so.

    G. The narrator leaves his village and is spotted by the pinching man.

    H. The narrator breaks a village rule and confesses to his mother what he did.

    I. The narrator leaves his cows with his friends while he goes to another village.

5 Why did the narrator's mother react differently when the warrior whipped him than when the pinching man was after him?

    A. because he had lied to the warrior

    B. because he had run away from the warrior

    C. because he had been disrespectful to the warrior

    D. because he had been tricked into leaving the hut by the warrior

6 From whose point of view was the story told?

    F. from an omniscient point of view

    G. from a third-person point of view

    H. from a young boy's point of view

    I. from the pinching man's point of view

7 What is the theme of the story?

    A. Children who are disobedient or disrespectful will pay the price.

    B. Children who are honest with their parents will always be protected.

    C. Children should be protected from adults who might hurt them.

    D. Children should be allowed to make mistakes while they are young.

8 What can you infer from the story about herding cows in the narrator's village?

    F. It is a boring chore.

    G. It is an entertaining pastime.

    H. It is an important responsibility.

    I. It is a way to keep children out of trouble.

9 Why did the narrator come out of the hut when he heard the warrior ask for him?

    A. He wanted to get his punishment over with.

    B. He believed his mother would protect him from harm.

    C. He thought the warrior wanted to send him on an errand.

    D. He wanted to ask the warrior if he had seen the pinching man.

Read the story "Johanna" before answering Numbers 1 through 9.

Johanna
by Jane Yolen

The forest was dark and the snow-covered path was merely an impression left on Johanna's moccasined feet.

If she had not come this way countless daylit times, Johanna would never have known where to go. But Hartwood was familiar to her, even in the unfamiliar night. She had often picnicked in the cool, shady copses and grubbed around the tall oak trees. In a hard winter like this one, a family could subsist for days on acorn stew.

Still, this was the first night she had ever been out in the forest, though she had lived by it all her life. It was tradition—no, more than that—that members of the Chevril family did not venture into the midnight forest. "Never, never go to the woods at night," her mother said, and it was not a warning so much as a command. "Your father went though he was told not to. He never returned."

And Johanna had obeyed. Her father's disappearance was still in her memory, though she remembered nothing else of him. He was not the first of the Chevrils to go that way. There had been a great-uncle and two girl cousins who had likewise "never returned." At least, that was what Johanna had been told. Whether they had disappeared into the maw of the city that lurked over several mountains to the west, or into the hungry jaws of a wolf or bear, was never made clear. But Johanna, being an obedient girl, always came into the house with the setting sun.

For sixteen years she had listened to that warning. But tonight, with her mother pale and sightless, breathing brokenly in the bed they shared, Johanna had no choice. The doctor, who lived on the other side of the wood, must be fetched. He lived in the cluster of houses that rimmed the far side of Hartwood, a cluster that was known as "the village," though it was really much too small for such a name. The five houses of the Chevril family that clung together, now empty except for Johanna and her mother, were not called a village, though they squatted on as much land.

Usually the doctor himself came through the forest to visit the Chevrils. Once a year he made the trip. Even when the grandparents and uncles and cousins had been alive, the village doctor came only once a year. He was gruff with them and called them "strong as beasts" and went away, never even offering a tonic. They needed none. They were healthy.

But the long, cruel winter had sapped Johanna's mother's strength. She lay for days silent, eyes cloudy and unfocused, barely taking in the acorn gruel that Johanna spooned for her. And at last Johanna had said: "I will fetch the doctor."

Her mother had grunted "no" each day, until this evening. When Johanna mentioned the doctor again, there had been no answering voice. Without her mother's no, Johanna made up her own mind. She *would* go.

If she did not get through the woods

and back with the doctor before dawn, she felt it would be too late. Deep inside she knew she should have left before, even when her mother did not want her to go. And so she ran as quickly as she dared, following the small, twisting path through Hartwood by feel.

At first Johanna's guilt and the unfamiliar night were a burden, making her feel heavier than usual. But as she continued running, the crisp night air seemed to clear her head. She felt unnaturally alert, as if she had suddenly begun to discover new senses.

The wind molded her short dark hair to her head. For the first time she felt graceful and light, almost beautiful. Her feet beat a steady tattoo on the snow as she ran, and she felt neither cold nor winded. Her steps lengthened as she went.

Suddenly a broken branch across the path tangled in her legs. She went down heavily on all fours, her breath caught in her throat. As she got to her feet, she searched the darkness ahead. Were there other branches waiting?

Even as she stared, the forest seemed to grow brighter. The light from the full moon must be finding its way into the heart of the woods. It was a comforting thought.

She ran faster now, confident of her steps. The trees seemed to rush by. There would be plenty of time.

She came at last to the place where the woods stopped, and cautiously she ranged along the last trees, careful not to be silhouetted against the sky. Then she halted.

She could hear nothing moving, could see nothing that threatened. When she was sure, she edged out onto the short meadow that ran in a downward curve to the back of the village.

Once more she stopped. This time she turned her head to the left and right. She could smell the musk of the farm animals on the wind, blowing faintly up to her. The moon beat down upon her head and, for a moment, seemed to ride on her broad, dark shoulder.

Slowly she paced down the hill toward the line of houses that stood like teeth in a jagged row. Light streamed out of the rear windows, making threatening little earthbound moons on the graying snow.

She hesitated.

A dog barked. Then a second began, only to end his call in a whine.

A voice cried out from the house farthest on the right, a woman's voice, soft and soothing. "Be quiet, Boy."

The dog was silenced.

She dared a few more slow steps toward the village, but her fear seemed to precede her. As if catching its scent, the first dog barked lustily again.

"Boy! Down!" It was a man this time, shattering the night with authority.

She recognized it at once. It was the doctor's voice. She edged toward its sound. Shivering with relief and dread, she came to

the backyard of the house on the right and waited. In her nervousness, she moved one foot restlessly, pawing the snow down to the dead grass. She wondered if her father, her great-uncle, her cousins had felt this fear under the burning eye of the moon.

The doctor, short and too stout for his age, came out of the back door, buttoning his breeches with one hand. In the other he carried a gun. He peered out into the darkness.

"Who's there?"

She stepped forward into the yard, into the puddle of light. She tried to speak her name, but she suddenly could not recall it. She tried to tell why she had come, but nothing passed her closed throat. She shook her head to clear the fear away.

The dog barked again, excited, furious.

"By gosh," the doctor said, "it's a deer."

She spun around and looked behind her, following his line of sight. There was nothing there.

"That's enough meat to last the rest of this cruel winter," he said. He raised the gun, and fired.

Now answer Numbers 1 through 9. Base your answers on the story "Johanna."

1 Read this sentence from the story.

> In a hard winter like this, a family could *subsist* for days on acorn stew.

What does the word *subsist* mean?

A. enjoy

B. starve

C. survive

D. grow fat

2 Why was Johanna forbidden from going into the forest at night?

F. because she would be changed into a deer

G. because she would become lost in the forest

H. because her mother became sick after going there at night

I. because her father disappeared when he went there at night

3 What is the MAIN conflict of the story?

A. Johanna must convince a doctor to come see her mother.

B. Johanna must overcome her fear of being alone in the forest.

C. Johanna must travel through a forest to get a doctor for her mother.

D. Johanna must find her father, who disappeared in the forest long ago.

4 Why did Johanna wait a long time before she decided to go for help?

F. Her mother kept telling her not to go.

G. She thought her mother was getting better.

H. She believed the doctor would come to see them soon.

I. Her mother had forbidden her from entering the forest.

The Plot Thickens

5 Which of the following was a clue that Johanna was changing physically?

    A. Johanna decided to go get the doctor.

    B. Johanna felt as if she had new senses.

    C. Johanna felt comforted by the full moon.

    D. Johanna ran as fast as she could through the forest.

6 How was the forest setting important to the plot of the story?

    F. It was why the doctor didn't see Johanna.

    G. It was where Johanna and her mother lived.

    H. It was the cause of Johanna's physical change.

    I. It was the reason Johanna's mother became sick.

7 Which word BEST describes the tone of the story?

    A. happy

    B. gloomy

    C. humorous

    D. suspenseful

8 Why didn't the doctor recognize Johanna?

    F. She had changed her physical form.

    G. She and the doctor had never met before.

    H. She had not seen the doctor for a long time.

    I. She had shown up at the doctor's late at night.

9 Why did Johanna spin around when the doctor said, "By gosh, it's a deer"?

    A. She wanted to run away before she was shot.

    B. She wanted to see the deer he was talking about.

    C. She wanted to run back into the forest after the deer.

    D. She wanted to show the doctor that it was really she.

MAKING SENSE OF IT

You can remember the terms discussed in this chapter by using them when you talk with your friends, family, and teachers about books and stories you have read, and movies, TV shows, and plays you have seen. Next time you read a short story or novel, ask yourself "Is the conflict man vs. man, man vs. society, man vs. nature, man vs. himself?" and "Could this story take place anywhere else, or is the setting too important to the plot for it to happen anywhere else?" Think about the other elements as well: the characters, the mood, the climax and resolution of the story. Here is a brief review of the elements you have learned:

- **Point of View:** a narrator may be part of the action or outside the action
- **Setting:** the place and time events unfold and the mood of the story; important to the plot
- **Characters:** who the story is about
- **Plot:** the action of the story; consists of a *conflict* that is worked out until it reaches a *resolution*
- **Tone/Mood:** the overall feeling or attitude suggested in a story; can be sarcastic, light-hearted, amused, cynical, dark; revealed by word choice and by what the characters say and do
- **Theme:** a universal truth the author expresses in the story

Practice Test One

Read the article "Is the Stress Getting to You?" before answering Numbers 1 through 8.

Is the STRESS Getting to You?

Finding yourself in a hectic situation, whether it's forgetting your homework or missing your ride home, can really stress you out. Are you looking for a safety net for those days that seem to get worse by the second? Could you really use some advice on how to de-stress both your body and your mind? Knowing how to deal with stress can be half the battle!

Check out these 10 tips to keep you cool, calm, and collected:

1. Put your body in motion.

Moving from the chair to the couch while watching TV is not being physically active! Physical activity is one of the most important ways to keep stress away by clearing your head and lifting your spirits. Physical activity also increases endorphin levels—the natural "feel-good" chemicals in the body that leave you with a naturally happy feeling.

Whether you like full-fledged games of football, tennis, or roller hockey, or you prefer walks with family and friends, it's important to get up, get out, and get moving!

2. Fuel up.

Start your day off with a full tank—eating breakfast will give you the energy you need to tackle the day. Eating regular meals (this means no skipping dinner) and taking time to enjoy them (nope, eating in the car on the way to practice doesn't count) will make you feel better, too.

Make sure to fuel up with fruits, vegetables, proteins (peanut butter, a chicken sandwich, or a tuna salad) and grains (wheat bread, pasta, or some crackers)—and these will give you the power you need to make it through those hectic days.

Don't be fooled by the jolt of energy you get from sodas and sugary snacks—this only lasts a short time, and once it wears off, you may feel sluggish and more tired than usual. For that extra boost of energy to sail through history notes, math class, and after-school activities, grab a banana, some string cheese, or a granola bar for some power—packed energy!

3. LOL!

Some say that laughter is the best medicine—well, in many cases, it is! Did you know that it takes 15 facial muscles to laugh? Lots of laughing can make you feel good, and that good feeling can stay with you even after the laughter stops. So head off stress with regular doses of laughter by watching a funny movie or cartoons, reading a joke book (you may even learn some new jokes), or even make up your own riddles. Laughter can make you feel like a new person!

Everyone has those days when they do something really silly or stupid. Instead of getting upset with yourself, laugh out loud! No one's perfect. Life should be about having fun. So lighten up!

4. Have fun with friends.

Being with people you like is always a good way to ditch your stress. Get a group together to go to the movies, shoot some hoops, or play a board game—or just hang out and talk. Friends can help you work through your problems and let you see the brighter side of things.

5. Spill to someone you trust.

Instead of keeping your feelings bottled up inside, talk to someone you trust or respect about what's bothering you. It could be a friend, a parent, someone in your family, or a teacher. Talking out your problems and seeing them from a different view might help you figure out ways to deal with them. Just remember, you don't have to go it alone!

6. Take time to chill.

Pick a comfy spot to sit and read, daydream, or even take a snooze. Listen to your favorite music. Work on a relaxing project like putting together a puzzle or making jewelry.

Stress can sometimes make you feel like a tight rubber band—stretched to the limit! If this happens, take a few deep breaths to help yourself unwind. If you're in the middle of an impossible homework problem, take a break. Finding time to relax after (and sometimes during) a hectic day or week can make all the difference.

7. Catch some zzzzz...

Fatigue is a best friend to stress. When you don't get enough sleep, it's hard to deal with stress. You may feel tired, cranky, or you may have trouble thinking clearly. When you're overtired, a problem may seem much bigger than it actually is. You may have a hard time doing a school assignment that usually seems easy, you don't do your best in sports or any physical activity, or you may have an argument with your friends over something really stupid.

Sleep is a big deal! Getting the right amount of sleep is especially important for kids your age. Because your body (and mind) is changing and developing, it requires more sleep to recharge for the next day. So don't resist; hit the hay!

8. Keep a journal.

If you're having one of those crazy days when nothing goes right, it's a good idea to write things down in a journal to get it off of your chest—like how you feel, what's going on in your life, and things you'd like to accomplish. You could even write down what you do when you're faced with a stressful situation, and then look back and think about how you handled it later. So find a quiet spot, grab a notebook and pen, and start writing!

9. Get it together.

Too much to do but not enough time? Forgot your homework? Feeling overwhelmed or discombobulated? Being unprepared for school, practice, or other activities can make for a very stressful day.

Getting everything done can be a challenge, but all you have to do is plan a little and get organized.

10. Lend a hand.

Get involved in an activity that helps others. It's almost impossible to feel stressed out when you're helping someone else. It's also a great way to find out about yourself and the special qualities you never knew you had. Signing up for a service project is a good idea, but helping others is as easy as saying hello, holding a door, or volunteering to keep a neighbor's pet. If you want to get involved in a more organized volunteer program, try working at a local recreation center or helping with an after-school program. The feeling you will get from helping others is greater than you can imagine!

Most importantly, don't sweat the small stuff. Try to pick a few really important things and let the rest slide. Getting worked up over every little thing will only increase your stress. So toughen up and don't let stressful situations get to you. Remember you're not alone—everyone knows what stress feels like. It's up to you to choose how to deal with it.

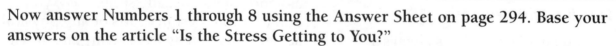

Now answer Numbers 1 through 8 using the Answer Sheet on page 294. Base your answers on the article "Is the Stress Getting to You?"

1 What was the author's MAIN purpose for writing this article?

    A. to explain the effects of stress

    B. to suggest ways to deal with stress

    C. to prove that some stress is good

    D. to show the different causes of stress

2 How is eating a banana DIFFERENT from eating sugary snacks?

    F. It boosts your energy with natural endorphins.

    G. It makes you feel tired after the energy wears off.

    H. It gives you energy for just a short period of time.

    I. It provides you with longer-lasting energy.

3 What is the MAIN idea of Tip 3?

    A. Laughter is a good way to lower your stress.

    B. Laughter is one way to relax your facial muscles.

    C. Laughter is the best way to react to silly mistakes.

    D. Laughter is one way to deal with not being perfect.

4 Which word BEST describes the tone of the article?

    F. joyful

    G. serious

    H. frightening

    I. encouraging

5 Which stress-related factor can cause a person to have problems thinking clearly?

    A. not exercising enough

    B. not finding time to relax

    C. not getting enough sleep

    D. not spending time with friends

6 What can you infer from BOTH Tip 5 and Tip 8?

    F. It is best to keep personal problems to yourself.

    G. It is not always easy to find someone you can talk to.

    H. It is always helpful to tell another person your problems.

    I. It is not a good idea to keep your feelings bottled up inside.

7 Which of the following would make Tip 9 more helpful?

    A. suggesting a few ways to get more organized

    B. telling what might happen if you are disorganized

    C. comparing the effects of a messy desk to that of a neat desk

    D. explaining a scientific study of teenagers and their busy schedules

8 With which statement would the author MOST likely agree?

    F. Helping others takes a lot of time and commitment.

    G. Volunteering is a good way to learn about other people.

    H. Being of service to others is hard work, but it is worth the effort.

    I. Doing things for others helps you as much as it helps other people.

The Open Window

by Saki (H. H. Munro)

"My aunt will be down presently, Mr. Nuttel," said a very self-possessed young lady of fifteen; "in the meantime you must try and put up with me."

Framton Nuttel endeavored to say the correct something which should duly flatter the niece of the moment without unduly discounting the aunt that was to come. Privately he doubted more than ever whether these formal visits on a succession of total strangers would do much toward helping the nerve cure which he was supposed to be undergoing.

"I know how it will be," his sister had said when he was preparing to migrate to this rural retreat; "you will bury yourself down there and not speak to a living soul, and your nerves will be worse than ever from moping. I shall just give you letters of introduction to all the people I know there. Some of them, as far as I can remember, were quite nice."

Framton wondered whether Mrs. Sappleton, the lady to whom he was presenting one of the letters of introduction, came into the nice division.

"Do you know many of the people round here?" asked the niece, when she judged that they had had sufficient silent communion.

"Hardly a soul," said Framton. "My sister was staying here, at the rectory, you know, some four years ago, and she gave me letters of introduction to some of the people here."

He made the last statement in a tone of distinct regret.

"Then you know practically nothing about my aunt?" pursued the self-possessed young lady.

"Only her name and address," admitted the caller. He was wondering whether Mrs. Sappleton was in the married or widowed state. An indefinable something about the room seemed to suggest masculine habitation.

"Her great tragedy happened just three years ago," said the child; "that would be since your sister's time."

"Her tragedy?" asked Framton; somehow in this restful country spot tragedies seemed out of place.

"You may wonder why we keep that window wide open on an October afternoon," said the niece, indicating a large French window that opened to a lawn.

"It is quite warm for the time of the year," said Framton; "but has that window got anything to do with the tragedy?"

"Out through that window, three years ago to a day, her husband and her two young brothers went off for their day's shooting. They never came back. In crossing the moor to their favorite snipe-shooting ground they were all three engulfed in a treacherous piece of bog. It had been that dreadful wet summer, you know, and places that were safe in other years gave way suddenly without warning. Their bodies were never recovered. That was the dreadful part of it." Here the child's voice lost its self-possessed note and became falteringly human. "Poor aunt always thinks that they will come back some day, they and the little brown spaniel that was lost with them, and walk in at that window just as they used to do. That is why the window is kept open every evening till it is quite dusk. Poor dear aunt, she has often told me how they went out, her husband with his white waterproof coat over his arm, and Ronnie, her youngest brother, singing 'Bertie, why do you bound?' as he always did to tease her, because she said it got on her nerves. Do you know, sometimes on still, quiet evenings like this, I almost get a creepy feeling that they will all walk in through that window—"

She broke off with a little shudder. It was a relief to Framton when the aunt bustled into the room with a whirl of apologies for being late in making her appearance.

"I hope Vera has been amusing you?" she said.

"She has been very interesting," said Framton.

"I hope you don't mind the open window," said Mrs. Sappleton briskly; "my husband and brothers will be home directly from shooting, and they always come in this way. They've been out for snipe in the marshes today, so they'll make a fine mess over my poor carpets. So like you menfolks, isn't it?"

She rattled on cheerfully about the shooting and the scarcity of birds, and the prospects for duck in the winter. To Framton it was all purely horrible. He made a desperate but only partially successful effort to turn the talk on to a less ghastly topic; he was conscious that his hostess was giving him only a fragment of her attention, and her eyes were constantly straying past him to the open window and the lawn beyond. It was certainly an unfortunate coincidence that he should have paid his visit on this tragic anniversary.

"The doctors agree in ordering me complete rest, an absence of mental excitement, and avoidance of anything in the nature of violent physical exercise," announced Framton, who labored under the tolerably widespread delusion that total strangers and chance acquaintances are hungry for the least detail of one's ailments and infirmities, their cause and cure. "On the matter of diet they are not so much in agreement," he continued.

"No?" said Mrs. Sappleton, in a voice which only replaced a yawn at the last moment. Then she suddenly brightened into alert attention—but not to what Framton was saying.

"Here they are at last!" she cried. "Just in time for tea, and don't they look as if they were muddy up to the eyes!"

Framton shivered slightly and turned toward the niece with a look intended to convey sympathetic comprehension. The child was staring out through the open window with dazed horror in her eyes. In a chill shock of nameless fear Framton swung round in his seat and looked in the same direction.

In the deepening twilight three figures were walking across the lawn towards the window; they all carried guns under their arms, and one of them was additionally burdened with a white coat hung over his shoulders. A tired brown spaniel kept close at their heels. Noiselessly they neared the house, and then a hoarse young voice chanted out of the dusk: "I said, Bertie, why do you bound?"

Framton grabbed wildly at his stick and hat; the hall door, the gravel drive, and the front gate were dimly noted stages in his headlong retreat. A cyclist coming along the road had to run into the hedge to avoid imminent collision.

"Here we are, my dear," said the bearer of the white mackintosh, coming in through the window, "fairly muddy, but most of it's dry. Who was that who bolted out as we came up?"

"A most extraordinary man, a Mr. Nuttel," said Mrs. Sappleton; "could only talk about his illness, and dashed off without a word of good-bye or apology when you arrived. One would think he had seen a ghost."

"I expect it was the spaniel," said the niece calmly; "he told me he had a horror of dogs. He was once hunted into a cemetery somewhere on the banks of the Ganges by a pack of pariah dogs, and had to spend the night in a newly dug grave with the creatures snarling and grinning and foaming just above him. Enough to make anyone lose their nerve."

Romance at short notice was her specialty.

Now answer Numbers 9 through 16 using the Answer Sheet on page 294. Base your answers on the story "The Open Window."

9 What is the author's purpose in the story?

    A. to share

    B. to inform

    C. to entertain

    D. to persuade

10 Which of these traits did the niece possess?

    F. a bad temper

    G. a gentle spirit

    H. a loving heart

    I. a lively imagination

11 Why was Mr. Nuttel visiting Mrs. Sappleton?

    A. to introduce himself to her

    B. to show his sympathy for her loss

    C. to deliver a letter from a mutual friend

    D. to find out if she was married or widowed

12 Which pair of words BEST describes the tone in the paragraph that begins "Out through that window, three years ago to a day, her husband and her two young brothers went off for their day's shooting"?

   F. tired and weary
   G. proud and happy
   H. hopeful and excited
   I. sad and mysterious

13 How would Mrs. Sappleton describe Mr. Nuttel?

   A. boring and strange
   B. intelligent and kind-hearted
   C. fascinating and funny
   D. overconfident and rude

14 Why did Mr. Nuttel run out of the house when he saw the three men?

   F. He believed they were ghosts.
   G. He feared they would be angry.
   H. He thought they would shoot him.
   I. He felt their dog might attack him.

15 Why did the author include the sentence "Romance at short notice was her specialty" at the end of the story?

   A. to prove that the niece had some kind of mental illness
   B. to show that the niece was amazed by the men's appearance
   C. to convey the idea that the niece had fallen in love with Mr. Nuttel
   D. to make it clear that the niece had made up the story she told Mr. Nuttel

16 Read this sentence from the story.

> In crossing the moor to their favorite snipe-shooting ground they were all three engulfed in a treacherous piece of bog.

What does *treacherous* mean?

   F. deep
   G. hidden
   H. protected
   I. dangerous

Read the article "Litter in the Water" before answering Numbers 17 through 24.

Litter in the Water

by Thomas F. Greene

During the summer of 1988, a tide of solid wastes washed up on the shore, from Massachusetts to Maryland. Much of the debris consisted of medical wastes, including hypodermic syringes and other products made of plastic. There was so much garbage in the water that many beaches had to be closed. The public was frightened and outraged.

No spot is too remote for seagoing trash. On Ducie Island, an uninhabited spot in the middle of the South Pacific nearly 500 km from the nearest inhabited island, scientists have discovered litter washed up on its beaches. On one occasion, a scientist counted 953 pieces of trash, most of it plastic, along a 2.5-km stretch of beach. Much of the garbage came from vessels, such as cruise ships, that had routinely dumped their trash overboard.

Litter is solid waste or garbage. Most litter consists of plastic, glass, and metal—materials that do not undergo natural decay. Litter that cannot be broken down by natural processes is called nonbiodegradable. Nonbiodegradable waste, such as plastic, may remain in the environment for hundreds of years.

Plastic waste is not only unsightly, but it often poses a threat to marine life. Some animals, particularly sea turtles that eat jellyfish, mistake plastic bags for food. The turtles then die—either of starvation (with plastic bags filling their stomachs) or of suffocation (after choking on the plastic bags). Carelessly discarded plastic rings from beverage six-packs trap and choke fish, birds, and other marine life when the animals swim, or put their heads in through the rings and are unable to get them off their bodies. And each year, thousands of fish, seabirds, turtles, and marine mammals die when they become entangled in plastic gill nets, fishing line, and huge drift nets that are discarded or lost at sea by fishing vessels.

The United States throws away more trash than does any other nation in the world. More than 150 million tons of solid wastes, or refuse, are thrown out each year—nearly 10 million tons of it into offshore waters. Among the items dumped into the sea are millions of old cars, along with old boats and military weapons. In addition, millions of glass, metal, paper, plastic, and plastic foam items are thrown into the ocean each year. Whereas many of these items may be harmful to marine life and the environment, sunken cars and ships sometimes serve as artificial reefs that attract fish, which is good for ocean life and for recreational activities.

Approximately 75 percent of all garbage is buried in landfill sites. But many U.S. cities and states are running out of such spaces to dump their solid wastes. Landfills are supposed to be constructed so that waste substances do not leach into the ground and contaminate groundwater. In spite of this, some landfills contain hazardous chemicals that seep through the ground into drinking water sources and into nearby waterways that are used for swimming and fishing. The proper disposal of solid wastes is a serious problem because as the U.S. population increases so too will the amount of garbage it generates.

Solutions to Pollution

What can communities do to dispose of garbage properly, without dumping it directly into the ground or the ocean? One method is incineration, the disposal of solid wastes by combustion. There are some 200 large incinerators now operating in the United States. Although the burning of wastes can be used to generate energy, it is not a perfect solution to waste disposal. Many towns cannot afford to build an incinerator. In addition, incineration of garbage can produce air pollutants, especially when plastics are burned.

There are valid environmental and economic concerns about the disposal of solid wastes in landfills and by incineration. A more ecologically sound method of handling solid wastes is *recycling*—the disposal of garbage by reusing it or by converting it into useful products. Some of the most commonly recycled items are paper, plastics, glass, and metal. The incentive of deposit payments for beverage cans and bottles has greatly diminished the number of such containers that are discarded. Billions of glass food jars and aluminum cans are recycled in the United States each year. Incentives for the recycling of paper have spawned about 2000 wastepaper dealers and brokers nationwide. Out of an estimated 27 million tons of waste paper, about 5 million tons have been recycled into packaging products and exported abroad. However, experts believe that recycling at best will involve only 25 percent of our trash. Hopefully, companies will use more biodegradable products, and the government will provide more economic incentives for companies and consumers to recycle. In Japan, 50 percent of solid wastes are recycled. Citizen participation in recycling programs is essential if we are to reduce the amount of litter we produce and discard.

Answer Numbers 17 through 24 using the Answer Sheet on page 294. Base your answers on the article "Litter in the Water."

 Read these sentences from the article.

> No spot is too remote for seagoing trash. On Ducie Island, an uninhabited spot in the middle of the South Pacific nearly 500 km from the nearest inhabited island, scientists have discovered litter washed up on its beaches.

What does the word *remote* mean?

    A. safe

    B. clean

    C. nearby

    D. far away

18 How are glass, plastic, and metal all ALIKE?

    F. They all present a danger to marine wildlife.

    G. They all cause chemicals to leach into the soil.

    H. They all create energy when they are recycled.

    I. They all stay in the environment for a long time.

19 How do plastic bags kill sea turtles?

    A. Turtles swim inside them and suffocate.

    B. Turtles think they are food and eat them.

    C. Turtles stick their heads through them and choke.

    D. Turtles get their legs caught up in them and drown.

20 Which of these ideas from the article weakens the author's argument that litter is bad?

    F. Japan recycles 50 percent of its solid wastes.

    G. Sunken cars and ships may become reefs for fish.

    H. The United States makes more trash than any other country.

    I. Billions of glass jars and aluminum cans are recycled every year.

21 What problem are U.S. landfills facing today?

    A. They are being replaced by incinerators.

    B. They are running out of room for garbage.

    C. They are losing money to recycling companies.

    D. They are getting fined for not preventing leaching.

22 What is the MAIN idea of the paragraph that begins "What can communities do to dispose of garbage properly, without dumping it directly into the ground or the ocean?"

    F. Incineration is a way to dispose of wastes by burning them.

    G. Incineration is too expensive to use as a way to dispose of garbage.

    H. Incineration is one way to get rid of garbage, but it has its problems, too.

    I. Incineration is the most popular way of getting rid of garbage in the United States.

23 According to the article, what has been the effect of charging a deposit on cans and bottles?

    A. People have been buying fewer drinks in cans and bottles.

    B. People have been less likely to throw away cans and bottles.

    C. A huge industry of can and bottle dealers and brokers has been created.

    D. A lot of money has been lost as people have continued to throw away cans and bottles.

24. What is the author's opinion of recycling?

    F. It is not as good a solution as incineration.

    G. It will take care of all our solid wastes someday.

    H. It will make biodegradable products unnecessary.

    I. It is only part of the solution to our garbage problems.

Read the passage "Lobbying 101" before answering Numbers 25 through 32.

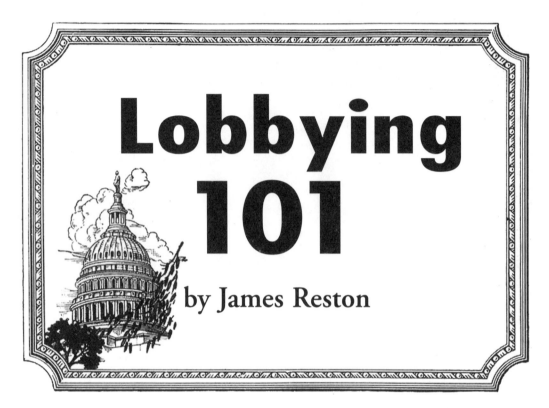

Lobbying 101
by James Reston

Lobbying is perceived as a difficult thing to do. It's not.

My first lobbying experiences occurred when I was just a teenager. I often took days off school, taking a 6 a.m. bus to my state capitol to spend the day pressing the flesh with legislators. It was an unusual experience for me—not the actual process of lobbying, but being the only teenager actually working there, rather than one who was taking the hour-long tour.

I will admit that, at first, I was scared to meet with my legislators, worrying that my comments might hurt my cause instead of helping it. But unfounded fears have a way of dissipating all on their own, and the more meetings I had, the more confident I felt about my lobbying abilities. My opinions on pending legislation had a profound effect on the voting records of my legislators. The entire lobbying experience was like a meeting with a friend. I also discovered legislators really do care about the feelings of their constituents. Even though I personally couldn't vote at the time, I was still a very influential lobbyist, because as president of Earth 2000, I was in contact with thousands of teens throughout Pennsylvania who had parents and older siblings who did vote. My lobbyist friend Laura summed it up best when she said, "No politician wants to be known as the legislator who made a group of kids cry."

Back in my school, I started recruiting other young people to come with me to the state capitol. At one point, we actually took the term lobbying literally: We set up a booth right in the lobby of the Capitol building, handing out brochures and pamphlets to passersby. Many of these people included politicians and the press who found it unusual to see a group of teenagers being so knowledgeable about pending environmental legislation.

As more and more of our peers got involved, we became aware of how important voting really is. When a local state representative refused to change his

The Lingo of Lobbyists: A Dictionary for Novices

As a lobbyist, there are some basic terms that you should know. These are words commonly used by elected officials, their staffs, and lobbyists. Don't use them just to impress a friend at a party; make them part of your lobbying vocabulary:

Act: A bill that has been passed by both houses and becomes law.

Bill: A proposed law introduced in either the House or Senate

Committee: Workshops composed of legislators who study new bills, dissect them to find problems, and hear concerns from lobbyists, constituents, and other legislators.

Constituent: A public citizen in a legislator's district.

District: A territory of the state that has one state senator and one state representative to represent its interest in the state legislature. Federal districts are larger and have one federal representative. Every state has two federal senators.

Filibuster: To deliberately take advantage of the freedom of debate—a law which allows a legislator unlimited time to debate a bill before a vote—in order to delay the vote on a bill.

Table: To postpone action or debate on a bill. If a legislator has a special interest in a certain bill (e.g., a bill that would force cattle ranchers to pay higher taxes in a district which has more cows than people), the legislator would try to table discussion—and therefore stall action—until he or she could find a way to gain support.

Veto: The power of the president of the United States and each state's governor to reject a bill that has already passed both legislative houses.

---

views on a bill, we rallied together in our small town, where only a tiny percentage of people would normally turn out to vote, and started swaying even hard-core Republicans to switch their vote. It was amazing to see so many of my peers feel passionate about politics. Today, voting is still a major priority for all of us; I've been known to hop on a red-eye flight back from the West Coast to cast my vote in New York (when I forgot to secure an absentee ballot).

I think schools should abandon the traditional route of a class field trip to teach students about politics and our government. Instead, young people should research legislation and bills that are pending on issues they care about, such as gun control, the environment, and health care. Schools should set up meetings with groups of young people, sit down with them, and have an unrehearsed conversation with them. Keep it real. I've always believed that when you take a hard-to-understand topic like lobbying and present it in a straightforward, understandable format, people will grasp the idea immediately. Imagine the possibilities if every young person had a one-on-one experience with the politicians.

Now answer Numbers 25 through 32. Base your answers on the passage "Lobbying 101."

25 What can you infer from the fact that the author took days off school to go lobby?

    A. His parents did not think school was very important.
    B. His teachers did not mind if their students skipped school.
    C. His school did not notice whether or not students missed school.
    D. His parents and teachers did not care if he missed school for a good reason.

26 How was the author DIFFERENT from the other teenagers visiting the state capitol?

    F. He was a tourist.
    G. He was a student.
    H. He was a lobbyist.
    I. He was a politician.

27 Why did the author feel scared at first about meeting with legislators?

    A. He feared he might do more harm than good.
    B. He thought they might not take him seriously.
    C. He believed the legislators were too busy to talk.
    D. He felt that his cause had little chance for support.

28 What was the author's opinion of the legislators he met?

    F. He felt they had more respect for nonvoters than for voters.
    G. He believed they did not care what people his age had to say.
    H. He thought they had real concern for the people they represented.
    I. He sensed they did not know how much influence teenagers can have.

29 Which fact from the story BEST supports the author's statement that voting was still important to him as an adult?

    A. He got his friends involved in politics.
    B. He disliked traditional class field trips.
    C. He learned about environmental legislation.
    D. He took a cross-country plane trip just to vote.

30 What is the MAIN idea of the article?

    F. People should get involved in politics by lobbying.
    G. People should feel comfortable talking with their legislators.
    H. People should understand how lobbyists influence lawmaking.
    I. People should lobby their representatives about environmental issues.

31 How does the information in the sidebar support the main article?

    A. by giving a definition of the term *lobbying*

    B. by teaching the words people need to know if they want to lobby

    C. by showing the steps to take when getting ready to lobby

    D. by explaining the methods that make lobbying effective

32 What happens to a bill when it is either filibustered or tabled?

    F. It is stalled.

    G. It is passed.

    H. It is defeated.

    I. It is introduced.

Read the article "What Is a Gene?" before answering Numbers 33 through 40.

What Is a Gene?

by Louis E. Bartoshesky, MD, MPH

The doorbell rings. Busy in the kitchen fixing dinner, Nancy's dad calls out, "Answer the door, Nancy! My hands are full!" Nancy opens the front door, and suddenly a bunch of people she hasn't seen in three years pours into the house.

Aunt Rita hands Nancy a wrapped package and says, "Well, look at you! How you've grown. And you've got such beautiful red, curly hair! It runs in the family, you know. You look just like my grandmother!" Uncle Michael adds, "And she's going to be tall, like her father. Only nine years old, and she looks like a basketball player already!"

Nancy makes a dash to the kitchen, wondering, "Huh? Aunt Rita's grandmother? Runs in the family? Basketball? What are they talking about?"

Genes (say: **jeenz**), that's what they're talking about. Genes are the things that determine physical traits—how we look—and lots of other stuff about us. They carry information that helps make you who you are; curly or straight hair, long or short legs, even how you might smile or laugh, are all passed through generations of your family in genes. Keep reading to learn more about genes and how they work.

What Is a Gene?

Each cell in the human body contains about 25,000 to 35,000 genes, which carry information that determines your **traits** (say: **trates**). Traits are characteristics you inherit from your parents; this means your

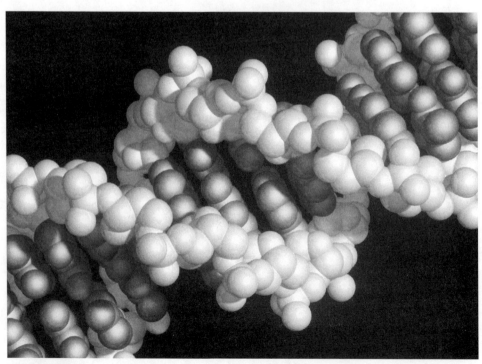

A DNA model

parents pass some of their characteristics on to you through genes. For example, if both of your parents have green eyes, you might inherit the trait of green eyes from them. Or if your mom has freckles, you might inherit that trait and wind up with a freckled face. And genes aren't just in humans—all animals and plants have genes, too.

Genes are lined up on thread-like things called **chromosomes** (say: **kro**-moh-somes). Chromosomes come in pairs, and there are hundreds, sometimes thousands, of genes in one chromosome. Together, all of the chromosomes and genes make up DNA, which is short for **deoxyribonucleic** (say: dee-**ox**-see-ri-bo-nyoo-**clay**-ik) **acid**.

Chromosomes are found inside cells, the very small units that make up all living things. A cell is so tiny that you can see it only through the lens of a strong microscope, and there are billions of cells in your body. Most cells have one **nucleus** (say: **noo**-clee-us). The nucleus, which is sort of egg-shaped, is like the brain of the cell. It tells every part of the cell what to do. How does the nucleus know so much? As tiny as it is, the nucleus has more information in it than the biggest dictionary you've ever seen.

In humans, a cell nucleus contains 46 individual chromosomes or 23 pairs of chromosomes (chromosomes come in pairs, remember? $23 \times 2 = 46$). Half of these chromosomes come from one parent, and half come from the other parent. But not every living thing has 46 chromosomes inside its cells. For instance, a fruit fly cell has only four chromosomes!

How Do Genes Work?

Each gene has a special job to do. It carries blueprints—the instructions—for making **proteins** (say: **pro**-teens) in the cell. Proteins are the building blocks for everything in your body. Bones and teeth, hair and earlobes, muscles and blood, all are made up of proteins (as well as other stuff). Those proteins help our bodies grow, work properly, and stay healthy. Scientists today estimate that each gene in the body may make as many as ten different proteins. That's over 300,000 proteins!

Like chromosomes, genes come in pairs. Each of your biological parents has two copies of each of their genes, and each parent passes along just one copy to make up the genes you have. Genes that are passed on to you determine many of your traits, such as your hair color and skin color.

Maybe Nancy's mother has one gene for brown hair and one for red hair, and she passed the red-hair gene on to Nancy. If her father has two genes for red hair, that could explain her red hair. Nancy ended up with two genes for red hair, one from each of her parents.

You can see genes at work if you think about all the breeds of dogs there are. They all have the genes that make them dogs instead of cats, fish, or people. But those same genes that make a dog a dog also make different dog traits. So some breeds are small, and others are big. Some have long fur, and others have short fur. Dalmatians have genes for curly fur. You get the idea.

When There Are Problems with Genes

Scientists are very busy studying genes. What do the proteins that each gene makes actually do in the body? What illnesses are caused by genes that don't work properly? Researchers think genes that have changed in some way, also known as altered (or mutated) genes, may be partly to blame for lung problems, cancer, and many other illnesses.

Take the gene that helps the body make **hemoglobin** (say: **hee**-muh-glow-bin), for example. Hemoglobin is an important protein that is needed for red-blood cells to carry oxygen throughout the body. If parents pass on altered hemoglobin genes to their child, the child may be able to make only a type of hemoglobin that doesn't work properly. This can cause anemia (say: un-**nee**-mee-uh), a condition in which a person has fewer healthy red-blood cells.

Anemias that are inherited can sometimes be serious enough to require long-term medical care. Sickle-cell anemia is one kind of anemia that is passed on through genes from parents to children. Kids with sickle-cell anemia sometimes need to go to the hospital to take care of their blood.

Cystic fibrosis (say: **sis**-tick fi-**bro**-sus), or CF, is another illness that some kids inherit. Parents with the CF gene can pass it on to their kids. People who have CF sometimes have trouble breathing because their bodies make a lot of **mucus** (say: **myoo**-kus)—the slimy stuff that comes out of your nose when you blow—that gets stuck in the lungs. They will need treatment throughout their lives to keep their lungs as healthy as possible.

For more articles like this one, visit www.KidsHealth.org or www.TeensHealth.org.

Now answer Numbers 33 through 40. Base your answers on the article "What Is a Gene?"

33 How did Nancy feel after greeting Aunt Rita and Uncle Michael?

    A. angry

    B. pleased

    C. confused

    D. embarrassed

34 What decides a person's physical traits?

    F. cells

    G. genes

    H. protein

    I. hemoglobin

35 How are humans, plants, and animals ALIKE?

    A. They all get sickle-cell anemia.

    B. They all share the same physical traits.

    C. They all have 23 pairs of chromosomes.

    D. They all pass on traits through their genes.

36 What information can you find in parentheses after each scientific term in the article?

    F. the term's origin

    G. the term's spelling

    H. the term's meaning

    I. the term's pronunciation

37 What does a gene do?

    A. gives instructions for making protein

    B. builds proteins for making chromosomes

    C. keeps mucus from forming in the lungs

    D. carries blood cells throughout the body

38 Why does the author compare the nucleus of a cell to a brain?

    F. to explain why it is shaped like an egg

    G. to show that it gives instructions to the rest of the cell

    H. to prove that it is more important than the other cell parts

    I. to demonstrate why a cell needs to hold so much information

39 Which two words from the article have about the same meaning?

    A. cell, nucleus

    B. gene, protein

    C. altered, inherited

    D. trait, characteristic

40 How does a child get sickle-cell anemia?

    F. from a parent that has the CF gene

    G. from a parent passing on a changed gene

    H. from a gene that mutates within the child

    I. from a gene that changes the mucus in the lungs

Read the article "Python vs. Pooch" before answering Numbers 41 through 49.

Python vs. Pooch

by Elizabeth Caram

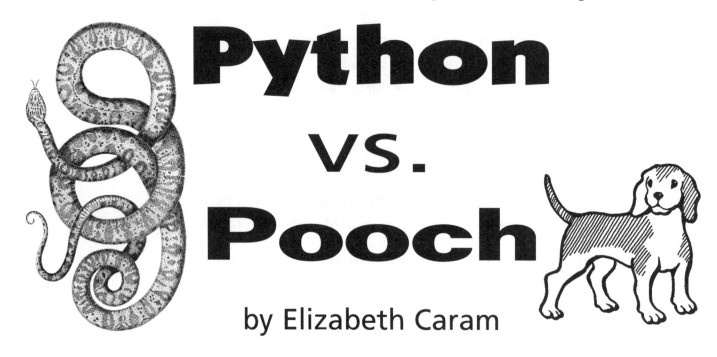

In the strange-but-true fight against giant pythons that increasingly are roaming the far reaches of the Florida Everglades, park officials have come up with an unlikely weapon: a beagle named Python Pete.

The 6-month-old puppy is being trained to track the snakes that biologists say have invaded Everglades National Park—discarded pets that have grown to science-fiction proportions.

"These are extraordinary times as the park faces a unique issue. We have to do what it takes to find these pythons," said Rick Cook, public affairs officer for the Everglades. "The hope is that the dog will be able to pick up the snakes' scent."

The experimental idea came from Lori Oberhofer, an Everglades wildlife technician who worked for the U.S. Department of Agriculture in Guam, where a similar program is still used.

Oberhofer brings the puppy to work with her every day, training him for his future snake-tracking duties by using a rag that smells like python.

"Although this has never been tried before in the Everglades, we have great plans for him," Oberhofer said.

Park biologist Skip Snow is hopeful that the experiment will turn into the solution the park needs.

"We do not know if Python Pete will be successful. He's still a puppy," Snow cautioned.

The problem of giant snakes in the Everglades is becoming more acute because the pythons are competing with native animals—including the federally threatened indigo snake—for food and living space. Burmese pythons, for example, typically grow to about 20 feet.

Already, park-goers have witnessed two headline-making battles between alligators and pythons. The first came in January 2003 when two reptiles engaged in an epic 24-hour battle. The snake finally managed to escape.

Nearly a year later, in February 2004, another snake wasn't as lucky. Park visitors saw an alligator catch one of the large snakes in its mouth and swim away victoriously.

Park biologists want to eradicate the Everglades' python population, euthanizing any that are found.

Daniel Vice, assistant state director for the U.S. Department of Agriculture, works in Guam with Jack Russell terriers that are used to detect and capture brown tree snakes.

"Studies indicate that a well-trained, experienced dog-and-handler team can expect to find about 75 percent of the snakes," Vice said. "With appropriate and adequate training and maintenance, this rate of detection is fairly consistent across time and locations."

Oberhofer, who paid for the dog herself, said she hopes that Pete will be just as productive in the Everglades.

"He is showing lots of potential and has already accomplished what much older dogs are trained to do. And he's still just a six-month-old puppy," she said.

The dog's training sessions generally last ten minutes, once or twice a day. Inside a plastic container in the corner of Oberhofer's office, a large, mesh laundry bag holds a large python. Pete's favorite rag, checkered and chewed on, is kept in the box, absorbing snake musk.

When it's time to train, Oberhofer puts a special red collar and matching leash on Pete—a combination used only when it is "work time." She leads him outside to a field with knee-high grass, carrying the mesh bag containing the python and musky rag. Oberhofer gently drags the mesh bag through the grass, creating a 50-foot scent trail for Pete. Then she tells him: "Find it!"

The puppy's ears perk up and he begins sniffing the grass. He finds the trail, which has been marked by stakes. As a reward when he has tracked the snake, Oberhofer lets him play tug of war with the musky rag.

"I want Pete to think that this scent means fun," she said.

So far, the beagle has been successful in finding the trail each time he has tried, she added.

When he's ready, Oberhofer will take Pete out into the field for the real thing: to hunt for pythons. To keep him from becoming a snake snack, Pete will always be kept on a leash, Oberhofer said.

"If Python Pete turns out to be very successful at finding pythons for us, I would anticipate that we would continue using him and perhaps expand the program and get more dogs," she said. "But that would depend on future funding for the program."

Now answer Numbers 41 through 49. Base your answers on the article "Python vs. Pooch."

41 What problem do park officials face in the Florida Everglades?

    A. Dogs are killing endangered snakes.

    B. Pet snakes are escaping from their owners.

    C. People are dumping their pet snakes in the Everglades.

    D. Giant snakes and alligators are having dangerous battles.

42 How did Lori Oberhofer come up with the idea of using Python Pete?

    F. from watching Pete track snakes

    G. from reading science-fiction novels

    H. from using dogs in Guam to hunt snakes

    I. from working as an Everglades technician

43 How will Python Pete find the snakes once he is trained?

    A. by seeing them

    B. by hearing them

    C. by smelling them

    D. by attracting them

44 What is the MAIN reason that park officials are concerned about giant snakes in the Everglades?

    F. The snakes are attacking humans.

    G. The snakes are feeding on people's pets.

    H. The snakes are crowding out other species.

    I. The snakes are eating the endangered indigo snake.

45 What will happen to the snakes once they are found?

    A. They will be sold as pets.

    B. They will be donated to zoos.

    C. They will be killed humanely.

    D. They will be returned to their owners.

46 How are the pythons in the Everglades and the brown tree snake in Guam ALIKE?

    F. Both are non-native species.

    G. Both are endangered species.

    H. Both are dangerous to humans.

    I. Both are protected by federal law.

47 What can you infer from the fact that Oberhofer paid for Pete herself?

    A. She has experience in raising and training beagles.

    B. She is not sure that Pete will be able to track snakes.

    C. She has confidence in the idea of using Pete to find snakes.

    D. She is training Pete against the advice of other park officials.

48 Why does Oberhofer keep a python in her office?

- F. to train Pete to track snakes
- G. to learn about python behavior
- H. to teach Pete not to fear snakes
- I. to educate the public about snakes

49 What makes Pete want to track the snake?

- A. He wants to kill the snake.
- B. He wants to play tug-of-war.
- C. He wants to protect Oberhofer.
- D. He wants to get a food reward.

Read the article "Acting" before answering Numbers 50 through 57.

Acting

"There is no teacher like performing."
—Ed Asner

No cinematographer or film editor, no matter how gifted, can turn a terrible performance into a great one.

The right actor can give a screenwriter's words exciting new depth and dimensions. Actors are essential for conveying emotions to an audience, for bringing the words and ideas in a script to life. Even animated characters rely on the personalities of behind-the-scenes performers.

Imagine that you are an actor. You've worked primarily in New York theater but have decided to try your hand at working in film. You pack your bags and head to Hollywood. In Hollywood, you meet other actors and enroll in workshops to hone your instruments: your voice, your body, and your imagination. You seek out an agent and have some publicity photos taken.

Once you're lucky enough to secure an agent, you are sent on interviews where you meet casting directors and read for parts. Over the course of two months, you try out for 23 roles and are chosen for none of them. Finally, you are cast in a film. It's a minor part, but substantial enough that if you do well, you will enjoy more work and exposure. After the shock wears off, you begin to prepare.

Understanding the Role

Your agent has been able to secure a copy of the script for you. It's a thriller called *Blueberry Hill*. You have been cast as Emily Grubowski, the plain, bitter wife of a has-been police officer. You have three scenes, which will give you approximately two minutes of screen time. Somehow you must connect closely with your character. You read and reread the entire script, not just your scenes. You try to understand the characters' relationships with each other. Here is the first of your scenes, which will be shot tomorrow:

[INT, Stan Grubowski's home. Night. Grubowski, seated on a sofa, stares into a blazing fire. Emily enters the room, hands him a mug of tea.]

GRUBOWSKI
Thanks.
[*Emily sits next to him. He makes no movement in her direction. There is ice between them.*]

EMILY
It's peculiar, isn't it?

GRUBOWSKI
What is?

EMILY
All this happening now. Ten years this month, that child disappeared.
[*Grubowski gets up, moves away from the sofa. Emily watches him closely.*]

GRUBOWSKI
I'm tired. I'm going to bed.
[*He leaves the room. Emily pokes the fire. It blazes up. She drops her head sadly.*]

EMILY
Turn down the thermostat, Stan.

As an actor, you must be able to become many different people. In order to make Emily come to life, you must bring to the role those parts of yourself that are similar to the character. You look deep inside yourself to find feelings that will help you come across as sad and bitter.

You study the role in depth. In order to learn your lines, you know you must learn the part. Memorizing lines without understanding the role will be of little help to you.

As you study Emily, you learn there is more to her than meets the eye. She is bitter because she has been hurt repeatedly by her husband. But she is also frightened of losing him and wants to protect him. She is a complex character, though her time on screen is brief.

You ask an actor friend to help you rehearse your lines, and after much study, you feel confident that you have done as much preparation as you can. You're ready to shoot the scene.

Now answer numbers 50 through 57. Base your answers on the article "Acting."

50 What is the MAIN idea of the first paragraph of the article?

    F. It takes good acting to make a good film.

    G. It takes good directing to bring out the best in an actor.

    H. No director can help an actor bring a bad script to life.

    I. No actor can make a bad screenplay into a good movie.

51 Why does the author use the pronoun *you* throughout the article?

    A. to demonstrate to the reader that anyone can be an actor

    B. to help the reader imagine himself or herself as an actor

    C. to prove that acting demands total involvement from a person

    D. to show the article was written as advice to one of the author's friends

52 What conclusion can you draw from the article about finding work as an actor?

    F. It is easy once you find an agent.

    G. It is easy if you already know the casting directors.

    H. It is difficult, and you will not get every role you try out for.

    I. It is hard but worthwhile because of all the friends you make.

53 At the beginning of the scene, what does INT most likely stand for?

    A. intense

    B. interior

    C. interest

    D. interview

54 Which word BEST describes Emily in the scene?

    F. angry

    G. unhappy

    H. suspicious

    I. frightened

55 What does the author believe an actor must do to make his or her character come to life?

    A. rehearse with an actor friend

    B. memorize the character's lines

    C. bring one's own feelings to the role

    D. dress in clothes the character would wear

56 What does the article suggest about minor roles in films?

    F. They may result in more screen time.
    G. They may pay more than major roles.
    H. They can be very complex and challenging.
    I. They can hurt an actor's chances at other roles.

57 Read this sentence from the article.

Your agent has been able to secure a copy of the script for you.

What definition of *secure* explains its meaning in this sentence?

    A. to guarantee payment
    B. to fasten something firmly in place
    C. to obtain or get something with effort
    D. to make something safe; not likely to be attacked

Practice Test Two

Read the article "Why Exercise Is Wise" before answering Numbers 1 through 8.

Why Exercise Is Wise

by Heidi Kecskemethy

You've probably heard countless times how exercise is "good for you," but did you know that it can actually help you *feel* good, too? Getting the right amount of exercise can rev up your energy levels and even help you to feel better emotionally.

Experts recommend that adults get 30 to 60 minutes of physical activity each day-and because most teens are no longer in the "child" category for exercise, these recommendations probably apply to you. There are three components to a well-balanced exercise routine: aerobic exercise, strength training, and flexibility training.

Rewards and Benefits

Exercise benefits every part of the body, including the mind. Exercising causes the body to produce endorphins, chemicals that lead a person to feel peaceful and happy. Exercise can help some people sleep better. It can also help with mental health issues, such as mild depression and self-esteem: If you feel strong and powerful, it can help you see yourself in a better light. Plus, exercise can give people a real sense of accomplishment and pride at having achieved a certain goal—like beating an old time in the 100-meter dash.

Exercising can help you look better, too. People who exercise burn calories and look more toned than those who don't. In fact, exercise is one of the most important ways of keeping your body at a healthy weight. When you exercise, you burn food calories as fuel. If a person eats more calories than he or she burns, the body stores them away as fat. Exercise can help burn these stored calories.

Exercising to maintain a healthy weight also decreases a person's risk of developing certain diseases, including type-2 diabetes and high blood pressure. These diseases, which used to be found mostly in adults, are becoming more common in teens.

Finally, it may not seem important now, but exercise can help a person age well. Women are especially prone to a condition called **osteoporosis** (a weakening of the bones) as they get older. Studies have found that weight-bearing exercise, like running or brisk walking, can help girls (and guys!) keep their bones strong.

Aerobic Exercise

Like other muscles, the heart likes a good workout. You can provide it with one in the form of aerobic exercise. Aerobic exercise is any type of exercise that gets the heart pumping and the muscles using oxygen (you'll notice your body using oxygen as you breathe faster). When you give your heart this kind of workout on a regular basis, your heart will get stronger and more efficient in delivering oxygen (in the form of oxygen-carrying blood cells) to all parts of your body.

In addition to being active every day, experts recommend that teens get at least three 20-minute sessions a week of vigorous activity. If you play team sports, you're probably doing more than that recommendation, which is great! Some team sports that give you a great aerobic workout are swimming, basketball, soccer, lacrosse, hockey, and rowing.

But if you don't play team sports, don't worry; there are plenty of ways to get aerobic exercise on your own or with friends. These include biking, running, swimming, dancing, in-line skating, cross-country skiing, hiking, and walking quickly. In fact, the types of exercise that you do on your own are easier to continue when you leave high school and go on to work or college, making it easier to stay fit later in life as well.

Strength Training

The heart isn't the only muscle to benefit from regular exercise—most of the other muscles in your body enjoy exercise, too. When you use your muscles and they become stronger, it allows you to be active for longer periods of time without getting worn out. Strong muscles are also a plus because they actually help protect you when you exercise by supporting your joints and helping to prevent injuries. Muscle also burns more energy when a person's at rest than fat does, so building your muscles will help you burn more calories and maintain a healthy weight.

Different types of exercise strengthen different muscle groups, for example:

- For arms, try rowing or cross-country skiing. Pull-ups and push-ups, those old gym-class standbys, are also good for building arm muscles.
- For strong legs, try running, biking, or skating.
- For shapely abs, you can't beat rowing, bike riding, and crunches.

Flexibility Training

Strengthening the heart and other muscles isn't the only important goal of exercise. Exercise also helps the body stay flexible, meaning that your muscles and joints stretch and bend easily. People who are flexible can worry less about strained muscles and sprains. Flexibility can also help improve a person's sports performance. Some activities, like dance or martial arts, obviously require great flexibility, but increased flexibility can also help people perform better at other sports, such as soccer or lacrosse.

Sports and activities that encourage flexibility are easy to find. Many high schools have gymnastics programs. Martial arts like karate also help a person stay flexible. Ballet, pilates, and yoga are other good choices. Warming up for a workout and doing simple stretching exercises after your workout also help you develop flexibility.

What's Right for Me?

One of the biggest reasons people drop an exercise program is lack of interest: If what you're doing isn't fun, it's hard to keep it up. The good news is that there are tons of different sports and activities that you can try out to see which one inspires you.

When picking the right type of exercise for you, it can help to consider your workout personality. For example, do you like to work out alone and on your own schedule (in which case solo sports like biking or snowboarding may be for you), or do you like the shared motivation and companionship that comes from being part of a team? You also need to factor in practical considerations, such as whether your chosen activity is affordable and accessible to you (activities like horse riding are harder for people who live in cities, for example) and how much time you can set aside for your sport.

For more articles like this one, visit www.KidsHealth.org or www.TeensHealth.org.

Now answer Numbers 1 through 8 using the Answer Sheet on page 295. Base your answers on the article "Why Exercise Is Wise."

1 Which sentence from the article BEST expresses the article's MAIN idea?

  A. If you feel strong and powerful, it can help you see yourself in a better light.
  B. When picking the right type of exercise, it can help to consider your workout personality.
  C. Getting the right amount of exercise can rev up your energy levels and even help you to feel better emotionally.
  D. There are three components to a well-balanced exercise routine: aerobic exercise, strength training, and flexibility training.

2 How do endorphins help a person feel better?

  F. They give a person a feeling of pride.
  G. They help a person to sleep more soundly.
  H. They make a person feel calm and cheerful.
  I. They bring a person a sense of power and strength.

3 What happens when a person burns fewer calories than he or she eats?

  A. The body becomes more toned.
  B. The body stays at a healthy weight.
  C. The body turns the calories into fat.
  D. The body works harder to burn the calories.

4 What can you infer from the fact that type-2 diabetes and high blood pressure have become more common in teenagers?

  F. Teenagers today mature at a faster rate.
  G. Some teenagers today do not exercise enough.
  H. Teenagers today experience more unhealthy stress.
  I. Many teenagers are pressured to stay at a healthy weight.

5 How are the heart and other muscles in the body ALIKE?

  A. They all need exercise.
  B. They all deliver oxygen.
  C. They all are prone to osteoporosis.
  D. They all need weight-bearing exercise.

6 What does the author think about teens getting more than the recommended three 20-minute sessions a week of aerobic exercise?

  F. It is a good idea.
  G. It is a waste of time.
  H. It is a dangerous practice.
  I. It is a good way to make friends.

7 According to the article, what makes many people stop doing an activity?

  A. having an accident
  B. becoming too busy
  C. reaching their fitness goal
  D. getting bored with the activity

8 Read the sentence from the article.

You also need to factor in practical considerations, such as whether your chosen activity is affordable and accessible to you (activities like horse riding are harder for people who live in cities, for example).

What does the word *accessible* mean?

  F. easy
  G. nearby
  H. practical
  I. interesting

Read the passage from *Black Boy* and the poem "The Swimming Lesson" before answering Numbers 9 through 16.

from Black Boy

by Richard Wright

Hunger stole upon me so slowly that at first I was not aware of what hunger really meant. Hunger had always been more or less at my elbow when I played, but now I began to wake up at night to find hunger standing at my bedside, staring at me gauntly. The hunger I had known before this had been no grim, hostile stranger; it had been a normal hunger that had made me beg constantly for bread, and when I ate a crust or two I was satisfied. But this new hunger baffled me, scared me, made me angry and insistent. Whenever I begged for food now my mother would pour me a cup of tea which would still the clamor in my stomach for a moment or two; but a little later I would feel hunger nudging my ribs, twisting my empty guts until they ached. I would grow dizzy and my vision would dim. I became less active in my play, and for the first time in my life I had to pause and think of what was happening to me.

"Mama, I'm hungry," I complained one afternoon.

"Jump up and catch a kungry," she said, trying to make me laugh and forget.

"What's a kungry?"

"It's what little boys eat when they get hungry," she said.

"What does it taste like?"

"I don't know."

"Then why do you tell me to catch one?"

"Because you said that you were hungry," she said, smiling.

I sensed that she was teasing me and it made me angry.

"But I'm hungry. I want to eat."

"You'll have to wait."

"But I want to eat now."

"But there's nothing to eat," she told me.

"Why?"

"Just because there's none," she explained.

"But I want to eat," I said, beginning to cry.

"You'll just have to wait," she said again.

"But why?"

"For God to send some food."

"When is He going to send it?"

"I don't know."

"But I'm hungry!"

She was ironing, and she paused and looked at me with tears in her eyes.

"Where's your father?"

I stared in bewilderment. Yes, it was true that my father had not come home to sleep for many days now and I could make as much noise as I wanted. Though I had not known why he was absent, I had been glad that he was not there to shout his restrictions at me. But it had never occurred to me that his absence would mean that there would be no food.

My mother finally went to work as a cook and left me and my brother alone in the flat each day with a loaf of bread and a pot of tea. When she returned at evening she would be tired and dispirited and would cry a lot.

One evening my mother told me that I would have to do the shopping for food. She took me to the corner store to show me the way. I was proud; I felt like a grownup. The next afternoon I looped the basket over my arm and went down the pavement toward the store. When I reached the corner, a gang of boys grabbed me, knocked me down, snatched the basket, took the money, and sent me running home in panic. That evening I told my mother what had happened, but she made no comment; she sat down at once, wrote another note, gave me more money, and sent me out to the grocery again. I crept down the steps and saw the same gang of boys playing down the street. I ran back into the house.

"What's the matter?" my mother asked.

"It's those same boys," I said. "They'll beat me."

"You've got to get over that," she said. "Now, go on."

"I'm scared," I said.

"Go on and don't pay any attention to them," she said.

I went out of the door and walked briskly down the sidewalk, praying that the gang would not molest me. But when I came abreast of them someone shouted.

"There he is!"

"They came toward me and I broke into a wild run toward home. They overtook me and flung me to the pavement. I yelled, pleaded, kicked, but they wrenched the money out of my hand. They yanked me to my feet, gave me a few slaps, and sent me home sobbing. My mother met me at the door.

"They b-beat m-me," I gasped. "They t-t-took the m-money."

I started up the steps, seeking the shelter of the house.

"Don't you come in here," my mother warned me.

I froze in my tracks and stared at her.

"But they're coming after me," I said.

"You just stay right where you are," she said in a deadly tone. "I'm going to teach you this night to stand up and fight for yourself."

She went into the house and I waited, terrified, wondering what she was about. Presently she returned with more money and another note; she also had a long heavy stick.

"Take this money, this note, and this stick," she said. "Go to the store and buy those groceries. If those boys bother you, then fight."

I was baffled. My mother was telling me to fight, a thing that she had never done before.

"But I'm scared," I said.

"Don't you come into this house until

you've gotten those groceries," she said.

"They'll beat me; they'll beat me," I said.

"Then stay in the streets; don't come back here!"

I ran up the steps and tried to force my way past her into the house. A stinging slap came on my jaw. I stood on the sidewalk, crying.

"Please let me wait until tomorrow," I begged.

"No," she said. "Go now! If you come back into this house without those groceries, I'll whip you!"

She slammed the door and I heard the key turn in the lock. I shook with fright. I was alone upon the dark, hostile streets and gangs were after me. I had the choice of being beaten at home or away from home. I clutched the stick, crying, trying to reason. If I were beaten at home, there was absolutely nothing that I could do about it; but if I were beaten in the streets, I had a chance to fight and defend myself. I walked slowly down the sidewalk, coming closer to the gang of boys, holding the stick tightly. I was so full of fear that I could scarcely breathe. I was almost upon them now.

"There he is again!" the cry went up.

They surrounded me quickly and began to grab for my hand.

"I'll kill you!" I threatened.

They closed in. In blind fear I let the stick fly, feeling it crack against a boy's skull. I swung again, slamming another skull, then another. Realizing that they would retaliate if I let up for but a second, I fought to lay them low, to knock them cold, to kill them so that they could not strike back at me. I flayed with tears in my eyes, teeth clenched, stark fear making me throw

every ounce of my strength behind each blow. I hit again and again, dropping the money and the grocery list. The boys scattered, yelling, nursing their heads, staring at me in utter disbelief. They had never seen such frenzy. I stood panting, egging them on, taunting them to come on and fight. When they refused, I ran after them and they tore out for their homes, screaming. The parents of the boys rushed into the streets and threatened me, and for the first time in my life I shouted at grownups, telling them that I would give them the same if they bothered me. I finally found my grocery list and the money and went to the store. On my way back I kept my stick poised for instant use, but there was not a single boy in sight. That night I won the right to the streets of Memphis.

The Swimming Lesson

by Mary Oliver

Feeling the icy kick, the endless waves
Reaching around my life, I moved my arms
And coughed, and in the end saw land.

Somebody, I suppose,
Remembering the medieval maxim,
Had tossed me in,
Had wanted me to learn to swim,

Not knowing that none of us, who ever came back
From that long lonely fall and frenzied rising,
Ever learned anything at all
About swimming, but only
How to put off, one by one,
Dreams and pity, love and grace,—
How to survive in any place.

Now answer Numbers 9 through 16 using the Answer Sheet on page 00. Base your answers on the passage from *Black Boy* and the poem "The Swimming Lesson."

9 How was the "new hunger" DIFFERENT from the hunger the narrator was used to?

   A. It made him weak.
   B. It gave him nightmares.
   C. It was easier to live with.
   D. It went away if he ate bread.

10 Why did the narrator's family suddenly have less food than before?

   F. His father lost his job.
   G. His father left the family.
   H. His mother was unable to find work.
   I. His mother was away looking for work.

11 What is the MAIN conflict of the story?

    A. The narrator has to find a way to get money to buy food.

    B. The narrator needs to help his mother after she is forced to get a job.

    C. The narrator needs to learn how to fight in order to protect his mother.

    D. The narrator must face a gang of boys who want to steal his grocery money.

12 Which pair of words BEST describes the narrator's mother?

    F. firm and loving

    G. fearful and timid

    H. selfish and mean

    I. uncaring and hurtful

13 How did the narrator's mother react the second time he came home without the groceries?

    A. She let him in the house and scolded him.

    B. She gave him a stick and told him to fight.

    C. She sent him back to the store without saying anything.

    D. She slapped him and told him never to come back home.

14 Read the sentence from the story.

> **Realizing that they would retaliate if I let up for but a second, I fought to lay them low, to knock them cold, to kill them so that they could not strike back at me.**

What does the word *retaliate* mean?

    F. get up

    G. run away

    H. fight back

    I. chase after

15 How did the speaker in the poem feel when she was tossed into the water?

    A. angry

    B. excited

    C. grateful

    D. terrified

16 Which sentence expresses the theme of both the story and the poem?

    F. Some of life's lessons can be very hard.

    G. Facing your fears is a rewarding experience.

    H. Learning to stand up for yourself is an important lesson.

    I. Those who try to teach us a lesson can do more harm than good.

Read the article "12 Keys to Your Future Career" before answering Numbers 17 through 24.

12 Keys to Your Future Career

An old saying goes, "If you don't figure out what you want to do with your life, someone else will." You don't have to decide right this second, but you can start making plans and exploring options. Try these ideas. Some you can do right now; others you may have to wait to do until you're older. Put them on your to-do list for the future.

1. **Stay in school.** Sticking it out can sometimes be tough, but don't give up. Get the help you need from teachers, counselors, and advisors. Your future will be very limited if you don't finish high school—and you should plan for college, too.

2. **Meet with your school counselor.** He or she is a good resource for figuring out where you want to go in life. Guidance counselors can give you valuable information about college and university programs, trade and technical schools, scholarships, internships, potential mentors, and leads on part-time jobs. They can also help you plan which classes to take and which extracurricular activities will boost your chances of getting into the college or trade school of your choice.

3. **Open your mind.** Try new things. Experience life. Explore as much as you can. Discover your talents. Learn a new skill. Volunteer. Be curious, and set your sights high.

4. **Read, read, read.** Books open up a world of knowledge. Read books on topics that interest you, even if they don't seem to have any direct connection to your future. You may be surprised. Read magazines and newspapers. Keep up with late-breaking news and information.

5. **Surf the Web.** The Internet is an electronic universe loaded with a wealth of information that didn't exist when your parents were thinking about careers. It's a fast and fun way to learn about any topic you can think of.

6. **Get real-world experience.** The only way to find out for sure what you like or what you're good at is to get out in the world and try things. Join a club, participate in student government, volunteer, try out for a sports team, play an instrument, be active in your community. You'll develop confidence, improve your interpersonal skills, and have plenty of things to list on your college applications and résumés when the time comes.

7. **Volunteer.** Offer your time and services to those who need them. Volunteering is good for the spirit, and it gives you a chance to make a positive contribution to your community, and it looks good on college and job applications. Volunteering is also a great way to explore potential careers.

8. **Find a mentor.** A mentor is someone who can offer you guidance in some or all facets of your life. A mentor is someone who can teach you, provide emotional support, help you with moral dilemmas, help you meet challenges and tackle obstacles, give advice, guide you with personal decisions, and impart wisdom. A mentor can be a teacher, a relative, a spiritual leader, a friend of your parents, a senior citizen, an older student, a coach, a neighbor, or anyone else who has time to offer you direction and encouragement. For more information, visit the National Mentoring Partnership's Web site: www.mentoring.org.

9. **Network.** Networking is all about talking to people who can point you in the right direction in your career path. It's an incredibly valuable skill. Put the word out to anyone you can think of—relatives, friends, classmates, teachers, neighbors—that you're interested in learning about a particular topic. They may know someone who knows someone, and before you know it, you've started your own network of connections.

10. **Find an internship.** An internship gives you hands-on experience in a real work environment. It gives you contact with people who could become mentors, references, or future employers. Some internships offer a small salary called a stipend; most don't. Your guidance counselor can help you find something in an area that interests you. Or go to a library and look at the latest edition of *The Internship Bible*, published by the Princeton Review.

11. **Become an apprentice.** An apprenticeship is very similar to an internship. The main difference is that apprentices usually get paid to learn a trade or craft by working side by side with a master craftsperson, technician, or supervisor. Especially if you don't plan to attend a four-year college, this type of experience can give you a head start into a better paying career. For more information about apprenticeships, talk with your guidance counselor. Or go to the library and look at the latest edition of *Ferguson's Guide to Apprenticeship Programs*.

12. **Get a part-time job.** If you're not old enough to do this officially, you can do it unofficially. Baby-sit or mow lawns in your neighborhood. Work after school, on the weekends, during breaks. You'll gain valuable work experience and job skills.

Now answer Numbers 17 through 24 using the Answer Sheet on page 295. Base your answers on the article "12 Keys to Your Future Career."

17 Why does the author begin the article with the quotation "If you don't figure out what you want to do with your life, someone else will"?

A. to explain why it is important to have a plan

B. to show how difficult it can be to set life goals

C. to demonstrate ways people will try to influence you

D. to prove that you should decide on a career right now

18 What conclusion can be drawn from Keys 3 and 6 of the article?

F. The author places value on real-life experience.

G. The author cares most about academic achievement.

H. The author believes in concentrating on one thing at a time.

I. The author thinks it is best to trust what you already know.

19 What is the MAIN idea of Key 7?

A. Volunteering should be done only with others' best interests in mind.

B. Volunteering helps others and can also help you achieve your career goals.

C. Volunteering gives you a chance to help the community and network for a job.

D. Volunteering should be done if it will help your chances of getting into college.

20 What can you infer from Key 8 about choosing a mentor?

F. A mentor should be a close, personal friend.

G. A mentor should work in the career field that interests you.

H. A mentor should be someone older with more experience.

I. A mentor should be someone in a leadership position.

21 How can networking help you explore career possibilities?

　　A. by giving you practice in asking for help
　　B. by letting you work on your interviewing skills
　　C. by increasing the number of people who can guide you
　　D. by showing you where to look on the Internet for help

22 How is being an apprentice DIFFERENT from being an intern?

　　F. An apprentice learns real job skills.
　　G. An apprentice meets future employers.
　　H. An apprentice gets on-the-job training.
　　I. An apprentice gets money for working.

23 What organizational method does the author use?

　　A. spatial order
　　B. numbered list
　　C. cause and effect
　　D. compare and contrast

24 Which two words from the article have about the same meaning?

　　F. facets, challenges
　　G. counselor, advisor
　　H. direction, encouragement
　　I. interpersonal, extracurricular

Read the article "Osceola" before answering Numbers 25 through 32.

Osceola

by Jan Glidewell

He wasn't really a chief; he wasn't really a Seminole; he wasn't even a native of Florida. And Osceola was an English vulgarization of his true Indian name.

But the man who led the Seminole Indian Tribe to several victories in the Second Seminole War stands as a symbol of Indian dignity and resistance—and as a reminder of America's duplicity toward its first inhabitants.

Osceola, also known as William Powell, was a Creek Indian from Georgia and, by some accounts, had at least one white ancestor. His real name was "Asiyahola," the cry given by those who took a ceremonial black drink that was meant to cleanse the body and spirit.

He was neither a hereditary nor elected chief, but was acknowledged as a leader because of his fierce opposition to the government. When Seminole chiefs agreed in 1835 to move the tribe to what is now Oklahoma, Osceola plunged his dagger through the treaty and vowed to stay and fight. Thus began a bloody, seven-year conflict, the end of which Osceola wouldn't live to see.

As with other Indian leaders of that era, fact and legend intertwine in accounts of his life. He is known to have punished Seminoles who cooperated with whites, murdered at least one U.S. Indian agent, and outwitted five Army generals on the battlefield.

By some accounts, he starved himself so he could slip through a narrow window and escape from Castillo de San Marcos at St. Augustine, only to be recaptured. Other accounts hold that he chose to remain in captivity as a martyr while Wild Cat and others escaped.

Although he was not present at the battle, Osceola is credited with masterminding the attack on Major Francis Langhorn Dade near Bushnell, in which nearly every member of Dade's command was killed.

Ironically, Osceola is not among the Floridians to be recognized and honored with plaques during a millennial project sponsored by the state. Dade—who led his troops into an ambush in which he and 108 others died—is.

In October 1837, Osceola came under a flag of truce to negotiate with Army officials, who promptly seized and imprisoned him—first at St. Augustine, then at Fort Moultrie, near Charleston, S.C. The shameful nature of his capture became a *cause célèbre* and sparked nationwide protests against the conduct of the Second Seminole War—125 years before such protests became commonplace.

He died at 34 from the combined effects of malaria, quinsy, and the treachery of his foes. Most historians agree that Osceola was, at his death, the most famous Indian in America, his demise noted on the front pages of newspapers around the world. Today, hundreds of cities, counties, schools and businesses across the country bear his name.

Now answer Numbers 25 through 32 using the Answer Sheet on page 295. Base your answers on the article "Osceola."

25 What can you infer from the first two sentences of the article?

   A. Not very much is known about Osceola.

   B. People have mistaken beliefs about Osceola.

   C. Osceola fooled many people into believing he was a Seminole.

   D. Osceola was not as important to Seminole history as many people think.

26 With which statement would the author MOST likely agree?

   F. The American Army treated Seminole warriors with respect.

   G. The American government often treated Native Americans unfairly.

   H. The Seminole chiefs all agreed with Osceola's position on the 1835 treaty.

   I. The American people approved of the way the Second Seminole War was run.

27 How did Osceola become a leader of the Seminoles?

   A. He was an elected Seminole chief.

   B. He was the son of a Seminole chief.

   C. He was strongly against the American government.

   D. He was clearly willing to work toward a peaceful solution.

28 Which pair of words BEST describes Osceola's reaction to the 1835 treaty?

   F. sly and crafty

   G. angry and defiant

   H. calm and cooperative

   I. curious and thoughtful

29 Which statement BEST describes how the author feels about Osceola?

    A. He admires him as a great warrior.

    B. He respects him for his love of peace.

    C. He dislikes him for his violent actions.

    D. He disrespects him for not cooperating.

30 Why was the capture of Osceola shameful?

    F. They made Osceola move from prison to prison.

    G. They starved Osceola during the time he was in prison.

    H. They arrested Osceola after an attack on Major Francis Langhorn Dade.

    I. They captured Osceola when he came to talk about a peace settlement.

31 Which of the following supports the idea that Osceola was the most famous American Indian in the country when he died?

    A. There were articles about his death in newspapers throughout the world.

    B. There were plaques in honor of the ambush that killed Dade and his soldiers.

    C. There were protests against the Second Seminole War throughout the nation.

    D. There were hundreds of schools and businesses that closed for a day in his honor.

32 Which two words from the article have about the same meaning?

    F. fact, legend

    G. foes, leaders

    H. duplicity, treachery

    I. outwitted, recognized

Read the story "Misery" before answering Numbers 33 through 40.

from Misery

by Anton Chekhov

"To whom shall I tell my grief?"

The twilight of evening. Big flakes of wet snow are whirling lazily about the street lamps, which have just been lighted, and lying in a thin soft layer on roofs, horses' backs, shoulders, caps. Iona Potapov, the sledge-driver, is all white like a ghost. He sits on the box without stirring, bent as double as the living body can be bent. If a regular snowdrift fell on him it seems as though even then he would not think it necessary to shake it off. . . .

It is a long time since Iona and his nag have budged. They came out of the yard before dinnertime and not a single fare yet. But now the shades of evening are falling on the town. The pale light of the street lamps changes to a vivid color, and the bustle of the street grows noisier.

"Sledge to Vyborgskaya!" Iona hears. "Sledge!"

Iona starts, and through his snow-plastered eyelashes sees an officer in a military overcoat with a hood over his head.

"To Vyborgskaya," repeats the officer. "Are you asleep? To Vyborgskaya!"

In token of assent Iona gives a tug at the reins which sends cakes of snow flying from the horse's back and shoulders. The officer gets into the sledge. The sledge-driver clicks to the horse, cranes his neck like a swan, rises in his seat, and more from habit than necessity brandishes his whip. The mare cranes her neck, too, crooks her stick-like legs, and hesitatingly sets off. . . .

"Where are you shoving, you devil?" Iona immediately hears shouts from the dark mass shifting to and fro before him. "Where the devil are you going? Keep to the r-right!"

"You don't know how to drive! Keep to the right," says the officer angrily.

A coachman driving a carriage swears at him; a pedestrian crossing the road and brushing the horse's nose with his shoulder looks at him angrily and shakes the snow off his sleeve. Iona fidgets on the box as though he were sitting on thorns, jerks his elbows, and turns his eyes about like one possessed as though he did not know where he was or why he was there.

"What rascals they all are!" says the officer jocosely. "They are simply doing their best to run up against you or fall under the horse's feet. They must be doing it on purpose."

Iona looks at his fare and moves his lips. . . . Apparently he means to say something, but nothing comes but a sniff.

"What?" inquires the officer.

Iona gives a wry smile, and straining his throat, brings out huskily: "My son . . . er . . . my son died this week, sir."

"H'm! What did he die of?"

Iona turns his whole body round to his fare, and says:

"Who can tell! It must have been from fever. . . . He lay three days in the hospital and then he died. . . . God's will."

"Turn round, you devil!" comes out of the darkness. "Have you gone cracked, you old dog? Look where you are going!"

"Drive on! drive on! . . ." says the officer. "We shan't get there till to-morrow going on like this. Hurry up!"

The sledge-driver cranes his neck again, rises in his seat, and with heavy grace swings his whip. Several times he looks round at the officer, but the latter keeps his eyes shut and is apparently disinclined to listen. Putting his fare down at Vyborgskaya, Iona stops by a restaurant, and again sits huddled up on the box. . . . Again the wet snow paints him and his horse white. One hour passes, and then another. . . .

Three young men, two tall and thin, one short and hunchbacked, come up, railing at each other and loudly stamping on the pavement with their galoshes.

"Cabby, to the Police Bridge!" the hunchback cries in a cracked voice. "The three of us, . . . twenty kopecks!"

Iona tugs at the reins and clicks to his horse. Twenty kopecks is not a fair price, but he has no thoughts for that. Whether it is a rouble or whether it is five kopecks does not matter to him now so long as he has a fare. . . .

"Well, drive on," says the hunchback in his cracked voice, settling himself and breathing down Iona's neck. "Cut along! What a cap you've got, my friend! You wouldn't find a worse one in all Petersburg. . . ."

"He-he! . . . he-he! . . ." laughs Iona. "It's nothing to boast of!"

"Well, then, nothing to boast of, drive on! Are you going to drive like this all the way? Eh? Shall I give you one in the neck?" . . .

Iona feels behind his back the jolting person and quivering voice of the hunchback. He hears abuse addressed to him, he sees people, and the feeling of loneliness begins little by little to be less heavy on his heart. The hunchback swears at him, till he chokes over some elaborately whimsical string of epithets and is overpowered by his cough. His tall companions begin talking of a certain Nadyezhda Petrovna. Iona looks round at them. Waiting till there is a brief pause, he looks round once more and says:

"This week . . . er . . . my . . . er . . . son died!"

"We shall all die, . . ." says the hunchback with a sigh, wiping his lips after coughing. "Come, drive on! drive on! My friends, I simply cannot stand crawling like this! When will he get us there?"

"Well, you give him a little encouragement . . . one in the neck!"

"Cabman, are you married?" asks one of the tall ones.

"I? He-he! Me-er-ry gentlemen. The only wife for me now is the damp earth. . . . He-ho-ho! . . . The grave that is! . . . Here my son's dead and I am alive. . . . It's a strange thing, death has come in at the wrong door. . . . Instead of coming for me it went for my son. . . ."

And Iona turns round to tell them how his son died, but at that point the hunchback gives a faint sigh and announces that, thank God! they have arrived at last. After taking his twenty kopecks, Iona gazes for a long while after the revelers, who disappear into a dark entry. Again he is alone and again there is silence for him. . . .

Iona drives a few paces away, bends himself double, and gives himself up to his misery. He feels it is no good to appeal to people. But before five minutes have passed he draws himself up, shakes his head as though he feels a sharp pain, and tugs at the reins. . . . He can bear it no longer.

"Back to the yard!" he thinks. "To the yard!"

And his little mare, as though she knew his thoughts, falls to trotting. An hour and a half later Iona is sitting by a big dirty stove. On the stove, on the floor, and on the benches are people snoring. The air is full of smells and stuffiness. Iona looks at the sleeping figures, scratches himself, and regrets that he has come home so early. . . .

"I have not earned enough to pay for the oats, even," he thinks. "That's why I am so miserable. A man who knows how to do his work, . . . who has had enough to eat, and whose horse has had enough to eat, is always at ease . . . ."

"Let's go out and have a look at the mare," Iona thinks. "There is always time for sleep. . . . You'll have sleep enough, no fear. . . ."

He puts on his coat and goes into the stables where his mare is standing. He thinks about oats, about hay, about the weather. . . . He cannot think about his son when he is alone. . . . To talk about him with someone is possible, but to think of him and picture him is insufferable anguish. . . .

"Are you munching?" Iona asks his mare, seeing her shining eyes. "There, munch away, munch away. . . . Since we have not earned enough for oats, we will eat hay. . . . Yes, . . . I have grown too old to drive. . . . My son ought to be driving, not I. . . . He was a real cabman. . . . He ought to have lived. . . ."

Iona is silent for a while, and then he goes on:

"That's how it is, old girl. . . . Kuzma Ionitch is gone. . . . He said good-by to me. . . . He went and died for no reason. . . . Now, suppose you had a little colt, and you were own mother to that little colt. . . . And all at once that same little colt went and died. . . . You'd be sorry, wouldn't you? . . ."

The little mare munches, listens, and breathes on her master's hands. Iona is carried away and tells her all about it.

Answer numbers 33 through 40. Base your answers on the story "Misery."

33 In the first paragraph, why doesn't Iona shake the snow off himself?

    A. He is too cold to move.

    B. He is too tired from the night's work.

    C. He is too worried about getting a fare.

    D. He is too sad to care if the snow covers him.

34 How do Iona's passengers treat him?

    F. with patience

    G. with kindness

    H. with sympathy

    I. with disrespect

35 Why do the people on the street get angry at Iona?

　　A. He is driving too slowly.
　　B. He is trying to run them off the street.
　　C. He is not paying attention to his driving.
　　D. He is driving on the right side of the street.

36 How does the setting help create the mood of the story?

　　F. The cold, snowy night helps create a sad mood.
　　G. The busy, crowded street helps create a lively mood.
　　H. The warm, cozy stable helps create a peaceful mood.
　　I. The snowy, dark night helps create a mysterious mood.

37 What is the MAIN problem Iona faces in the story?

　　A. He is too distracted by grief to be able to work.
　　B. He is forced to work even though his son just died.
　　C. His son just died and he doesn't know why.
　　D. His son just died and he has no one to talk to about it.

38 Why does Iona go back to the yard?

　　F. He has earned enough money for the night.
　　G. He has become tired from working all night.
　　H. He has had enough of driving rude passengers around.
　　I. He has had no luck in finding someone to listen to him.

39 How does Iona solve his main problem?

　　A. by talking to his horse
　　B. by talking to his passengers
　　C. by working hard to earn more money
　　D. by working hard to take his mind off his son

40 Which of the following statements BEST expresses the story's theme?

　　F. People need to share their feelings after a tragic experience.
　　G. People should not be too busy to stop and help those in need.
　　H. It is hard to understand why bad things happen to those we love.
　　I. It is best to get back to your normal routine after losing a loved one.

Armed But Not Dangerous

by Doug Stewart

Is the octopus really the invertebrate intellect of the sea?

Frequently, we humans look down on invertebrates as inferior forms of life. But at least one invertebrate, the octopus, may possess enough brainpower to alter this biological prejudice.

Octopuses are mollusks, like snails, clams and oysters, but they are smarter, nimbler, more curious and more resourceful than any oyster. They have to be: Like their fellow cephalopods, squid and cuttlefish, they lost their external shells millions of years ago, but what they lack in armor, experts say, they make up for in brains. The central nervous system of the octopus is among the largest and most complex in the invertebrate world, rivaling that of many vertebrates, including birds and fish. How intelligent that nervous system makes the octopus is still a matter of scientific debate, however.

Over the years, scientists have tested octopus intelligence by teaching captive specimens to slither through simple mazes and to tell squares from crosses. Octopuses even learn to unscrew lids to get at food.

The most dramatic evidence for octopus intelligence came in 1992. A pair of researchers in Naples, Italy, Graziano Fiorito and Pietro Scotto, used conventional means—food as a carrot, mild electric shock as the stick—to train a group of captive common octopuses to grab a red ball instead of a white one. The scientists then let untrained animals watch from adjoining tanks as their experienced confreres reached for red balls over and over. Thereafter, Fiorito and Scotto reported, most of the watchers, when offered a choice, pounced on red balls. In fact, they learned to do so more quickly than had the original group. The octopuses, according to the researchers, were doing something invertebrate had never been known to do before: learning by watching.

Or so it seemed. Critics since then have weighed in with a list of complaints about the experiment. Controls were sloppy: Fiorito and Scotto themselves concede that untrained octopuses at the outset already preferred red balls by more than three to one. Gerald Biederman of the University of Toronto's Learning Laboratory wrote that octopuses typically "are reluctant to attack novel stimuli." Having watched trained octopuses repeatedly snatch the red ball, the untrained animals may simply have gotten used to watching that ball and so were more apt to pounce on it themselves.

What perplexed scientists most about Fiorito and Scotto's paper, however, was the assumption that the animals would do something in captivity that they would never do in nature. An ability to learn by watching makes sense, in evolutionary terms, only for animals that live in social groups. But octopuses do not.

Indeed, an octopus leads a remarkably solitary life. It never knows its parents. In most species, the mother stops eating while brooding her eggs and dies almost as soon as they hatch. Newborn common octopuses, flealike creatures the size of rice grains, spend their first weeks as ocean plankton, drifting at the surface. After gaining weight, they drop to the bottom, where they spend most of their lives hiding watchfully in dens, which can be rocky crevices, abandoned shells, holes scooped in the sand, even the odd oil drum or mayonnaise jar.

From 150 to 200 species of octopus inhabit the world's oceans. The common octopus, the species best known to scientists, thrives in warm rocky shallows off the coasts of the southeastern United States, western Central America and Japan, as well as in the Mediterranean and the Caribbean. It can weigh up to 50 pounds and have a 10-foot arm span. The species that comes closest in size to the monsters of science fiction is the giant Pacific octopus, found off the western coast of North America and across the northern Pacific to Japan. The biggest ever captured weighed more than 600 pounds and measured 31 feet from arm tip to arm tip. Despite their impressive growth, Pacific giants rarely live longer than three years. At the other extreme, adults of some pygmy species weigh less than a penny, grow to an arm span of less than two inches and are lucky to live six months.

"Out of the water, an octopus feels very loose and slimy," says Roland Anderson, a biologist at the Seattle Aquarium. "It's almost like holding a jellyfish. Underwater, though, their arms feel quite muscular, and they're very, very strong." At the aquarium one night, he reports, a 40-pound octopus smashed the sealed, quarter-inch-thick Plexiglas lid of its tank and crawled out. "A night biologist came in and found it slithering around on the floor," he says.

Octopus literature is filled with tales of naturalists briefly leaving animals in open tanks and returning to find them scaling a bookcase, hiding in a teapot or expired on the carpet. Astonishingly compressible, an octopus can ooze through an opening no bigger than one of its eyeballs. Its yen to get loose is probably linked to an instinctive urge to change dens every week or two. But on dry land, an octopus is doomed: Within half an hour, it will die from lack of oxygen.

An octopus in the open sea might seem easy pickings for predators such as moray eels, sea lions and bigger octopuses, but the octopus can marshal a dazzling array of defenses. Like a squid, it can disorient a pursuer with a burst of purplish-black ink. Should it lose an arm to the jaws of a predator, it can grow a new limb. More impressive still, an octopus can change color in less than a second.

"When it comes to camouflage, it's the most capable organism on the planet without question," says Roger Hanlon, a cephalopod-behavior expert at the Marine Biological Laboratory in Woods Hole, Massachusetts. "Chameleons are just dead-boring compared to octopuses." The octopus' secret is cells in its skin called chromatophores, which are under muscular control: Different pigments come into view as the cell walls are stretched or squeezed.

Although scientists have learned a great deal about octopus biology, no one yet knows what and how these animals think. Roger Hanlon of the Woods Hole marine lab points out that explanations other than higher intelligence can account for much of the size of an octopus brain. To camouflage itself, for instance, the octopus must gauge its surroundings and transform its body shape, pattern, color, texture, and brightness in a fraction of a second. "It takes a lot of brain tissue to coordinate all that," says Hanlon.

Then there are all those suckers, which not only grip things but taste them. Each sucker may have 10,000 neurons to handle both taste and touch, and an octopus has thousands of suckers. "You've got to have a big brain to handle all that, too." And the animal needs brainpower to coordinate the movements of its eight long arms. "That's not trivial," says Hanlon. "They use their arms to walk, crawl, burrow, dig, swim, eat, mate—those arms do everything."

Jean Geary Boal is a researcher at the cephalopod center in Galveston who spent a year at Graziano Fiorito's lab in Naples. Having reviewed in depth the evidence for learning in octopuses, she sides with the skeptics. "Hard and fast data about the intelligence of octopuses are not very good," she says. Still, she understands what drives people to establish a sense of kinship with these creatures. "It's extremely easy to anthropomorphize octopuses. They make eye contact with you. They respond to you. They reach toward you. There's just something mesmerizing for people about octopuses."

Now answer Numbers 41 through 48. Base your answers on the article "Armed But Not Dangerous."

41 How are octopuses DIFFERENT from other mollusks?

A. They are less active.

B. They are more intelligent.

C. They have a smaller external shell.

D. They have a simpler nervous system.

42 What was the goal of Fiorito and Scotto's experiment with octopuses?

F. to see if octopuses prefer some colors over others

G. to see if octopuses could tell a red ball apart from a white ball

H. to find out if trained octopuses were smarter than untrained octopuses

I. to find out if octopuses could learn from seeing what other octopuses did

43 Why do naturalists think that octopuses try to escape from their aquariums?

    A. In the ocean, they like to hide in dark places.
    B. In captivity, they can die from lack of oxygen.
    C. In the lab, they like to squeeze through small holes.
    D. In the wild, they often move from one den to another.

44 According to the article, how are octopuses and squid ALIKE?

    F. Both are intelligent invertebrates.
    G. Both can grow a new arm if they lose one.
    H. Both change colors to help them hunt prey.
    I. Both use ink as a defense against predators.

45 What does an octopus use to taste things?

    A. its arms
    B. its beak
    C. its mouth
    D. its suckers

46 What is the MAIN idea of the article?

    F. Scientists agree that octopuses learn by observation.
    G. Scientists are not sure how intelligent octopuses are.
    H. Research has shown that invertebrates are able to learn.
    I. Research has proved that octopuses are highly intelligent.

47 What does Jean Geary Boal mean when she says that it is easy for people to "anthropomorphize" octopuses?

    A. It is easy to make pets out of octopuses.
    B. It is easy to see invertebrates as less intelligent.
    C. It is easy to think of invertebrates as inferior animals.
    D. It is easy to view octopuses as having human qualities.

48 Read these sentences from the article.

Frequently, we humans look down on invertebrates as inferior forms of life. But at least one invertebrate, the octopus, may possess enough brainpower to alter this biological prejudice.

What does the word *alter* mean?

    F. show
    G. prove
    H. change
    I. disprove

Read the article "The History of the Pony Express" before answering Numbers 49 through 56.

The History of the Pony Express

The Pony Express actually began as an advertisement. Its purpose was to draw public attention to the Central Route in hopes of gaining the million-dollar government mail contract for the Central Overland California and Pikes Peak Express Company (COC&PP). By 1860, over a half-million people lived west of the Rocky Mountains. It was difficult for these people to communicate with friends and family in the east and they were demanding better and faster mail service.

Before 1860, there were three mail routes in use. Two were overland routes, and one was by sea. The route by sea was the most popular one. Mail was carried to Panama by ship, then taken across the isthmus of Panama by wagons, mules, or stagecoaches. The mail was then loaded onto a second ship for transport to California. On the most popular overland route, the Southern or Butterfield Route, the mail was carried by stagecoach. Although the Central Route was 2,000 miles long, it was the shortest of the three mail routes. It was also the least used route because people did not believe it could be traveled year round.

The COC&PP was a freighting company operated by William H. Russell, Alexander Majors, and William B. Waddell. This company held the monopoly on the Central Route. The company wanted the $1,000,000 government mail contract held by the Overland Mail Company on the Southern Route. Russell, Majors, and Waddell set out to prove that winter was not a factor in traveling the Central Route.

The COC&PP had suffered heavy losses of supplies and equipment during the Mormon War in 1857. Congress refused to pay for the supplies and other freighting the company had done for the government. The result was that Russell, Majors, and Waddell were heavily in debt. They hoped to save the company from bankruptcy by using the Pony Express as a way of advertising to the country and Congress the benefits of the Central Route.

The COC&PP chose St. Joseph, Missouri, as the eastern terminus of the Pony Express because both the telegraph and railroad had reached this far west. St. Joseph was well known as a jumping off point for the Oregon-California Trails. The citizens of St. Joseph also offered incentives of land, office space, and free railroad passage for company personnel and freight.

At 7:15 P.M., on April 3, 1860, Johnny Fry left the Pike's Peak Stables in St. Joseph and headed west. In the early morning hours of April 4, Billy Hamilton left Sacramento in a driving rain headed east. They had ten days to get the mail through. On April 13, Johnny Fry returned to St. Joseph with the eastbound mail. The Pony Express had done it! Ten days to get the mail over the Central Route. This beat the fastest times on the Southern Route and the Panama Route.

At any given time, there were two riders on the trail, one headed east and one headed west, day and night. The mail was carried in relays with each rider covering 75 to 100 miles. In that distance, he would change horses at relay stations spaced ten to twelve miles apart. The horses could average ten miles per hour and each rider changed horses eight to ten times.

From April 3, 1860, to October 24, 1861, almost 35,000 letters were carried by Pony Express riders. Letters were written on lightweight paper and wrapped in oiled silk to protect the paper from the elements. When the Pony Express began, it cost $5.00 per 1/2 ounce to send one letter. By the time the Pony Express ended, the price had dropped to $1.00 per 1/2 ounce. The mail was carried in specially designed saddlebags called a *mochila*. The *mochila* was thrown over the saddle and held in place by the weight of the rider. Each corner of the *mochila* had a *cantina*, or pocket. Bundles of mail were placed in each *cantina*. The *mochila* could hold twenty pounds of mail.

On October 24, 1861, the transcontinental telegraph line was completed. Now that messages could be sent in minutes by telegraph, the Pony Express was no longer the fastest method of communication and was ended.

Financially, the Pony Express was a huge failure. However, its successes are numerous. It proved that the Central Route could be traveled through all seasons, blazed the trail for the transcontinental railroad across the mountains, provided the fastest communication between the east and west coasts until the transcontinental telegraph line was completed, and kept communication open to California at the beginning of the Civil War.

Now answer Numbers 49 through 56. Base your answers on the article "The History of the Pony Express."

49 What made the Central Overland California and Pikes Peak Express Company want to begin the Pony Express?

    A. It wanted to receive its company mail faster.

    B. It hoped to get a mail contract from the government.

    C. It wanted to put the Overland Mail Company out of business.

    D. It needed to communicate more easily with people in California.

50. How was the Central Route DIFFERENT from the Southern Route and the sea route?

   F. It was the shortest route.

   G. It was the most popular route.

   H. It carried mail by stagecoach.

   I. It took the longest time to travel.

51. What did the COC&PP need to prove to people?

   A. that the Central Route could be used in the winter

   B. that the Central Route could be used to transport mail

   C. that the Central Route was cheaper than the sea route

   D. that the Central Route was faster than the Southern Route

52. What was the MAIN reason the COC&PP picked St. Joseph, Missouri, as the starting point for the Pony Express?

   F. The city gave them free office space.

   G. The citizens of St. Joseph gave them land.

   H. The railroad let them ship freight for free.

   I. The railroad and telegraph lines west ended at St. Joseph.

53. Why did the Pony Express always have two riders on the trail at one time?

   A. so that they would be able to carry twice as much mail

   B. so that they would cut the time it took to deliver mail in half

   C. so that they would have a back-up rider in case of accidents

   D. so that they would be able to defend themselves against robbers

54. What did the Pony Express riders use a *mochila* for?

   F. carrying the mail

   G. weighing the mail

   H. saddling the horse

   I. waterproofing the letters

55. What was the MAIN reason the Pony Express ended?

   A. It was too expensive to operate year-round.

   B. It was replaced by the transcontinental railroad.

   C. It was taken over by the Overland Mail Company.

   D. It was no longer the quickest way to communicate.

56. Based on the last paragraph of the article, what is the author's point of view toward the Pony Express?

F. It failed financially and was a waste of time.
G. It failed in some ways but succeeded in others.
H. It made money and led to the creation of the telegraph.
I. It made money and connected the east and west coasts.

Answer Sheet

Name _____

Answer all the questions that appear in Practice Test One on this Answer Sheet.

1. Ⓐ Ⓑ Ⓒ Ⓓ
2. Ⓕ Ⓖ Ⓗ Ⓘ
3. Ⓐ Ⓑ Ⓒ Ⓓ
4. Ⓕ Ⓖ Ⓗ Ⓘ
5. Ⓐ Ⓑ Ⓒ Ⓓ
6. Ⓕ Ⓖ Ⓗ Ⓘ
7. Ⓐ Ⓑ Ⓒ Ⓓ
8. Ⓕ Ⓖ Ⓗ Ⓘ
9. Ⓐ Ⓑ Ⓒ Ⓓ
10. Ⓕ Ⓖ Ⓗ Ⓘ
11. Ⓐ Ⓑ Ⓒ Ⓓ
12. Ⓕ Ⓖ Ⓗ Ⓘ
13. Ⓐ Ⓑ Ⓒ Ⓓ
14. Ⓕ Ⓖ Ⓗ Ⓘ
15. Ⓐ Ⓑ Ⓒ Ⓓ
16. Ⓕ Ⓖ Ⓗ Ⓘ
17. Ⓐ Ⓑ Ⓒ Ⓓ
18. Ⓕ Ⓖ Ⓗ Ⓘ
19. Ⓐ Ⓑ Ⓒ Ⓓ
20. Ⓕ Ⓖ Ⓗ Ⓘ

21. Ⓐ Ⓑ Ⓒ Ⓓ
22. Ⓕ Ⓖ Ⓗ Ⓘ
23. Ⓐ Ⓑ Ⓒ Ⓓ
24. Ⓕ Ⓖ Ⓗ Ⓘ
25. Ⓐ Ⓑ Ⓒ Ⓓ
26. Ⓕ Ⓖ Ⓗ Ⓘ
27. Ⓐ Ⓑ Ⓒ Ⓓ
28. Ⓕ Ⓖ Ⓗ Ⓘ
29. Ⓐ Ⓑ Ⓒ Ⓓ
30. Ⓕ Ⓖ Ⓗ Ⓘ
31. Ⓐ Ⓑ Ⓒ Ⓓ
32. Ⓕ Ⓖ Ⓗ Ⓘ
33. Ⓐ Ⓑ Ⓒ Ⓓ
34. Ⓕ Ⓖ Ⓗ Ⓘ
35. Ⓐ Ⓑ Ⓒ Ⓓ
36. Ⓕ Ⓖ Ⓗ Ⓘ
37. Ⓐ Ⓑ Ⓒ Ⓓ
38. Ⓕ Ⓖ Ⓗ Ⓘ

39. Ⓐ Ⓑ Ⓒ Ⓓ
40. Ⓕ Ⓖ Ⓗ Ⓘ
41. Ⓐ Ⓑ Ⓒ Ⓓ
42. Ⓕ Ⓖ Ⓗ Ⓘ
43. Ⓐ Ⓑ Ⓒ Ⓓ
44. Ⓕ Ⓖ Ⓗ Ⓘ
45. Ⓐ Ⓑ Ⓒ Ⓓ
46. Ⓕ Ⓖ Ⓗ Ⓘ
47. Ⓐ Ⓑ Ⓒ Ⓓ
48. Ⓕ Ⓖ Ⓗ Ⓘ
49. Ⓐ Ⓑ Ⓒ Ⓓ
50. Ⓕ Ⓖ Ⓗ Ⓘ
51. Ⓐ Ⓑ Ⓒ Ⓓ
52. Ⓕ Ⓖ Ⓗ Ⓘ
53. Ⓐ Ⓑ Ⓒ Ⓓ
54. Ⓕ Ⓖ Ⓗ Ⓘ
55. Ⓐ Ⓑ Ⓒ Ⓓ
56. Ⓕ Ⓖ Ⓗ Ⓘ

Answer Sheet

Name _____

Answer all the questions that appear in Practice Test Two on this Answer Sheet.

1	Ⓐ	Ⓑ	Ⓒ	Ⓓ	**21** Ⓐ Ⓑ Ⓒ Ⓓ				**39** Ⓐ Ⓑ Ⓒ Ⓓ			
2	Ⓕ	Ⓖ	Ⓗ	Ⓘ	**22** Ⓕ Ⓖ Ⓗ Ⓘ				**40** Ⓕ Ⓖ Ⓗ Ⓘ			
3	Ⓐ	Ⓑ	Ⓒ	Ⓓ	**23** Ⓐ Ⓑ Ⓒ Ⓓ				**41** Ⓐ Ⓑ Ⓒ Ⓓ			
4	Ⓕ	Ⓖ	Ⓗ	Ⓘ	**24** Ⓕ Ⓖ Ⓗ Ⓘ				**42** Ⓕ Ⓖ Ⓗ Ⓘ			
5	Ⓐ	Ⓑ	Ⓒ	Ⓓ	**25** Ⓐ Ⓑ Ⓒ Ⓓ				**43** Ⓐ Ⓑ Ⓒ Ⓓ			
6	Ⓕ	Ⓖ	Ⓗ	Ⓘ	**26** Ⓕ Ⓖ Ⓗ Ⓘ				**44** Ⓕ Ⓖ Ⓗ Ⓘ			
7	Ⓐ	Ⓑ	Ⓒ	Ⓓ	**27** Ⓐ Ⓑ Ⓒ Ⓓ				**45** Ⓐ Ⓑ Ⓒ Ⓓ			
8	Ⓕ	Ⓖ	Ⓗ	Ⓘ	**28** Ⓕ Ⓖ Ⓗ Ⓘ				**46** Ⓕ Ⓖ Ⓗ Ⓘ			
9	Ⓐ	Ⓑ	Ⓒ	Ⓓ	**29** Ⓐ Ⓑ Ⓒ Ⓓ				**47** Ⓐ Ⓑ Ⓒ Ⓓ			
10	Ⓕ	Ⓖ	Ⓗ	Ⓘ	**30** Ⓕ Ⓖ Ⓗ Ⓘ				**48** Ⓕ Ⓖ Ⓗ Ⓘ			
11	Ⓐ	Ⓑ	Ⓒ	Ⓓ	**31** Ⓐ Ⓑ Ⓒ Ⓓ				**49** Ⓐ Ⓑ Ⓒ Ⓓ			
12	Ⓕ	Ⓖ	Ⓗ	Ⓘ	**32** Ⓕ Ⓖ Ⓗ Ⓘ				**50** Ⓕ Ⓖ Ⓗ Ⓘ			
13	Ⓐ	Ⓑ	Ⓒ	Ⓓ	**33** Ⓐ Ⓑ Ⓒ Ⓓ				**51** Ⓐ Ⓑ Ⓒ Ⓓ			
14	Ⓕ	Ⓖ	Ⓗ	Ⓘ	**34** Ⓕ Ⓖ Ⓗ Ⓘ				**52** Ⓕ Ⓖ Ⓗ Ⓘ			
15	Ⓐ	Ⓑ	Ⓒ	Ⓓ	**35** Ⓐ Ⓑ Ⓒ Ⓓ				**53** Ⓐ Ⓑ Ⓒ Ⓓ			
16	Ⓕ	Ⓖ	Ⓗ	Ⓘ	**36** Ⓕ Ⓖ Ⓗ Ⓘ				**54** Ⓕ Ⓖ Ⓗ Ⓘ			
17	Ⓐ	Ⓑ	Ⓒ	Ⓓ	**37** Ⓐ Ⓑ Ⓒ Ⓓ				**55** Ⓐ Ⓑ Ⓒ Ⓓ			
18	Ⓕ	Ⓖ	Ⓗ	Ⓘ	**38** Ⓕ Ⓖ Ⓗ Ⓘ				**56** Ⓕ Ⓖ Ⓗ Ⓘ			
19	Ⓐ	Ⓑ	Ⓒ	Ⓓ								
20	Ⓕ	Ⓖ	Ⓗ	Ⓘ								

Index

A

Active reading, 34
Adjective suffixes, 39
Almanacs, 137
Analysis, 34
   of information, 163
   of word parts, 36–39
Antagonism, 206
Antagonists, 209–210
Arguments
   as organizational method, 89, 91
   strong, 163, 164–166, 184
   weak, 163, 164–166, 184
Atlases, 136–137
Author card, 138
Author's point of view, 103, 104, 118–119, 132
Author's purpose, 58, 103, 104, 109, 121, 132

B

Biases, 118
Bibliography, 144
Biographical reference books, 139
Book Review Digest, 140
Bulleted list, 89, 91, 102

C

Card catalog, 137–139
   author card in, 138
   subject card in, 138
   title card in, 138
Cause, 187, 204. *See also* Cause and effect
Cause and effect, 85–86, 91, 102, 185, 187, 188–189, 204
Cause and effect chart, 86
Characters, 58, 206, 209–210, 219, 234
   antagonists as, 209–210
   protagonists as, 209–210
Charts, cause and effect, 86
Chronological order, 88
Climax, 206, 215–216
Comparison, 59, 60, 61, 65, 76
   words that signal a, 59, 76
Comparison and contrast, 57, 86–87, 91, 102
Comparison table, 87
Computer catalogs, 139
Conclusions
   drawing, 34, 144, 160
   effect of personal values on, 184
Conflict, 206, 210–212, 219, 234
   types of, 210
Context, 39
Context clues, using, 39–43
Contrast, 41, 59, 65, 76. *See also* Comparison and contrast
   words that signal, 59, 76
Current Biography, 140

D

Descriptions, 119
Details, 78, 80–82, 91, 102
   choice of, 119
   factual, 80–81
   on note cards, 143
   sensory, 81
   web in organizing, 84–85

297

Dictionary, 135–136, 136
  multiple definitions in, 136
  origin or etymology in, 136
  part of speech in, 136
  pronunciation in, 136
  spelling in, 136
  Webster's Biographical, 140
Documentation of sources, 144

E

Education Index, 140
Effect, 187, 204. *See also* Cause and effect
Encyclopedia, 136
Entertains, writing that, 106–107, 132
Etymology in dictionary, 136
Evaluation, 34
Exposition, 213–214

F

Facts, 163, 184
  as basis for inferences, 35
  distinguishing, from opinions, 163–164
Factual details, 80–81
Falling action, 217
First-person point of view, 207–208
Flashback, 89, 91, 102
Foreshadowing, 89, 91, 102

G

Guide to Reference Books, 140

I

Implied main idea, 79–80
Inciting incident, 214
Index
  education, 140
  newspaper, 141
  periodic, 141
Inferences, 34–35, 56, 144, 160
Inform, 132
Information
  analysis of, 163
  checking validity of, 164
Informational writing, 106, 132

K

Keyword searches, 138

L

Libraries, 137
  reference sources in, 139–142

M

Main idea, 78–80, 91, 102, 160
  on note cards, 143
  stated versus implied, 79–80
  web in organizing, 84–85
Main idea questions, 83
Mood, 207, 208, 219, 234
Multiple-choice questions, 58, 107
Multiple definitions in dictionary, 136

N

Newspaper indexes, 141
Note cards, 141–143
  details on, 143
  main idea on, 143
Noun suffixes
  people, 38
  places or things, 39
Number-related prefixes, 37

O

Omniscient, 207
Opinions, 163, 164, 184
  distinguishing facts from, 163–164
Organizational methods, 58, 78, 85, 89, 91
  argument/support, 89, 91
  bulleted list, 89, 91, 102
  cause and effect, 85–86, 91, 102
  comparison and contrast, 86–87, 91, 102
  flashback, 89, 91, 102
  foreshadowing, 89, 91, 102
  question/answer, 89, 91, 102
  spatial order, 87–88, 91, 102
  time order, 88, 91, 102

Origin of word in dictionary, 136

P

Parts of speech in dictionary, 136
Periodicals, 140
Periodic Index, 141
Personal experience, writing that shares a, 107, 132
Personal judgments, 118
Personal values, 163, 184
  recognizing influence of, 166–168
Persuasive writing, 105–106, 132
Place, 208
Plot, 58, 206, 212–213, 219, 234
  climax in, 215–216
  development of, 217
  exposition in, 213–214
  falling action in, 217
  inciting incident in, 214
  resolution in, 217
  rising action in, 215
Point of view, 58, 121, 207, 219, 234
  author's, 103, 104, 118–119, 132
  first-person, 207–208
  third-person, 207–208
Position-related prefixes, 37
Prefixes, 33, 36, 37, 44, 56, 104
  commonly used, 38
  number-related, 37
  position-related, 37
  time-related, 37
Pronouns
  in first-person point of view, 207
  in third-person point of view, 207
Pronunciation in dictionary, 136
Protagonists, 206, 209–210

Q

Question/answer
  as organizational method, 89, 91, 102
Questions

Index

asking, 204
main idea, 83
multiple-choice, 58, 107

R

Readers' Guide to Periodic Literature, 141
Reference materials
  almanacs as, 137
  atlases as, 136–137
  card catalogs as, 137–139
  computer catalogs as, 139
  dictionaries as, 135–136
  encyclopedias as, 136
  in libraries, 137, 139–142
  World Wide Web as, 137
Reference sources in the library, 137, 139–142
  biographical reference books as, 139
  Book Review Digest as, 140
  Current Biography as, 140
  Education Index as, 140
  Guide to Reference Books as, 140
  newspaper indexes as, 141
  periodicals as, 140
  Periodic Index as, 141
  Readers' Guide to Periodic Literature as, 141
  Webster's Biographical Dictionary as, 140
  Who's Who and *Who's Who in America* as, 140
Resolution, 206, 210–212, 217, 219, 234
Rising action, 215
Root, 36, 56, 104

S

Sensory details, 81
Setting, 58, 206, 208–209, 219, 234
  mood in, 209
  place in, 209
  time in, 208–209
Sources
  documenting, 144
  step-by-step approach to combining information from, 144–146

Spatial order, 87–88, 91, 102
Spelling in dictionary, 136
Stated main idea, 79–80
Story elements
  characters as, 206, 209, 219, 234
  conflict as, 206, 219, 234
  mood as, 207, 219, 234
  plot as, 206, 219, 234
  point of view as, 207, 219, 234
  resolution as, 206, 219, 234
  setting as, 206, 208–209, 219, 234
  theme as, 207, 218, 219, 234
  tone as, 207, 208, 219, 234
Story line, 212
Strong arguments, 163, 164–166, 184
Subject card, 138
Suffixes, 33, 36, 38, 56, 104
  adjective, 39
  noun (people), 38
  noun (places or things), 39
Synthesizing, 34

T

Tables, comparison, 87
Theme, 58, 207, 218, 219, 234
Third-person point of view, 207–208
  limited, 208
  omniscient, 207
Time, 208–209
Time order, 88, 91, 102
  words that signal, 88
Time-related prefixes, 37
Title card, 138
Tone, 58, 207, 208, 219, 234
Topic, 79, 91
Troubleshooting, 187

W

Weak arguments, 163, 164–166, 184
Web in organizing main idea and details, 84–85
Webster's Biographical Dictionary, 140
Who's Who and *Who's Who in America*, 140

Words
  analyzing parts of, 36–39
  choice of, 119
  origin of, in dictionary, 136
  prefixes of, 33, 36, 37, 44, 56, 104
  roots of, 36, 56, 104
  suffixes as, 33, 36, 38, 56, 104
  that signal comparison, 59, 76
  that signal contrast, 59, 76
  that signal time order, 88
World Wide Web, 137
Writing
  for entertainment, 106–107, 132
  for information, 106, 132
  personal experience, 107, 132
  persuasive, 105–106, 132

Acknowledgements

Grateful acknowledgement is made to the following sources for permission to reprint copyrighted materials. Every effort has been made to obtain permission to use previously published materials. Any errors or omissions are unintentional.

"Adventures on the Everglades Trail" by Christopher Percy Collier. From *The Nature Conservancy*, Winter 2004. Copyright © 2004. Reprinted by permission of the author. Page 2.

Excerpt from *Looking Good, Eating Right* by Dr. Charles A. Salter. Copyright ©1991 by Dr. Charles A. Salter. Reprinted by permission of the author. Page 6.

"History of Chocolate." National Confectioners Association, CandyUSA.org. Copyright © 2005. Reprinted by permission. Page 10

From ROSA PARKS: MY STORY by Rosa Parks with Jim Haskins, copyright © 1992 by Rosa Parks. Used by permission of Dial Books for Young Readers, A Division of Penguin Young Readers Group, A Member of Penguin Group (USA) Inc., 345 Hudson Street, New York, NY 10014. All rights reserved. Page 14.

"Cloud Cover" by Nick Walker, meteorologist for the Weather Channel. Copyright © 2004. Small Gate Media. Page 18.

"The Wolf and the Cow" by Emily Sohn. Reprinted with permission from SCIENCE NEWS for Kids, copyright © 2005 by Science Service. Page 22.

"The American Cowboy," from *Preparing for TAAS Reading Exit Level* by Amy Bunin Kaiman, pages 50–51. Copyright © 1999 by Amsco School Publications, Inc. Page 47.

Excerpt from *Triumph of the Imagination: The Story of Writer J. K. Rowling* by Lisa A. Chippendale. Copyright © 2002, Chelsea House Publishers. Reprinted with permission of Chelsea House Publishers, a subsidiary of Haights Cross Communications®. Page 50.

"Manatees Introduction and Background; Manatees, People, and the Buddy System." Copyright © 2005. Reprinted with permission of Courter Films & Associates. Page 53.

"In the Beginning," from *The Story of Baseball* by

Acknowledgements

Lawrence Ritter. Text copyright © 1983, 1990, 1999 by Lawrence Ritter. Used by permission of HarperCollins Publishers. Page 69.

Robert Francis, "The Base Stealer," in *The Orb Weaver* © 1960 by Robert Francis and reprinted by permission of Wesleyan University Press. Page 71.

"Animal Fat" by Stephen James O'Meara. From ODYSSEY's May 2004 issue: *Weighing In*, © 2004, Carus Publishing Company, published by Cobblestone Publishing, 30 Grove Street, Suite C, Peterborough, NH 03458. All Rights Reserved. Reprinted by permission of the publisher. Page 73.

"Conquering Mount Everest" by Phyllis Raybin Emert. From *Mysteries of People and Places*. Copyright © 1992 by the author and reprinted by permission of Tom Doherty Associates, LLC. Page 92.

"Mars Mission Offers Clues in Hunt for New Worlds" by Randal Jackson reprinted courtesy of NASA/JPL/Caltech. Page 96.

"Tech-Trash Tragedy" by Liam O'Donnell. From ODYSSEY's September 2004 issue: *Wired, Wired World*, © 2004, Carus Publishing Company, published by Cobblestone Publishing, 30 Grove Street, Suite C, Peterborough, NH 03458. All Rights Reserved. Reprinted by permission of the publisher. Page 99.

"Internet Safety: Safe Surfing Tips for Teens". From www.KidsHealth.org. Copyright © 2004. Page 122.

"The door." Miroslav Holub, *Poems Before & After: Collected English Translations*, trans. Ian & Jarmila Milner, Ewald Osers & George Theiner (Bloodaxe Books, 1990). Reprinted by permission of Bloodaxe Books. Page 126.

"You're It!" from *Made You Look: How Advertising Works and Why You Should Know* by Shari Graydon, Annick Press, copyright © 2003, pages 17–18. Page 129.

"History and Geography of the Olympic Games in Ancient Greece" by Rick Price. From www.experienceplus.com. Copyright © 2005. Reprinted by permission of the author. Page 150.

"Florida Panther," from www.defenders.org. Copyright © 2005. Adapted with permission from Defenders of Wildlife. Page 154.

"Be a Nutrition Detective" by Jeanne Miller. From ODYSSEY's May 2004 issue: *Weighing In*, © 2004, Carus Publishing Company, published by Cobblestone Publishing, 30 Grove Street, Suite C, Peterborough, NH 03458. All Rights Reserved. Reprinted by permission of the publisher. Page 157.

Excerpt from *Night Siege: The Hudson Valley UFO Sightings* by Philip Imbrogno, Dr. J. Allen Hynek, and Bob Pratt © 1998. *Llewellyn Worldwide, Ltd.*, P.O. Box 64383, St. Paul, MN 55164. All rights reserved. Page 173.

"Evidence Supporting Continental Drift" by Randal Jackson reprinted courtesy of NASA/JPL/Caltech. Page 177.

"Are Computers a Benefit or a Risk to Children?" from *MCAS English Language Arts Grade 7* by Amy Bunin Kaiman, page 94. Copyright ©1999 by Amsco School Publications, Inc. Page 181.

"Ten Things You Can Do to Help Curb Global Warming," from www.sierraclub.org. This article has been reprinted with the Sierra Club's permission. Article copyright © 2005 Sierra Club. All Rights Reserved. Page 194.

"The Early Years," from *Yao Ming: Gentle Giant of Basketball* by Richard Krawiec. Copyright © 2004 by Avisson Press Inc. Reprinted by permission of Avisson Press. Page 198.

"Airborne" by Jesse Davidson. Copyright © 1982. Reprinted courtesy of the Jesse Davidson Aviation Archives, Great Neck, NY 11024. Page 222.

"The Pinching Man," from the book *Facing the Lion: Growing Up Maasai on the African Savanna* by Joseph Lemasolai Lekuton with Herman Viola. Copyright © 2003 Joseph Lemasolai Lekuton with Herman Viola. Reprinted with permission of National Geographic Books. Page 226.

Johanna Copyright ©1987 by Jane Yolen. First appeared in TALES OF WONDER, published by Random House, Inc. Reprinted by permission of Curtis Brown, Ltd. Page 230.

"Litter in the Water," from *Marine Science: Marine Biology and Oceanography* by Thomas F. Greene, pages 559–560. Copyright ©2004 by Amsco School Publications, Inc. Page 244.

"Lobbying 101," from "Understanding Government: If Mr. Smith Goes to Washington, So Can You," by James Reston. From *Be the Difference: A Beginner's Guide to*

Acknowledgements

Changing the World by Danny Seo. Copyright © 2001, New Society Publishers. Reprinted by permission of the publisher. Page 248.

"What is a Gene?" by Louis E. Bartoshesky, MD, MPH. From www.KidsHealth.org. Copyright © 2005. Page 252.

"Python vs. Pooch" by Elizabeth Caram. From *Miami Herald*, January 1, 2005. Permission granted by Copyright Clearance Center. Page 256.

"Acting." This selection, from www.learner.org, is reprinted with permission from Annenberg/CPB. All rights reserved. Page 260.

"Why Exercise Is Wise" by Heidi Kecskemethy, RD, CSP. From www.KidsHealth.org. Copyright © 2004. Page 266.

Excerpt from *Black Boy* by Richard Wright. Copyright © 1993 by Harper Perennial. Used by permission of HarperCollins Publishers. Page 270.

"The Swimming Lesson." Copyright © 1965, 1993 by Mary Oliver. From *No Voyage and Other Poems*. Page 273.

"12 Keys to Your Future Career." Excerpted from *Life Lists for Teens: Tips, Steps, Hints, and How-Tos for Growing Up, Getting Along, Learning, and Having Fun* by Pamela Espeland © 2003. Used with permission of Free Spirit Publishing Inc., Minneapolis, MN; 1-866-703–7322; www.freespirit.com. All rights reserved. Page 275.

"Osceola, ca. 1804–1838, Warrior" by Jan Glidewell. Copyright © St. Petersburg Times 1999. Reprinted by permission of the publisher. Page 279.

"Armed But Not Dangerous" by Doug Stewart. From *National Wildlife*, Volume 35, Number 2. Copyright ©2005. Reprinted by permission of the author. Page 286.

Illustrations

Rosa Parks Riding the Bus. Bettmann/Corbis. Page 14.

Cloud illustration. Copyright, University Corporation for Atmospheric Research. Reproduced by permission. Page 19.

J.K. Rowling. Reuters/Corbis. Page 50.

Fat Manx Cross Cat. Renee Stockdale/Animals, Animals, Earth Scenes. Page 74.

Pitcairn Airwing. Reproduced by permission of the Jesse Davidson Aviation Archives. Page 223.

Molecular model of DNA. Kenneth Eward/Photo Researchers. Page 252.